World Citizenship

World Citizenship

Cosmopolitan Thinking and Its Opponents

Derek Heater

continuum
LONDON • NEW YORK

Continuum
The Tower Building, 11 York Road, London, SE1 7NX
370 Lexington Avenue, New York, NY 10017-6503

First published 2002

British Library Cataloguing in Publication Data
A catalogue record for this book is available from the British Library.

ISBN 0-8264-5891-2 (hardback)
     0-8264-5892-0 (paperback)

Typeset by YHT Ltd, London
Printed and bound in Great Britain by Biddles Ltd, Guildford
and King's Lynn

Contents

Preface

Scholarly interest in the topic of cosmopolitan political thought has recently developed to a remarkable degree and generated a literature of high quality. The reader will be introduced to some of this work; however, this book, it must be made immediately clear, has no pretensions to participate in this academic debate. It has, rather, its own more modest two-fold purpose. First, it is offered as an interpretive textbook: useful to students at various levels, yet throwing out some suggestions for analysing the great range of material of which the topic is composed in order the more readily to comprehend its meaning and significance. Second, and as one of the interpretive devices, the chapters are arranged according to a basic breakdown of the concept of citizenship. The purpose of this approach is to insist that, if world citizenship is to be seriously accepted, it must stand alongside and be comparable with citizenship in the traditional, state-embedded sense. The content of the chapters has two particular features. These are: the generous use of historical material to exemplify the arguments; and the presentation of the case hostile to the idea and practice of world citizenship as well as the case marshalled in its favour, because the latter case cannot be fully understood without this context.

My perennial thanks to my wife for her support in my work must be augmented on this occasion by a record of my gratitude for her gallant mastery of a computer, whose arcane mysteries are beyond the comprehension of her husband, but whose workings are, I understand, essential for the metamorphosis of my mound of pencilled manuscript into the currently required tiny compass of a floppy disk.

Derek Heater
Rottingdean

CHAPTER 1

Introduction

Significance

World citizenship is an enigma. It has never existed in any of the defined legal or political senses that are the accepted signifiers of citizenship in the usual state context; yet the notion, the ideal, the hope, the expectation that there is or should be a world citizenship to parallel state citizenship, in a moral sense at the very least, has doggedly persisted in human minds and consciences for two and a third millennia. Failure to achieve an institutional setting has not led to the death of the ideal through despondency. On the contrary, as the second millennium of the Common Era drew to a close, awareness of the venerable tradition of cosmopolitanism revived; its adherents presented vigorous demonstrations of its relevance and worth to our own age, while delivering forcefully argued denunciations of what they perceived to be the blinkered obsolescence of its detractors' arguments. The sudden burgeoning of interest in cosmopolitanism since the 1990s invites an attempt both to explain it as a scholarly phenomenon and to indicate why it is a significant development.

A considerable number of events and trends may be identified as stimulants to this academic activity, which has generated a plethora of articles, essays and books. In 1992 Thomas Pogge made an illuminating comment:

The human future suddenly seems open. This is an inspiration;

1

> we can step back and think more freely. Instead of contain-
> ment or détente, political scientists are discussing grand
> pictures: the end of history, or the inevitable proliferation and
> mutual pacifism of capitalist democracies. And politicians are
> speaking of a new world order. My inspiration is a little more
> concrete. After developing a rough, cosmopolitan specification
> of our task to promote moral progress, I offer an idea for
> gradual global institutional reform. (Pogge, 1992: 48)

In other words, the pervasively haunting shadow of the Cold War
had so concentrated the minds of the students of international
relations on this strategic and ideological issue that studies
envisaging a future relieved of this dark presence seemed to require
fantasy, not scholarship. Then the disintegration of the Soviet bloc,
precipitately followed by that of the Soviet Union itself, in 1989–91
suddenly dispersed that shadow. Innovative political thinking again
became possible in both ethical and institutional spheres.

Moreover, a global scope for this new liberated thought became
increasingly pertinent. For there was still little mental room for
utopian thinking. Although the apocalyptic menace of thermo-
nuclear war was in all likelihood dispelled for the foreseeable future,
another terrifying threat was impressing itself on human consciousness. This was the possibility of economic and environmental
collapse of global extent. If the Cold War chasm that divided a great
proportion of the world was being so comfortably bridged by post-
Communist détente as to allow of the feasibility of productive
cosmopolitan thinking, the accelerating economic-environmental
crisis rendered such work of imperative importance.

Although we may accept that the will to engage with problems
of global extent is a measure of one's moral commitment as a world
citizen, that determination is but an impotent desire if there are no
effective institutions through which to channel one's moral energies.
Since the UN is the only united nations organization we have, old
thoughts were revived of improving its efficacy and injecting some
democratic element into its structure. Hopes were pinned on the
possibility of such a project by the ending of the bitter US–Soviet
quarrels in the Security Council and President George Bush's
proclamation of a UN-based 'New World Order'. The New World
Order soon proved a mirage, yet the vision of a reformed UN did
not fade: it was pronounced to be more than an ocular trick when
the idea was reiterated at the UN's fortieth anniversary in 1995 and

at the Millennium Summit in 2000. Accordingly, proponents of world citizenship felt that writing about the institutionalization of that concept was justified by its plausibility.

Furthermore, discussion started around a broader and more flexible concept, that of global governance. It was brought fully into the political and academic domains by the Stockholm Initiative on Global Security and Governance, the initial outcome of which was a report, *Common Responsibility in the 1990s*, published in 1991. The Initiative gave rise to the Commission on Global Governance, which produced its report, *Our Global Neighbourhood*, in 1995. This work defined governance as 'the sum of the many ways individuals and institutions, public and private, manage their common affairs' (Commission on Global Governance, 1995: 2). But the whole world has 'common affairs'. Hence the need, already apparent, for *global* governance; hence the need for individuals to think and act as world citizens to develop and participate in this emerging system. Hence, too, the scholarly interest in the nature of world citizenship as it relates to these practical institutional proposals.

Just as the need for more effective political authority of a global extent was being voiced in the 1990s, so too was the realization that economic and cultural trends were becoming increasingly 'globalized' (to use the inelegant term). The word 'globalization' had already existed since around 1970, but it was in the 1990s that the phenomenon became subjected to an extraordinary amount of scholarly analysis. The fact of globalization and the academic commentary it engendered could hardly fail to arouse interest in the question of world citizenship. For example, a book of Canadian provenance on the topic of citizenship, recognizing the very incomplete state of work on world citizenship, gives the opinion that 'The debate over globalization is ... complex and an adequate discussion of cosmopolitan citizenship would have to come to terms with this complexity' (Isin and Wood, 1999: 92). Insofar as globalization has undermined the sovereignty and cultural distinctiveness of the nation-state, it has weakened the former uniqueness of state citizenship and opened up the possibility of a complementary world citizenship. Yet, at the same time, by strengthening the powers of multinational companies, it undermines the autonomy of the person, which lies at the heart of the citizenly concept.

Even so, globalization has not been the only factor in forcing a reconsideration of the nature of citizenship. From about 1990 (see, e.g., Heater, 1990: 314–47) the concept of 'multiple citizenship' became recognized. If state citizenly codes have to be adapted to accommodate multicultural needs, and if one can simultaneously have a state citizenship, a regional citizenship in a federal state, dual citizenship, citizenship of one's own city or town and, in some states of Europe, EU citizenship, then the prospect of an added world citizenship does not seem so extraordinary. Indeed, the formal creation of EU citizenship in 1993 gave heart to some advocates of world citizenship as a model to be extended. However, the more interesting question is how world citizenship can slot into the whole variegated pattern.

By the 1990s, then, the traditional concept of citizenship as being a particular relationship that, for most of its history, connected the individual to his or her state was fast unravelling. For those politicians and academics who value the original nature and purpose of citizenship, this has been at best an unfortunate adaptation; at worst, it portends moral, social, even political collapse, because in this age it is the citizenly bond that, above all, holds the national community together. The case for retaining a strong sense of moral commitment to one's state has often been argued under the name of 'communitarianism', and any tendency that weakens or diverts this allegiance must therefore be suspect. The need to defend their position against this suspicion – also to attack their opponents – has consequently mobilized the advocates of world citizenship to extra efforts in order to present the cosmopolitan case more forcibly.

Having established the reasons for the rising interest in the subject, let us now examine why it is of such great import. To start with the most basic reason: the concept of world citizenship and its realization have significant implications for both the meaning of the term 'citizenship' and the life of the individual. This concept diversifies further the nature of citizenship; moreover, potentially, depending on the cosmopolitan style envisaged or achieved, it could even be a greater challenge to the integrity of traditional state citizenship than the other expressions of multiple citizenship just listed. True, in a federal state like the USA or a quasi-federal state as in the form of the EU, tension between the higher and lower planes of citizenship can be divisive, not to say dangerous. Local state autonomy *v.* federal authority has torn citizenly allegiance in the USA on a number of occasions, even to the ultimate rending of civil war, and, in incomparably milder form, the relationship between national citizenship and 'European' identity for EU citizens is a contentious issue in several member states, notably the UK. However, national citizenship has prevailed and is prevailing as the tighter mode of allegiance for the great bulk of the world's population, even though, because of the strengthening of multi-cultural identities, it must now exhibit greater elasticity than hitherto. However, world citizenship, certainly in its extreme or fundamentalist form (which will be explained below), presents the possibility of particularly severe strain in both quantitative and qualitative ways. Obviously, in one's capacity as a world citizen, the feeling of identity and the psychological process of bonding with one's fellow-citizens involves consideration in principle for a hugely larger number compared with any other levels of citizenship. And qualitatively, the cosmopolitan ethic (again as we shall see below) posits the moral equality of all human beings, whereas every other version of citizenship presupposes a distinctiveness between citizen and non-citizen or stranger, and the allocation of preference to the citizen.

World citizenship therefore affects the individual. It inserts another, highest, ultimate layer of rights for the individual's protection and of responsibilities for the individual to discharge. It imposes the need to know about and understand world issues as well as local and national ones, and to be concerned about, even involved in, the problems facing the planet and its inhabitants, especially those most disadvantaged. The role of the individual *qua* world citizen is, however, not quite as simple as this outline would suggest. Individuals are affected by the presumed status of world citizen in different ways because they may exercise the role in different ways, depending on circumstances or personal inclination – in the case of the latter, a choice is made. (Admittedly, the different ways available for exercising the function of world citizen are no different in principle from the options open to state citizens at the national level, but they must still be explained in our context here.)

First, the world citizen needs to relate in that capacity both to global institutions and to the human world community (leaving aside for our purpose here the environmental element in the citizenly ethic): thus, citizenship operates both 'vertically' and 'horizontally'. For example, a world citizen may wish to concentrate on campaigning for the reform of the UN or on supporting organizations devoted to relieving world poverty. Second, individuals may choose to commit themselves with greater or lesser zeal to the cosmopolitan ideal and/or have more or fewer opportunities to behave in accordance with its precepts. There is a precedent. The notion that some state citizens will live that status more fully than others – to be either 'active' or 'passive' citizens' – has an ancient lineage, in both constitutional law and personal inclination. So, there is no reason to doubt that the same should apply to world citizens, although in this democratic age there would be little if any support for a legal gradation of world citizens. At the same time, needless to say, relatively few individuals would wish to perform a very active role, for the majority of the world's population would surely settle for being 'passive' world citizens. Michael Walzer (1994) has popularized the distinction between 'thick' and 'thin' moralities; this distinction is very germane to the matter of world citizenship identity. The minority who are world citizens in the fullest sense that is currently possible may be referred to as 'a world citizen elite', or 'world citizen pilgrims', or 'pioneer' or 'vanguard world citizens'. These images do not in fact convey the same meanings. The elite are the favoured, the wealthy financiers, business people, senior administrators and academics, for instance, who enjoy the privileges of a cosmopolitan lifestyle. The pilgrims – a term coined, as will be shown later, by Richard Falk – are journeying to an imagined new global 'land' where higher ethical principles may be found. And the vanguard – the term that we wish to introduce here as seeming to be the most apt – are those making progress in constructing a cosmopolis but in advance and on behalf of all those who in due course of time will follow.

But who are all these world citizens, passive as well as active, followers as well as vanguard? Are all human beings world citizens? If so, what is the difference – merely that 'human being' is a biological term and 'world citizen' is an ethical-political term? The assumption, sometimes the assertion, of writers in the cosmopolitan tradition is that all human beings are endowed with the moral capacity to be world citizens. But the matter cannot be left there, for moral capacity is not enough: the essence of citizenship is the individual's relation to a state. Yet there is no *world* state. If, however, we can interpret the increasingly interdependent condition of the planet as a global community or world society, then, surely, the term 'world citizen' is a legitimate one. Thus, the concept is significant not only for our understanding of the changing nature of the state as a political-ethical unit and of the individual as a political-ethical animal, but also for our understanding of the nature of the world. If the modern state has needed citizens for its legitimacy and stability, so too does the emerging global community.

All these considerations about the nature and significance of world citizenship nevertheless give rise to two kinds of sharp disputes. One is engaged within the cosmopolitan camp itself; the other pits the cosmopolitans against their antagonists, who may be conveniently labelled the 'communitarians'. These are the topics of the second and third sections of this chapter.

Interpretations

In the scholarly eagerness to establish world citizenship as an honourable and viable idea, unfortunately the confused usage of the term was revealed, thus preventing any possibility of coming to a definition that would be succinct, comprehensive and generally agreed (Scheffler, 1999: 255 also makes this point). Or perhaps this was, rather, a fortunate outcome of the burgeoning literature, because we now understand much more thoroughly just how complex the concept is and how many components are contained in the simply written term. So, instead of starting the reader off with a definition of our subject, it is better to outline a few recent attempts at presenting the multiform nature of world citizenship. Six interpretations will be surveyed, drawing upon Pogge (1992), Falk (1994), Beitz (1999), Heater (1999), Scheffler (1999) and Delanty (2000). We shall take each in turn, then try to draw some conclusions from these distinct approaches.

However, before starting on this survey, two comments are necessary about the key words. The terms 'world citizenship' and 'cosmopolitan citizenship' are used interchangeably, though in the literature the latter appears to be increasingly favoured. 'World citizenship' is used in the present book on the grounds that 'cosmopolitan citizenship' has a hint of tautology: *kosmopolitēs*, the Greek word from which 'cosmopolitan' derives, means 'world citizen'.

The other point of etymology to make is that 'world citizen'/ 'world citizenship' have no convenient adjectival forms, so that 'cosmopolitan' does service when an adjective is needed in the global context. This practice is used in this book. Admittedly, this is not very satisfactory, for three reasons. One is that the word has meanings quite innocent of the moral, legal and political content of the quality of citizenship. To give two different examples: Marx asserted that the bourgeoisie had 'given a cosmopolitan character to production and consumption in every country' (Marx, 1948: 124), and the term 'a cosmopolitan city' is now common, meaning ethnically or culturally variegated. Second, and related to this point, is the trend among scholars in the field of cosmopolitanism to stress, in post-modernist fashion, the disintegration of even the fragile unity of meaning it might formerly have enjoyed. Because cosmopolitan experiences in the generalized sense are becoming increasingly real, attention must be concentrated on the extra-ordinarily diverse nature of these experiences. Accordingly, some scholars write in terms of many cosmopolitanisms. Bruce Robbins, in introducing a collection of essays on this theme, has declared that

> Like nations, cosmopolitanisms are now plural and particular. Like nations, they are both European and non-European, and they are weak and underdeveloped as well as strong and privileged. And again like the nation, cosmopolitanism is *there* – not merely an abstract idea, like loving one's neighbour as oneself, but habits of thought and feeling that have already shaped and been shaped by particular collectivities, that are socially and geographically situated, hence both limited and empowered. (Cheah and Robbins, 1998: 2)

These considerations divert us from the unity of legal status and of political purpose that are the hallmarks of citizenship. The third reason for using the word 'cosmopolitan' with reluctance is that, even in the moral-political sense, discussion on political cosmopolitanism can so concentrate on policies or institutional structures that the role of the individual *qua* world citizen seems to be at best a subsidiary consideration. So, this extended parenthesis brought to an end, we can now turn to the real purpose of this section, namely, to survey different analyses of the nature and content of world citizenship.

It will be most helpful to start with Charles Beitz's simple model. He distinguishes between what he calls institutional and moral cosmopolitanism. The first 'holds that the world's political structure should be reshaped so that states and other political units are brought under the authority of supranational agencies of some kind' (Beitz, 1999: 287). This form of cosmopolitan thinking argues that current institutions – the UN, human rights regimes, for example – are inadequate to provide human beings with effective means to act and be treated as world citizens. They therefore need to be reformed, supplemented or replaced. In defining the other, moral, expression of cosmopolitanism, Beitz quotes Thomas Pogge's phrase 'that every human being has a global stature as the ultimate unit of moral concern' (*ibid.*; Pogge, 1992: 49). To put the notion negatively: it is unethical to ignore the interests of anyone, wheresoever they might live, when actions are taken that could affect them. But it is crucial to understand the relationship between institutional and moral cosmopolitanism. As Beitz asserts, 'Cosmopolitanism about ethics does not necessarily imply cosmopolitanism about institutions' (Beitz, 1999: 287). What it does seek to provide is a moral basis for judging the aptness of particular kinds of institutions for ensuring that the cosmopolitan ethical principle of the equal worth of all human beings as world citizens is honoured in both political theory and practice.

Thomas Pogge offers a variant on the basic moral/institutional distinction, which he calls moral and legal cosmopolitanism. By legal cosmopolitanism he means commitment 'to a concrete political ideal of a global order under which all persons have equivalent legal rights and duties, that is, are fellow citizens of a universal republic' (Pogge, 1992: 49). In contrast, moral cosmopolitanism 'imposes limits upon our conduct and, in particular, upon our efforts to construct institutional schemes' (*ibid.*). However, Pogge's main theoretical intent is to present his subdivision of moral cosmopolitanism into 'institutional' and 'interactional' forms. Institutional moral cosmopolitanism concerns the laying down of rules of justice to be adhered to by social practices, and the individual's responsibility lies in his/her membership of or involvement in these institutions. Interactional cosmopolitan morality, on the other hand, constrains the individual's conduct when acting personally or in a group.

Samuel Scheffler, also working to a basic two-fold distinction – which he calls 'cosmopolitanism about justice and cosmopolitanism about culture' – writes at a deeper level of analysis than any of the other authors surveyed here. His purpose is to investigate the differences between the extreme and moderate versions of each of these expressions of the cosmopolitan idea. He discerns the two basic interpretations in recent writings on the subject, and defines them as follows:

Cosmopolitanism about justice is opposed to any view that posits principled restrictions on the scope of an adequate conception of justice. In other words, it opposes any view which holds, as a matter of principle, that the norms of justice apply primarily within bounded groups comprising some subset of the global population ...

Cosmopolitanism about culture and the self, meanwhile, is opposed to any suggestion that individuals' well-being or their identity or their capacity for effective human agency normally depends on their membership in a determinate cultural group whose boundaries are reasonably clear and whose stability and cohesion are reasonably secure. (Scheffler, 1999: 256)

From these two definitions Scheffler draws, somewhat repetitively, the two notions of world citizenship that derive from them. Thus, world citizenship as justice 'means that the norms of justice must ultimately be seen as governing the relations of all human beings to each other, and not merely as applying within individual societies or bonded groups of other kinds'; while world citizenship as culture 'means that individuals have the capacity to flourish by forging idiosyncratic identities from heterogeneous cultural sources, and are not to be thought of as constituted or defined by ascriptive ties to a particular culture, community or tradition' (*ibid.*: 258).

Scheffler's main purpose, however, is to examine what he calls an ambiguity in the idea of world citizenship that expresses itself in both forms. This ambiguity lies in the division between writers on the topic who take an extreme and those who take a moderate view of world citizenship. The extreme interpretation argues that one is justified in giving special attention to particular groups, such as family or compatriots, only if they are viewed as examples or parts of the totality of equal human beings; that, since one cannot behave as a good world citizen to all six billion other human beings, one needs for practical reasons, not reasons of principle, to exercise one's global civic virtue on the accessible sample. In contrast, the moderate version of world citizenship recognizes that the individual has a multiplicity of legitimate, separately justifiable, allegiances, among which, however, must be a commitment to humankind beyond one's nearer circles of contact. Also, to stress the cosmopolitan requirement, one's commitment to those closest must be tempered by the need to accommodate a consideration for those more distant. This differentiation, it goes without saying, colours and is replicated in cosmopolitan writers' interpretations of both the justice and culture forms of world citizenship.

The existence of these competing delineations of the cosmopolitan case, Scheffler continues, needs further investigation, despite the commonsense reaction that, 'Whereas the moderate versions of cosmopolitanism may strike some people as being so obvious as to be platitudinous, the extreme versions may seem so implausible as to be difficult to take seriously' (*ibid.*: 262). He believes that the persistence of the seemingly implausible extreme view is due to what he terms 'Nussbaum's dilemma'. Martha Nussbaum is one of the most influential scholars in the field of cosmopolitan writing, in particular through her essay 'Patriotism and Cosmopolitanism' (Nussbaum *et al.*, 1996: 2–17). Scheffler explains that she suggests the acceptance of separate affiliations must inevitably deny the principle of the equal worth of persons: this means, he argues, that, 'extreme cosmopolitanism is simply the inevitable consequence of a serious commitment to equality' (Scheffler, 1999: 262). In plain, blunt terms, patriotism and cosmopolitanism are mutually incompatible: therefore, moderate cosmopolitanism is an untenable confusion. However, Scheffler argues that 'Nussbaum's dilemma' is flawed, in both conception and application: specific relations between individuals, whatever the connections, will always carry with them particular values, or personal relations would be pointless. Also, individuals will always need to be flexible in their relations with institutions, depending on circumstances. Therefore, if the dilemma is ill-founded, rejection of the moderate form of world citizenship is also unwarranted. This is not to dismiss, though, the obvious inevitability of tensions between the competing demands on individuals' feelings and conduct. Scheffler concludes:

> Ultimately, however, the viability of moderate cosmopolitanism must depend on the success of human beings in negotiating a series of ineliminable distinctions – between justice and loyalty, tradition and choice, past and future, ourselves and others – without allowing those distinctions to calcify into rigid and destructive dichotomies. (*ibid.*: 276)

My own interpretation is much more superficial than Scheffler's but slightly more complicated than the simple distinction between moral/cultural and institutional/legal cosmopolitanism, recognizing not only a larger number of components but placing them in a spectrum from vague to precise, stretching from identity to morality, to law, to politics. The vaguest form of world citizenship is the sense of identity with the whole of humanity, of membership of the human race. Less vague is acceptance of some moral responsibility for the condition of the planet and its inhabitants, human and even non-human. A development of this ethical position, one rather more precise, is the recognition that 'one is subject to and should live by the codes of supra- and trans-national laws (i.e. natural and international) and possibly, in due time, to a universal world law' (Heater, 1999: 136). And the most precise commitment to the idea, indeed ideal, of world citizenship is that which embraces the need for some effective form(s) of supra-national political authority and for political action beyond the nation-state. This is a spectrum also in the sense that the four main 'tones' of world citizenship shade into their neighbours and that all are essential to the understanding and realization of world citizenship.

Richard Falk proffers a similar pattern of four 'levels' of the extension of citizenship globally and five 'images' of global citizenship. He starts with an approach which he calls 'aspirational in spirit ... [and] that posits for the planet as a whole a set of conditions of peace and justice and sustainability ... A normative perspective' (Falk, 1994: 131). Falk's second level is produced by the forces of globalization, which he views as strengthening the global mode of thinking of the first. His third level he calls 'a politics of impossibility based on ... attitudes of necessity' (*ibid.*: 132). This level of world citizenship derives from a recognition that more effective global political behaviour and control of the onrushing environmental disasters are imperative for the survival of the human race. The fourth level follows as 'a politics of mobilization ... to make "the impossible" happen' (*ibid.*): not just to be aware, to think, but to do, to take action to force change. Falk expands on the ways in which these attitudes generate five images or views of the global citizen. The first is the individual who advocates institutional reform, usually mixing utopianism with pragmatism. The second is the 'man or woman of transnational affairs' (*ibid.*: 134), the globe-trotting business elite, who are taking on a cosmopolitan identity because of their work- and lifestyles. The third view of world citizenship according to Falk is demonstrated by the person who adapts his or her lifestyle in accordance with the precept of global economic and environmental sustainability. The fourth image is provided by the integrative process of the European Union, a regional version of a transnational citizenship. Falk's fifth style is provided by the activities of grassroots organizations through pressure groups that have global agendas and a global reach.

Individuals engaged in this work are creating a global civil society. Falk explains their significance:

> Traditional citizenship operates spatially, global citizenship operates temporally, reaching out to a future to-be-created, and making such a person 'a citizen pilgrim', that is, someone on a journey to 'a country' to be established in the future in accordance with more idealistic and normatively rich conceptions of political community. (*ibid.*: 138–9; see also Chapter 6 below)

We move on now to Gerard Delanty's interpretation. He identifies four 'conceptions' of cosmopolitanism – legal or internationalism, political or globalization, cultural or transnationalism, and civic or post-nationalism. His first conception is a weak, Kantian cosmopolitanism centred on a system of states constrained by law. By political cosmopolitanism he means the emergence of a global civil society and the power of globalization in generating non- (even anti-) state modes of politics, including environmental consciousness. Delanty contrasts legal and political cosmopolitanism by associating the former with *government* and the latter with *governance*. In identifying cultural cosmopolitanism, he refers to the phenomenon of the world's peoples becoming increasingly mobile for reasons both fortunate and unfortunate, the result of which is the multiplication of the experience of diaspora, with many millions of people retaining their original cultures yet being territorially displaced. The term 'rooted cosmopolitanism' is used by other writers for this condition. For his fourth form of global citizenship, Delanty borrows from the work of Habermas (which we shall outline in Chapter 3 below) and develops from this his own idea of 'civic cosmopolitanism': he seeks to relate cosmopolitanism to a non-national sense of community. ('Rooted cosmopolitanism' and 'civic cosmopolitanism' are outlined in the Conclusion below.)

Before attempting to derive some general understanding about the nature of world citizenship and the complexities of both the concept and the academic debate, it will be helpful to return briefly to Pogge's article because he also provides a kind of highest common factor of the differing interpretations. As he says:

> Three elements are shared by all cosmopolitan positions. First, *individualism*: the ultimate units of concern are human beings, or persons. ... Second, *universality*: the status of the ultimate

unit of concern attaches to every living human being equally
... Third, *generality*: this special status has global force.
Persons are ultimate units of concern for everyone – not only
for their compatriots, fellow religionists, or such like. (Pogge,
1992: 48–9)

Even so, as we have seen, this triple covering of agreement needs to
be lifted in order to examine the varieties of disagreements and
complications that would otherwise be concealed. This detail also
clusters into a three-fold pattern. Let us label these features: range,
intensity and status.

By range we mean the basic divisions of moral/cultural and legal/
institutional/justice as identified by Beitz, Scheffler and (with his
subdivisions of moral cosmopolitanism) Pogge. In addition, we have
noticed the longer lists of Delanty, Falk and Heater, which, in
essence, are more detailed breakdowns of the moral and institutional
distinction. However, these fuller lists also trespass into the
intensity category (e.g. Heater) and the status category (e.g.
Delanty). So, what do we mean by intensity? This is the depth of
commitment the world citizen has in performing that role. In
Heater's outline terminology it is vague-to-precise; in Scheffler's
thorough argument it is the partition between the extreme and
moderate forms of cosmopolitan thinking. Range and intensity
clearly exercise the minds of the half-dozen contributors to the issue
who have been selected here. However, at least implicit in the
presentation of their analyses is the third matter – the issue of the
status of world citizenship. There are three positions: one is that,
however embryonically, it *exists*; the second is that it might or *will
exist* in the future; and the third is that it *should exist*. By connecting
these three positions with the issue of intensity, all can be held
simultaneously. The reason is that it is possible to argue that world
citizenship already exists in a partial form; that one can envisage, in
the light of current trends, its expansion into a fuller form, while
believing that some kind of 'complete' world citizenship is an
outcome devoutly to be desired.

Disputes

Intellectual awareness and pricked consciences have episodically
stimulated into life the idea and ideal of world citizenship for more

than two thousand years. There is clearly a human need to hang on to the cosmopolitan principle, a need that has grown from the conviction and hope that by living in accord with the principle, humankind can ascend to a higher plane of felicity and morality. Yet, attractive as this promise must seem, it has been the object of considerable hostile criticism, some quite virulent. World citizenship, these opponents argue, is neither desirable nor practicable. The debate between the two camps has been engaged with particular vigour since the mid-1990s, epitomized by the harsh words of Danilo Zolo, who speaks of 'the empty rhetoric of "cosmopolitan citizenship"' (Zolo, 1997: 133), expanding on this judgement thus:

> On both the cultural and the economic level, phenomena of globalization appear to be destined to produce further differentiation and fragmentation of the international arena over the next few decades. Thus terms such as global civil society, universal citizenship, world constitutionalism and transnational democracy may be said to belong to a normative vocabulary which draws strongly on wishful thinking. Furthermore, not only are the objectives they refer to almost certainly unrealisable in the foreseeable future, they are also of limited desirability. (Zolo, 1997: 153)

So, although the prime purpose of this book is to present the arguments in favour of accepting the concept and status of world citizenship, it cannot be gainsaid that powerful objections have been arrayed to reject the cosmopolitans' stance. Consequently, for the rest of this chapter we shall be examining the main planks in the debate, though leaving the detail to Chapters 3 to 7. For convenience we shall call the supporters of world citizenship 'cosmopolitans' or 'cosmopolites' (not following the useful, though not universally accepted, distinction drawn by Tuan (see Cheah and Robbins, 1998: 3)). Their opponents we shall call 'communitarians' – i.e., those who believe that the central role of the community (usually equated with the state) as the provider of ethical political standards should at all costs be preserved. We shall look in turn at the ways in which the communitarians argue that world citizenship is both undesirable and unworkable (or non-existent), followed by rebuttals from the cosmopolitan side. By displaying these cases we shall be able to discern the strengths and weaknesses of each.

Two major propositions can be advanced for preserving state citizenship against any diversion of allegiance to a notional world citizenship. These are the claimed positive need for retaining the state as the main source of authority, security and stability, and for sustaining the traditional community values including patriotism as an essential contribution to this purpose. The ethical argument, indeed, has two aspects. The root theory is that the state is the source of human social morality; the practical corollary is that firm allegiance to the state is an essential requirement for the maintenance of a moral communal life. This proposition renders cosmopolitanism undesirable because it questions the assumption about moral identity. The dispute between the communitarians and cosmopolitans on this issue is so central to the subject of world citizenship that it is examined at some length in Chapter 3. Let it suffice here to quote one authority, who sums up with clarity the crucial value of retaining traditional forms of community which might be under threat from cosmopolitanism. Samuel Scheffler explains that individuals, as members of established communities,

> are typically confronted with a reasonably well-articulated set of expectations concerning the content of [the responsibilities required of them]. Furthermore, the community provides an institutional framework within which those responsibilities may be discharged, as well as a set of mechanisms ... which serve to nurture and support the motivations that individuals must have if they are reliably to fulfil their responsibilities. In short, the community ... provides for them what might be called the 'infrastructure of responsibility'. (Scheffler, 1999: 270–1)

The communitarian case is also based on the practical benefits that the state provides for the individual and the international community, and which are so desirable that they must be protected against weakening through a siphoning-off of any authority in the interests of pursuing the cosmopolitan agenda. Gertrude Himmelfarb, for instance, is adamant about this. She declares:

> The social programs associated with a welfare state, or public education, or religious liberty and tolerance, or the prohibition of racial and sexual discrimination ... depend not on a nebulous cosmopolitan order but a vigorous administrative and legal order deriving its authority from the state. ... So too the first requirement of international cooperation ... essential

for economic development, environmental protection, and 'quality-of-life issues', is the existence of states capable of undertaking and enforcing international agreements. (Nussbaum *et al*, 1996: 76)

One of the most controversial and commented upon features of our increasingly complex and changing world, as we have already noted, is globalization. There is considerable dispute about the strength of this transforming tendency and consequently its effects on the desirability and practicality of world citizenship. At this stage we need to focus on the argument that the state, even in this new economic, financial and communications environment, still retains its function as a – indeed the – key actor on the world stage. Accepting that change is happening and will happen at an accelerating rate, the case for upholding the central function of the state is that its legitimacy and power alone can effect the changes in the least disruptive way possible. This belief also affects judgements on the allied matter of governance. Globalization, however it is assessed, and the felt need for new and flexible means of governance combine to force a rethinking of the role of the state. For the opponents of cosmopolitanism, the state, adaptable and adapted to these novel needs, is still vital in order to perform a 'pivotal' role, to use Hirst and Thompson's word. As they say, 'Nation-states should no longer be seen as "governing powers" ... but as loci from which forms of governance can be proposed, legitimated and monitored' (Hirst and Thompson, 1999: 275). Furthermore, globalization may well not be undermining the state's purpose and value as much as is often suggested. Even in the economic sphere, where the globalizing thrust of multinational companies is seen as a threat to the state, the need for the nation-state to retain as much authority as it can is in fact reinforced by this development. Monitoring, authorization and control – governance in fact – are cardinal roles of the state, to protect the world community as a whole, as well as the interests of its own citizens.

But even if world citizenship were not so evidently undesirable, continues the communitarian, it is certainly an idea incapable of being translated into practice; moreover, the cosmopolitan's assertion that the status already exists is a gross exaggeration. Before proceeding to the main analysis of this aspect of the anti-cosmopolitan case, however, we must take note of the stark realities of international politics. The USA has been notoriously dragging its heels on two key issues, namely, the creation of a world criminal court and measures to reduce the pace of global warming. China is notoriously dismissive of the concept of universal human rights. These examples are significant because the two states are so powerful. Many lesser examples could be cited. If governments are so determined to block progress on the central issues upon which the evolution of world citizenship depends, how can anyone expect that the idea can possibly be realized?

To proceed now with the components of the communitarians' case. Three major prongs in their attack on the practicability of world citizenship relate to identity, human rights and law. These are dealt with in their subject contexts in Chapters 3 and 4, so are only very briefly considered here. First, on the matter of identity, the communitarian argues that the deep roots of national and ethnic consciousness are evident throughout the world. Replacing or even overlaying them with a cosmopolitan identity is a virtual impossibility, not just because of the strength of traditional roots, but also because any additional or replacement roots would take such a very long time to grow to any effective strength. We may cite Anthony Smith on this viewpoint: 'A timeless global culture answers to no living needs and conjures no memories. . . . It strikes no chord among the vast masses of peoples divided in their habitual communities' (Smith, 1995: 24). Second, the communitarian holds that human rights are not world citizens' rights, are not evidence that a world citizenship status exists in embryo. Human rights regimes depend for their operation on individual states and on the state system protecting persons either as *state* citizens or as *human beings*. Third, in international law there is no such status as world citizenship; the 'person' is the state, and citizenship is defined as nationality. So much, at this juncture, for the arguments treated in the specialized core chapters.

What we need to treat in greater detail in this chapter is the denial of the claimed workability of world citizenship through analogies drawn from the status and practice of sub-global citizenship. This portion of the antis' case can be conveniently divided into four, namely, the fallacy of the 'domestic analogy' as a general problem; the proposition that world citizenship as envisaged by the cosmopolitans is not *real* citizenship; the canvassed notion of a global civil society is not a true parallel to civil societies within states; and even the use of citizenship of the European Union as a model for extrapolation to the global plane is misleading.

A succinct definition of the domestic analogy has been provided by Hidemi Suganami:

> The 'domestic analogy' is presumptive reasoning which holds that there are certain similarities between domestic and international phenomena; that, in particular, the conditions of order within states are similar to those of order between them; and that therefore those institutions which sustain order domestically should be reproduced at the international level. (Suganami, 1989: 1)

The domestic analogy has been widely criticized by International Relations scholars and since some of the academic debate concerns the validity of this kind of intellectual procedure it is therefore germane to its use in the world citizenship issue. By examining the three examples of world citizenship itself, global civil society and EU citizenship, it is hoped that the doubts about the use of the domestic analogy in this field of study will become clear.

The purpose of the citizen–state nexus is to distinguish citizens from non-citizens, the latter being aliens or, historically, the lower strata of the state's population. Yet these crucial distinctions cannot be true for so-called world citizens because in this context there are no aliens outside the realms of science fiction, and in our egalitarian age there can be no admission that lower, excluded strata exist either. This distinguishing function of citizenship in fact goes further than that, for the act of distinction is a two-way force. While the force of differentiation excludes the non-citizen, an opposite-and-equal force integrates the body of individuals who are citizens. And this integrative force is patriotism or nationalism, the very vigour of which cosmopolitanism is designed to emasculate. In the modern world, David Miller has asserted, the consolidation of national identities alone has 'enabled large masses of people to work together as citizens' (Miller, 1999: 68). Without the power of a bonding force such as this, the vastly greater mass of the total world population could not conceivably work together; they could not be world citizens. Yet, the communitarians argue, the sheer vastness of the world's total population would preclude the creation of such a cohesive force.

Moreover, even if one accepts the fundamental homogeneity of humankind, that does not denote a universal citizenship in any proper sense of the term. Because citizenship as a status and as a sense of identity relates the individual to the state, it follows that a world citizen could hold that title only as a member of a world state. Yet (with the exception of Dante, in a totally different, medieval setting) no cosmopolitan thinker of any distinction – neither Marcus Aurelius, nor Kant, nor present-day scholars – has envisaged a single global state. Marcus, for instance, uses the notion of a cosmopolis as a figure of speech: he referred to 'the Universe *as it were* a state' (Marcus Aurelius Antoninus, 1961: IV, 4, emphasis added). And Martha Nussbaum's case, as Michael Walzer has pointed out (Nussbaum *et al.*, 1996: 126), is no more than an argument by analogy: that we should *regard* all human beings as fellow-citizens, not that they *are* in any real sense.

Even the weaker sense of citizenship that is sometimes recommended, namely, membership of a civil society below the formalized level of the state, has been rejected as an exemplification of world citizenship when individuals act on a transnational plane. The equation of the activities of non-governmental organizations (NGOs), particularly of a humanitarian nature, with a global civil society has been denied. The core reason is that these 'are ultimately depending on shelter in and protection from "decent, democratic states", in order to help victims of war or victims of political oppression in undemocratic and conflict-ridden states. Instead of the dream of global citizenship, we face the grim reality of what could be called "selective humanitarianism"' (Hettne, 2000: 36). More fundamentally, it must be remembered, the term 'civil society' has been used to indicate a socio-economic homogeneous base upon which can be built the legal and political components of state citizenship. Is this process, it must therefore be asked, being replicated on the global level, or can it be? To argue thus is a clear example of domestic analogy; and, to its critics, it is just as clearly 'fallacious and misguided' because the required cultural and political cohesion does not exist (see Zolo, 1997: esp. 130–1).

If, however, these powerful arguments against the domestic analogy can be so successfully mobilized against the cosmopolites, surely they can call upon the example of the European Union as an actual achievement of the analogic process. Not so, say the communitarians: Europe cannot be thought of or used as a stepping-stone to the world (see, e.g., Bańkowski and Christodou-lidis, 1999: 93–8). Theirs is a dual attack. One prong is the basic communitarian argument that citizenship in its true meaning requires a tightly knit community to which citizens can display an effective allegiance, and that the EU, *pace* the legal status of citizenship of the Union, is no such bonded community. Reference to the concept of a European citizenship is therefore a distortion of the term 'citizenship' on a par with the use of the term 'world citizenship'. Furthermore, if a group of countries with so much in common has not evolved a proper unified citizenship, how much less likely is the construction of a real world citizenship? The second prong of the attack on the EU analogy is the demonstration that, ironically, it in truth *undermines* the cosmopolites' own agenda. The reason is that, if the EU is solidifying to the extent of rendering its own citizenship credible, then that form of the status will become a 'bounded citizenship' just like national citizenship but on a bigger scale, perhaps that of a 'fortress Europe', thus even more resistant to an open, worldwide citizenship.

Although much of the communitarian argument has been passed over in just a few sentences because of the separate treatment under the headings especially of identity, morality and law in Chapters 3 and 4, it is hoped that there is sufficient indication in the above pages to show the reader the strength of the case against world citizenship. And, to capture the hesitations of academics faced with the request to embrace the cosmopolitan thesis, let us conclude this survey of the opposition's case with the succinct assertion of Michael Walzer:

> No one has ever offered me citizenship [of the world], or described the naturalization process, or enlisted me in the world's institutional structures, or provided me with a list of the benefits and obligations of citizenship, or shown me the world's calendar and the common celebrations and commemorations of its citizens. (Nussbaum *et al.*, 1996: 125)

And one may add the communitarians' clinching rider that few people would be willing to adapt the famous adage of Horace – '*dulce et decorum est pro patria mori*' – by substituting '*mundo*' for '*patria*', to die for the world.

Communitarian thinkers have built up a formidably solid case to protect their conviction that the community of a people forming a state must be preserved. This intellectual and emotional defence has been erected and counterattacks launched against what they see as the false allurements of the cosmopolites' vision of the capacity of the individual to feel a holistic and mutual kinship with and responsibility for the human race. There follows then the inevitable question: can the cosmopolitans so undermine these communitarian defences and so resist their attacks as to confirm the validity of their own convictions? The cosmopolitan argument can be followed through in three thrusts: that the communitarians have constructed their case on misrepresentation of the cosmopolitan objective; that the cosmopolitan alternative to the communitarian is indeed desirable; and that it is both workable and, in albeit primitive form, already evolving.

Generalizations about each of the sides in the debate are not easy because there are differences of emphasis among the writers in both camps. However, it is reasonably fair to suggest that some communitarians have done less than justice to the subtlety of the modern cosmopolitan recommendations. Part of the problem lies in the variety of meanings that have become attached to the term 'world citizenship', as we have seen in the second section of this chapter. The point to stress here is that any criticism of the idea of world citizenship that takes little or no account of this complexity can be challenged as misleading. In fact, communitarian criticisms of cosmopolitanism often focus on the latter's weakening, even displacement, of patriotism as a cohering virtue and of the nation-state as an absolutely essential sovereign political unit. Now, although it is true that in the past world citizenship has been reckoned by some as necessitating a federal world state (or *vice versa*), many other advocates of world citizenship have denied this, and it would be difficult today to find serious scholars who would enjoin such a radical political development. As Chris Brown has written: 'the cosmopolitan position is perfectly compatible with the pragmatic acceptance of a world of divided jurisdictions' (Brown, 1992: 13). The extraordinary persistence of the image of concentric circles of identity and loyalty, as will be explained in Chapter 2, is assuredly powerful evidence that world citizenship presupposes complementing and not replacing state citizenship. Basing their arguments on the broad and non-exclusive meaning of world citizenship, cosmopolites are able to insist that the development of this status is in fact both desirable and workable. We take each of these justifications in turn.

World citizenship, it can be asserted, is desirable for both negative and positive reasons. The negative reasons derive from what are perceived as certain undesirable features of the modern nation-state. For all the signal services it has provided in securing internal stability within its territory and defence and welfare for its citizens, the nation-state as a political institution has its faults, faults that are becoming increasingly evident. The evils of nationalist ideology have grown from the identification of the political state with the cultural nation and the concentration of loyalty as patriotism to the state and the state alone has sometimes degenerated to a xenophobic intolerance. A form of multiple allegiance would dilute these unhealthy concentrated emotions. Also, on sheer pragmatic grounds, it is advisable for citizens to diversify their attachments in recognition of the inability of the presentday nation-state to secure its citizens' interests, rights even, quite as effectively as hitherto. The social contract interpretation of the citizen–state relationship is starting to lose its credibility. Specifically, the individual's economic interests are more and more determined by the effects of globalization; and his or her rights are, in moral terms, safeguarded in principle by the list of human rights, which are universally recognized and one aspect of which, in Stanley Hoffmann's words, is 'an incipient cosmopolitanism' (Hoffmann, 1981: 95).

Yet the cosmopolitans' reaction to the communitarians' position also has its positive side. Unique state citizenship is not just inadequate, obsolete even, in its self-sufficiency: world citizenship is a good in itself. By enlarging the individual's communal perspective, cosmopolitanism supplies the inestimable benefit of increasing each person's quantum of tolerance and empathy. Can the attainment of this goal or even a better approximation to it be anything but a social good?

If the ancient Stoics understood this, as we shall see in Chapter 2, how much more is it not evident today, living as we are in the shadow of recent totalitarian and genocidal horrors and caught up inextricably in the networks of globalization? It has moreover often been said, and bears repeating, that globalization has a deeply ambivalent relationship with world citizenship. Transnational financial and commercial business may give those engaged in these activities a sense of being world citizens, in Falk's second meaning. Nevertheless, not only is this experience confined to just a tiny proportion of the world's population, it can be argued – and was by the participants in the anti-capitalist demonstrations in Seattle, London and Prague at the close of the twentieth century – that economic globalization is severely detrimental to the vast majority of the world's population. If that is so, then a fuller, truer world citizenship is needed, and speedily. Human lives are being inexorably shaped by the forces of global integration, yet the institutions exerting these forces are unaccountable for their actions.

Citizenship is a political device, *inter alia*, for demanding and ensuring accountability. That process is missing from the global level; in all justice, the gap should be filled.

All very well; but are these, albeit desirable, hopes likely to be realized outside the realm of an Aristophanean cloud-cuckoo land? Again, we can approach this question by presenting the cosmopolites' negative and positive arguments. The negative case is that, for all the communitarians' persistence that the nation-state is still the uniquely sovereign political institution, there is mounting evidence that it cannot in fact perform all the functions it has accumulated since the seventeenth century: the Westphalian system is crumbling. If the state is not guaranteeing its citizens' rights, perhaps it also has not the strength to resist attempts to supplement its duties. In truth, in the socio-economic sphere, poor, disadvantaged and disaster-stricken peoples are already being helped by the international community.

This observation takes us on to the positive case for arguing that world citizenship is feasible. What modern cosmopolites are asking is that humankind and its institutions should adapt to changing conditions, not necessarily by adopting any completely new way of thinking, but by recovering and acting upon a venerable philosophical tradition. Because the basic principles of cosmopolitanism are not novel and because adaptation has been a constant feature of human history, the cosmopolitans' agenda should not be totally rejected as impossible. Indeed, building upon established ways of thinking, behaviour and institutional practice is precisely what the cosmopolitans require. International law is now edging towards the acceptance of a world law under which supranational courts can try and commit for punishment citizens of any state who violently transgress the universal code of human rights and humane behaviour. Indeed, the very acceptance of the notion of universal human rights reveals a belief that a higher code than that delineated for state citizens is expected and obedience to it can be required of individuals. What is more, a form of transnational civil society can be said to exist through the activities of international non-governmental organizations (INGOs), a base from which to develop other forms of participation in global affairs. So, embryonic legal and political modes of world citizenship exist and can be strengthened (see Chapters 4 and 6 below). Social and economic world citizenship is also implicit in active concern for the plight of so many in the so-called developing nations (see Chapter 5 below).

And, finally, if the existence of nation-states is thought to be a cast-iron argument for the indispensability of bounded, national citizenship, the sub-continental, admittedly young and weak experiment of citizenship of the European Union is evidence that supranational citizenship is possible.

The reader was promised no more than an outline in this section of the cosmopolitans' plan of campaign against the communitarians' defence of their traditional position. The following chapters provide some of the detail. For there is sufficient strength in the communitarians' arguments to warrant further, consolidating thinking by the cosmopolitans; and there is sufficient validity in the cosmopolitans' arguments to justify that further intellectual investment.

CHAPTER 2

Historical Patterns

The history of cosmopolitan thinking is a fascinating story, though it cannot detain us too long, partly because it is available elsewhere (Schlereth, 1977: xvii–xxv; Heater, 1996) and partly because the purpose of this book is to analyse the idea with a focus on the present. Nevertheless, an awareness of some patterns that may be discerned in the overall long span of time since the notion of world citizenship first emerged will help to place the present in perspective and further illuminate the major issues in the controversies between the camps of the cosmopolitans and communitarians. Expositions and interpretations of three very different kinds of historical patterns form the content of this chapter. We start with the most influential, the Stoic concept of the cosmopolis.

The Stoic Tradition

The belief – assertion, indeed – that individuals could consider themselves to be and behave as citizens of the world did not, in truth, have a very auspicious beginning. It is possible that Diogenes of Sinope coined the term that we now render as 'citizen of the world', yet it was he who gained notoriety by his shameless behaviour, for example, living in a capacious jar in the market-place, excreting in public and behaving, it was said, like a dog. He and his followers were called 'Cynics', a word deriving from the Greek word for dog. Even so, this lifestyle was itself a deliberate proclamation of his world citizenship – challenging by shock tactics the narrow conventions of the *polis*. He rejected the status of a *politēs*, a citizen, in favour of that of a *kosmopolitēs*, a citizen of the 'cosmos', the universe. Man, he was proclaiming, is not, as his contemporary Aristotle asserted, a political animal; he is, as a species, a multicultural animal. The culture of any given state or people is not the only one; no mode of behaviour is necessarily right. It is this openness of mind, the very negation of xenophobia and of the *hubris* of conceited patriotism, that is one of the crucial characteristics of the citizen of the world. One authority has summed up Diogenes' significance as follows: 'Diogenes' unique achievement of cosmopolitanism, whereby the whole world was his country, found expression both in his concern for his fellow men and in his submission to God' (Stanton, 1968: 186).

His most distinguished follower was Crates of Thebes who, in turn, taught Zeno of Citium. Zeno had migrated from his Cypriot home, then, in 310 BC, established his own school in Athens in the painted porch (*stoa poikelē*) of his house, thus inaugurating a system of thought consequently called Stoicism. Stoicism provided an extraordinarily durable philosophical support for the cosmopolitan idea (a mere portion of its total thought system), even though we must be on our guard against attributing too precise and modern an interpretation of the concept from its ancient expositions. Interest in and commitment to Stoicism lasted for half a millennium in the ancient world from its foundation to about AD 200, and it enjoyed a revival from about 1500 to 1800; although it must be said that in each of these blocks of time its influence waxed and waned so that we should refer more precisely to a pattern of five periods: Old Stoa, Middle Stoa, Late Stoa, Renaissance Neostoicism and the Enlightenment.

The key name after Zeno was Chrysippus, who developed Stoicism into a full philosophical system. With his death, *c.* 206 BC, the Old Stoa phase came to an end. Roughly half a century later the school of thought was revived (the Middle Stoa) by Panaetius (d. 109 BC) and then Posidonius (d. 51 BC), the most famous pupil of the latter being Cicero (d. 43 BC). So the political context of Stoic thinking had by this time shifted to Rome. Something under a century after Cicero's death, Seneca (d. AD 65) expounded the Stoic beliefs, which were formulated more systematically by Epictetus (d. AD 135) and more memorably by the Emperor Marcus Aurelius, with whose death, in 180, the Late Stoa effectively ended.

One of the most crucial concepts handed down by the Stoics was the notion of Natural Law, which underlay much Roman and medieval Christian thinking, without the Stoic consolidation of the concept being explicitly recognized. Not until the late fifteenth century did the study of the Stoic texts start to revive with their publication, at first in the original Greek and Latin and then in translation. The idea of world citizenship appears in essays by Montaigne (d. 1592) and Bacon (d. 1606). In his *Second Treatise of Civil Government*, published in 1690, Locke expresses Stoic-like cosmopolitan thoughts. But it was the mid-to-late eighteenth century that witnessed the claims by so many notable Enlightenment figures that they were 'citizens of the world' – for instance, Diderot, Schiller, Paine. And some openly expressed their intellectual debt to the ancient Stoics – we may instance the influence of Cicero and Seneca on Franklin and Marcus Aurelius on Voltaire. But these were no more than attitudes of mind, all paling in comparison with Kant's intellectual commitment to the cosmopolitan ideal at the very end of the century.

So much for basic chronology. Against this background we need to sketch the answers to four questions. How did cosmopolitanism arise out of the Stoic philosophy? How does one explain the episodic nature of its appearances? What was the content of Stoic cosmopolitanism? What, if any, is its relevance for today?

Of all the branches of philosophy, the Stoics gave primacy to ethics. And in developing their ethical principles they stressed two ideas that are particularly germane to the topic of world citizenship. One is the naturalness of virtue; the other is their concept of the relationship between self-centredness and concern for others. Stoics urged that one should 'live according to nature'. One's actions should be shaped according to the laws of nature, according to the will of God (or the gods) and, by so doing, live a good life, which is itself the path to true happiness. But what could be more natural than self-preservation? And what, then, of ethical principles? Yet the Stoics resolved this apparently contradictory argument for selfishness by construing concern for one's own well-being as embracing the well-being of the extensions of one's self, that is, one's kin. It was then but a series of ethical steps to encompass the whole of humanity in one's concern in a pattern of relationships we shall examine in the third section of this chapter. This pattern is one of concentric circles.

How – our second question – may we explain the fact that

interest in Stoicism burgeoned in five separate periods of history? Explanations must necessarily be tentative, but it may be noted that each era shared two characteristics: heightened awareness of the wider world, and of the role of individuals and texts in broadcasting the notion of world citizenship. In the late fourth century BC, the Greek *poleis* came under Macedonian dominion and became part of Alexander's great empire; and in 336 Zeno started teaching. By 146 Rome had expanded beyond the confines of Italy, let alone Latium, and had acquired the overseas territories of Spain, the west Mediterranean islands, Carthage and its hinterland, the east Adriatic littoral, Macedonia and Greece, and in 144 Panaetius arrived in Rome. By the first century AD, when Seneca was writing, the Empire stretched from Britain to Mauretania, Lusitania to Cappadocia. One and a half millennia later, Renaissance Neostoicism was spurred by the translation of the ancient texts, while the voyages of discovery unveiled not only greater knowledge of the Asian and African continents but revealed the very existence of a New World. Subsequently, increased colonization and commerce in the eighteenth century triggered a fascination with 'exotic' peoples and lands so different from Europe, while Paris, the cosmopolitan capital, provided the venue for *philosophes* captivated by the teachings of the ancient Stoics and Renaissance Neostoics. Moreover, as the use of the word 'exotic' indicates, the expansion of geographical awareness in each of these five eras included a recognition of the extraordinary ethnic and cultural complexity of peoples who were, even so, all members of the human race.

And so to address our third question, namely, what is the content of Stoic cosmopolitanism? This is no easy question to answer, partly because the cardinal works and ideas of Zeno and Chrysippus survive only in fragments or secondary references; partly because, inevitably over a period of five hundred years, expositions and emphases changed; and partly because modern scholarly exegesis has generated differing interpretations.

Now, although Zeno and Chrysippus probably codified the notion of the *kosmopolis*, the elements in this original Greek Stoic interpretation contained neither much originality nor a meaning of much practical use (see Baldry, 1965). This statement is not meant as a churlish denial of the significance of the Old Stoa, but rather an attempt to place it in historical context: to recognize its drawing upon earlier Greek thought, yet not denying the obvious fact that the pinning down of cosmopolitan thinking by the Stoics of the

Roman periods could scarcely have happened if Zeno had not organized a school in his decorated porch. The early Stoics took ideas from the intellectual climate of their time and used them to lay down certain basic principles that can be thought of as components of world citizenship. Let us imagine them as six tesserae of a mental mosaic.

One was the notion of an essential global unity, that human beings, for all their cultural differences, are of but a single species and may be perceived as living in one great world society, the *oikoumenē*.

The second and third ideas, in combination the most powerful of the Stoic concepts, were their notions of *logos* (speech and rational thought) and of a universal law. In fact, that wise philosopher of Ephesus, Heraclitus, had fused these two ideas some two centuries before Zeno. He declared that:

> Those who speak with understanding must rely on what is common to all, as a city relies on its law, and with far greater reliance. For all human laws are nourished by one law, the divine law, which has all the power it desires and is enough, and more than enough, for all. (quoted in Baldry, 1965: 26–7)

Those English words, 'speak' and 'understanding', are encapsulated in the Greek word '*logos*'. Man, alone of all the animals, has the power of speech, by means of which faculty he is able to frame his unique capacity for rational thought, a capacity which, in turn, he is able to use to comprehend the universal law.

But – and this is the fourth element in Greek cosmopolitan thinking – that universal law is divinely delivered. The gods (or God) are part of the universe, and man's endowment with *logos* gives him access to the numinous. Hence the more accurate rendering of the word '*kosmopolitēs*' as 'citizen of the universe' rather than 'of the world'. Only by comprehending the divine natural law can a man be a *kosmopolitēs*. This links to the fifth and sixth elements in the cosmopolis of the Old Stoa, namely, that only the wise can be regarded as its citizens, and only the wise are able to use their rational capacity, not just to live in accordance with the divine code of law but also, by so doing, to live in harmony. For *homonoia*, harmony or concord, is the chief end of association, whether within a *polis*, in the relationships between *poleis*, or in the metaphysical *polis* of the *kosmos*.

Does the mosaic of the Greek Stoic cosmopolis turn out to be, therefore, nothing but a metaphor? We have certainly come to think so. Just compare these two statements, the first published initially in 1935, the second in 1951:

[The Stoics] thought of a larger world than the little old republic; they pictured all the universe as one great polity. Who taught them that? It was Alexander. So they thought of all mankind as one republic of human beings, all citizens, Greeks or barbarians, women or slaves, all one great state of Humanity, where every citizen has a man's duty to do, to serve all mankind. (Glover, 1944: 215)

When [the Stoics] speak of a cosmic city, they mean nothing comparable to an empire of Alexander extending to the ends of the earth; it is a question for them of human relationships, free of all political form. But, in order to explain these relation-ships, they employ political vocabulary, having no other at their disposal. (Bréhier, 1951: 263)

Thus, although the word 'metaphor' is a little hard, perhaps, the message of the Old Stoa is now thought to be much nearer to being a figure of speech than a literal 'blueprint' for a world state. The *kosmopolitēs* – the citizen of the world, if you wish – neither inhabited nor ever conceived of inhabiting a gigantic *polis* (a contradiction in terms in any case because a *polis* was defined by its compact dimensions). The world citizen was a man who believed that the local laws and customs of his *polis* led to a one-dimensional moral life. The Stoic, in contrast to the Cynic, did not renounce his citizenship, even though the *polis* structure was decaying and was being superseded in the late fourth century BC. He did, however, grasp what he believed to be the truth of a higher set of principles to supplement his civic life and by which to live a more richly moral existence, a divinely ordained morality learned through the precious gift of reason.

How, we must now ask, was this handful of principles received and accommodated by the Roman Stoics and how did they add to them? Let us pursue each of the six fundamental concepts into the eras of the Middle Stoa and Late Stoa. The notions of the essential oneness of mankind was strengthened by developments unconnected with Stoic philosophy. For the Greeks, the awareness of mankind as a single species was always under threat of challenge by the deep-seated belief in the unbridgeable distinction between Greek and barbarian. The Romans entertained no such xenophobia. And so the extensive Roman Empire, irrespective of its multicultural composition, could, to Posidonius' mind, be equated with the Greek vision of the *oikoumenē*.

This was, however, a superficial development compared with the consolidation of the ideas of *logos* and natural law, which crucially accepted the rational foundation of morality and the moral foundation of natural law. Cicero and Marcus Aurelius were equally succinct in asserting that all human beings are linked by the reasoning faculty: 'that bond of connection,' declared Cicero, 'is reason and speech, which ... associate men together and unite them in a sort of natural fraternity' (Cicero, 1956: I, xvi, 50); while Marcus, stressing the strength of the kinship, explained that 'it is a community based not on blood or seed, but on mind' (XII, 26, quoted in Stanton, 1968: 189). Cicero also provided a very famous definition of natural law, the importance and influence of which it would be difficult to exaggerate. A portion of this informs the reader that:

> True law is right reason in agreement with nature; it is of universal application, unchanging and everlasting; it summons to duty by its commands, and averts from wrongdoing by its prohibitions. ... We cannot be freed from its obligations by senate or people, and we need not look outside ourselves for an expounder or interpreter of it. (Cicero, 1959: III, 22)

This passage contains the very quintessence of classical cosmopolitanism: law, nature, morality, reason are all tightly intertwined, with the result that all human beings who develop their innate reasoning capacity can live moral lives and, moreover, that this code of right conduct transcends the authority of any immoral state decrees.

Furthermore, in accord with Stoic teaching, Cicero explains that God 'is the author of this law, its promulgator and its enforcing judge'. Nevertheless, it is a weaker theological formulation than the religious content of Greek Stoicism, which posited the kinship of man and gods as world citizens. Panaetius and Posidonius started to shift to the position of distinguishing between men and gods, a position reflected in this passage of Cicero. Yet the older interpretation was never completely displaced. Epictetus refers to a government of men and God and suggests that it is only this kinship that makes men world citizens, 'being intertwined with him through the reason' (Epictetus, 1961: I, ix, 5). Moreover, both Cicero (in reporting Stoic beliefs) and Marcus Aurelius used each of the images in a different context.

Just as the Old Stoa axiom that men and gods exist in a close relationship was declining by the time of the Middle Stoa, so was the earlier elitism of a world citizenship confined to the wise. Cicero, for instance, wrote of men enlarging their reasoning capacity, learning through teaching and discussion (Cicero, 1956: I, xvi, 50). And, as to the Greek concept of a universal *homonoia*, this became easily translated into the quasi-universal *pax Romana*; even though that was based on the power of the legions, not the morality of the Stoics. On the other hand, while some of the features of the Old Stoa concept of world citizenship were weakening in the Roman era, other ideas were rendered more explicit. One pertinent idea of Seneca's seems to foreshadow Voluntary Service Overseas. If there are insufficient outlets for a man's virtuous commitment to public service in his own state, he says, 'Look how many broad stretching countries lie open behind you, how many peoples' (Seneca, 1961: IV, 4).

However, it is to Marcus Aurelius that we must turn for Stoic cosmopolitan thought in its most mature form. Living in accordance with natural law affords the potential for true freedom and equality (Marcus Aurelius, 1961: IV, 4.5; XII, 36), even though that ideal is so hard to achieve: 'Will you ever [my soul] be so fit to live as a fellow citizen with gods and man as never to find fault with them and never incur their reproach?' (X, 1, quoted in Stanton, 1968: 191). He does not, indeed, falter from his cosmopolitan beliefs for, like Cicero, all the interconnecting elements in his thought form a structure of solid truth, which he demonstrates in the following characteristically logical manner:

If the intellectual capacity is common to us all, common too is the reason, which makes us rational creatures. If so, that reason is common which tells us to do or not to do. If so, law is common. If so, we are citizens. If so, we are fellow-members of an organised community. If so, the Universe is as it were a state – for of what other single polity can the whole race of mankind be said to be fellow-members? – and from it, this common State, we get the intellectual, the rational, and the legal instinct, or whence do we get them? (Marcus Aurelius, 1961: IV, 4)

The ancient Stoic writers were eagerly read by men of like mind in the sixteenth to eighteenth centuries. And although the Renaissance and Enlightenment responses differed in some details, there was no hiatus in the purveying of the idea of world citizenship during those three centuries. Moreover, the *philosophes* were influenced by the Renaissance Neostoics as well as the philosophers of the ancient Stoa. For example, Francis Bacon was held in particularly high regard into the eighteenth century. It must be said nevertheless that, with two very notable exceptions, little was achieved in advancing the Stoic cosmopolitan principles as distinct from simply reiterating them.

All six of the ingredients we have identified in the Stoic tradition may be discerned in this modern period. Recognition of the essential oneness of humanity is basic to this thinking, while the power of the human rational faculty to understand the implications of that truth is encapsulated in the label for the period approximately 1680–1790 as the Age of Reason. Furthermore, despite the humanist and rationalist threads in the work of the thinkers in the three centuries here under review, they retained the belief that the unified and harmonious order of the cosmopolis derived from a divine being. For instance, Adam Smith, writing on universal benevolence, asserts that men should be willing to sacrifice lower-order private and public interests 'to the greater interest of the universe, to the interest of that greater society of all sensible and intelligent beings, of which God himself is the immediate administrator and director' (Smith, 1982: VI, ii, 3.3). (He is later at pains, however, to warn against neglect of our more mundane responsibilities.) There is a suggestion, too, in his use of the word 'intelligent', of the Stoic elitism. Like the Greeks, the *philosophes* more than hinted that only the wise could be citizens of the world: that is, themselves!

In presenting the components of Stoic cosmopolitanism as they were adopted by the Renaissance and the Enlightenment, the concept of universal natural law has still to be explained. This topic needs special treatment because the notion of a code of law or morality above state laws was developed in the eighteenth century along two different paths to become contributions of cardinal and lasting importance of that age.

The idea of a natural law did not die with the decay of ancient Stoicism; it enjoyed a Christianized life in the Middle Ages. Seventeenth-century thinkers secularized the idea; eighteenth-century thinkers built upon it the notion of natural rights. In

1741, the international lawyer Christian Wolff asserted that 'whenever we speak of natural law (*ius naturae*), we never intend the law of nature, but rather the right which belongs to man on the strength of that law, that is, naturally' (quoted in Wight, 1991: 112). Nevertheless, it was Locke's list of natural rights as life, liberty and property that was more influential in the eighteenth-century revolutions in America and France. For example, the Americans in their Declaration of Independence cited as justification for defending their 'unalienable rights' 'the laws of Nature and of Nature's God'. The natural-law line of thought could thus be taken to mean that God's law is superior to any state's civil law. There was, however, an alternative interpretation, namely, that a cosmopolitan law sits beside state and international law. This was Kant's view.

But can Kant be slotted into the Stoic tradition? Albeit with some reservations, Martha Nussbaum (1997b) has demonstrated that he not only knew the Stoic literature, but was influenced by their cosmopolitan thinking, most notably by Cicero's *De Officiis*. She summarizes:

> In general, we may say that Kant's conception of a world politics in which moral norms of respect for humanity work to contain aggression and to promote solidarity is a close adaptation of Cicero's Stoic ideas to the practical problems of his own era. (*ibid.*: 15)

The following remarks inevitably rely heavily upon Nussbaum's paper.

Kant shares with the Roman Stoics the belief that we all belong to a common humanity endowed with the capacity for reason and moral behaviour, and consequently our status as citizens of the world requires us to empathize with other peoples' different *moeurs*. More significantly, in his *Grundlegung*, Kant follows Cicero (in *De Officiis*, III) in linking respect for humanity with living in accordance with a universal natural law. Kant's concept of *ius cosmopoliticum* (which we shall discuss in Chapters 3 and 4) bears a close resemblance to the Stoics' *ius naturae*. However, whereas the Stoics' virtual cosmopolis existed in the mind and conscience, Kant, more dubious of the strength of man's moral reason and propensity to pacific behaviour, wanted tangible institutional structures (though not a world government) to support the cosmopolitan law. Even so, Kant retained a certain belief in a beneficent providence to generate universal harmony, a reflection perhaps of the Greeks' extension of their concept of *homonoia* (concord) onto a world plane. 'The mechanical process of nature,' wrote Kant in his *Perpetual Peace*, 'visibly exhibits the purposive plan of nature of producing concord among men, even against their will' (Reiss, 1991: 108). To cite Nussbaum again:

> We are told that our moral acts must take their bearings from the equal worth of humanity in all persons, near or far, and that this moral stance leads politics in a cosmopolitan direction; we are told that morality should be supreme over politics, giving political thought both constraints and goals. Following Cicero, Kant focuses on that moral imperative and its basis in reverence for humanity, and adds the appeals to providence only as a kind of reassurance to the faint-hearted. (Nussbaum, 1997b: 18)

Kant has been a great inspiration to cosmopolitan thinkers since about 1990, when serious work was resumed on the issue of world citizenship. The shocks of the two World Wars and the production of nuclear weapons had set many people to argue the need for a more harmonious world order, including some who spoke and wrote in terms of world citizenship. Thinking in global terms, therefore, did take place earlier in the century, but, until the 1990s, most of this work was heavily institutional – how to construct what would today be called collaborative world governance. References to world *citizenship* were slight or lacking the depth of a grounding in any academic discipline. Two exceptions to this generalization were the contributions of Jonathan Cohen (1954) and L. C. Green (1987), works based respectively on philosophy and international law.

Yet neither of these publications nor the major symposium edited by Hutchings and Dannreuther (1999) makes a great deal of the Stoic tradition. It has been left mainly to Martha Nussbaum (1996, 1997a, 1997b) to stress the significance of this heritage. At one point she chides those who question that world citizenship can exist without an (undesirable) world state:

> This question seems a little odd to me, given the fact that a very long tradition in concrete political thinking, beginning with Cicero's *De Officiis* and extending through Grotius to Kant and Adam Smith and straight on to modern international law, has appealed to Stoic norms to justify certain

maxims of both domestic and international political conduct. (Nussbaum *et al.*, 1996: 133–4)

What, then, is the relevance to our own world of the six components we have used as a working definition of Stoic world citizenship? The wisdom of the ancients in conceiving of the world as a unity is becoming increasingly obvious. We are in all probability descended from African hominids; we are all dependent upon sustaining a healthy planet. Reason, or in modern parlance, scientific enquiry, enables us to comprehend these truths; traditional myths, whether of fundamentalist creationism or of emotional and fissile religious dogma and nationalist ideology, endanger the achievements of rationalist thought. And endanger also the Greek ideal of harmony: sectarian conflict splits the human community in bloody war; economic competitiveness and uncontrolled population increase are straining the natural ecological balance of our planet. Even the elitism of the Stoics, for which they have been much criticized, is replicated in our own cosmopolitan scene – again much criticized. It is the educated and privileged of the 'Western' countries who can afford to think in a cosmopolitan mode: the cruelly impoverished and ill-educated billions in the so-called developing world neither know what world citizenship means nor would care if they did.

Even so, the ideal of a natural law with concomitant natural rights – human rights – has persisted and taken hold, though of assumed human rather than divine provenance. The Preamble to the Universal Declaration of Human Rights states that 'recognition of the inherent dignity and of the equal and inalienable rights of all members of the human family is the foundation of freedom, justice and peace in the world'. Would such a proposition have been possible if Stoic philosophy had never evolved?

Classical Compatibilities

Stoic cosmopolitanism did not preclude the holding of other identities simultaneously with world citizenship. Most notably, the Roman Stoics were highly conscious that their stern philosophy enjoined a strict adherence to civic duty alongside their commitment to the cosmopolitan code of conduct. The thesis of this next section is that during the periods of cosmopolitan consciousness just reviewed, the separate identities of state citizenship, world citizenship and nationhood were mutually compatible, co-existing without the felt need for any to obliterate or incorporate any other(s). Let us call this 'the classical tradition of compatibility'. Then, for about two centuries, between around 1800 and 2000, nationalism absorbed citizenship and effaced world citizenship. However, at the turn of the twentieth century, the conflation of nationalism and citizenship began to loosen and the cosmopolitan idea started to enjoy a revival in a mood which we may call 'the new classicism'.

But, an admission: this broad pattern is clearly perceptible only if one filters out the contradictory evidence. For instance, it is easy to show that the distinction between Greeks and barbarians rendered nationhood and world citizenship incompatible; or that the bitter wars between the Greek *poleis*, notably the Peloponnesian War, indicate an incompatibility between citizenship and nationhood; or that Aristotle's famous assertion that man is an animal designed to live in a *polis* is incompatible with world citizenship. Even so, there is enough evidence to sustain the thesis of classical compatibilities to demonstrate that tension between these three forms of political identity is at least not inevitable. Thus, if the three ideas and statuses can independently and harmoniously co-exist, then it is possible to interpret the two-century hegemony of national citizenship as an aberration. So, we can put a little factual flesh on this interpretive skeleton, though there is no space here for more than the lightest covering of the bones.

As our subject is world citizenship, we are concerned only tangentially with showing that citizenship and nationhood were separate and not in tension, therefore a very brief corroboration of the assertion will suffice. Herodotus was keenly aware of a Panhellenic national identity and famously defined it as 'the common blood, the common language; the temples and religious ritual; the whole way of life we understand and share together' (Herodotus, 1954: Ch. 8, 550). Yet, as we have already noted, *poleis* were so consciously distinct from each other as sometimes to be bitter enemies; and even in the Hellenistic age the *poleis* jealously guarded as much autonomy as they could under the Macedonian conquerors and the Successor Kings. From the Roman republic until as late as the mid-eighteenth century, nations were ethnic or *cultural* subdivisions of states, whereas citizenship related an individual *legally* and *politically* to the city or the state. For example, it was common in the eighteenth century to speak of the nations (sic) of

France. Citizenship and nationhood in the classical tradition provided individuals with separate identities for living in separate spheres so that there was no occasion for the two to clash.

Now to the relationship between world citizenship on the one hand and citizenship and nationhood on the other. It is a chronological fact (and there may be a causative link) that cosmopolitan thinking emerged in late fourth-century Greece as the *polis*, the key political unit, was in decline. But we must guard against concluding from these conditions that the notions of state citizenship and world citizenship did not co-exist in the minds of Greek thinkers. One individual and one general reference may be used to confirm this. Socrates famously held to his duty to the *polis* by disdaining flight and drinking the hemlock as commanded. Yet, over many later centuries, Epictetus, Plutarch, Montaigne and Lipsius all used him as an exemplar of the world citizen: he took the course, 'when asked of what country he belonged, never to say "I am an Athenian", or "I am a Corinthian", but "I am a citizen of the universe"' (Epictetus, 1961: 63).

The second reference to substantiate the co-existence of state citizenship and world citizenship in Greek thought is that the *polis* not only continued into Hellenistic and Roman times, but more *poleis* were founded under the aegis of the successive empires, even though the military independence of the citizen-body of the *polis* was inevitably lost. Thus, while Zeno, Chrysippus and their successors were teaching Stoic cosmopolitanism, the status of citizen of the state continued to be prized and practised.

In contrast, the conviction that the world was populated by two categories of peoples, namely, Greeks and barbarians, unknown in the Archaic age (see Baldry, 1965: 8–16) but which gelled into a consciousness of Greek nationhood in the Persian Wars, was thrown into question by the rise of cosmopolitan thinking. In the Hellenistic period, there was no reason for a pride in the Greek way of life to conflict with a belief in an overarching sense of identity with and duty towards mankind as a whole. For Greeks were part of the (assumed) universal multi-ethnic empire of Alexander (albeit fleetingly) and, through that and succeeding political arrangements, were able to infiltrate their incomparable culture into new lands.

Even Rome succumbed, when captive Greece took captive her fierce captor, as Horace put it. But, as we have already explained, nationhood for the Romans, in contradistinction to the Greeks, was not a pan-Roman identity, rather an indication of provincial ethnicities: therefore, there was no clash with world citizenship. For example, of the leading Stoics of the Roman period, Panaetius was born in Rhodes, Posidonius in Syria and Seneca in Spain.

Nor did the Roman Stoics by any means discard their citizenly identities and duties in favour of their commitment to world citizenship. Indeed, they felt the conscious need to accommodate the two identities simultaneously and comfortably. 'Let us grasp the idea that there are two commonwealths,' Seneca urged (Seneca, 1958: iv, I); while Marcus Aurelius was adamant that both roles were necessary for the fulfilment of a man's virtue: 'my nature is rational and civic,' he wrote; 'my city and country, as Antoninus, is Rome; as a man, the world' (Marcus Aurelius, 1961: VI, 44). (For a detailed survey of the Roman Stoic accommodation of the two identities, see Hill, 2000.)

During the periods of the Renaissance and Enlightenment, as indicated already, nationhood was a cultural, not a political, attribute. That distinguished cosmopolitan Erasmus, for example, was a sharp observer of national character, even though prone to stereotyping, as this summary by John Hale indicates:

> Germans were easy-going and crude, the French violent under a veneer of refinement, the Italians vain and carried deviousness too far. He made Charon declare that he did not mind ferrying Spaniards across the Styx because they were abstemious, but the English were so crammed with food that they nearly sank the boat. (Hale, 1994: 52)

Yet these observations did not prevent Erasmus from insisting that 'all men ... are sprung from the same parents', and to ask, controversially, 'is not the Turk a man – a brother?' (Erasmus, 1917: 76, 69).

By the eighteenth century, the word 'nation' was coming to mean one's own country, and therefore the state. Consequently, a sense of nationality and of citizenship were becoming conflated. We can, therefore, find in the writings of the men of the Enlightenment the view that world citizenship co-exists in harmony with nationhood or state citizenship, these terms being used interchangeably. One example, therefore, of each. First, Thomas Paine: 'The true idea of a great nation is that which extends and promotes the principles of universal society ... and considers mankind of whatever nation or profession they may be as the work of one Creator' (quoted in Schlereth, 1977: 106). The second is from the *Aufklärer*, Christophe Wieland, who pointedly wrote that 'Only the true cosmopolitan can be a good citizen, only he can do the great work to which we have been called: to cultivate, to enlighten and ennoble the human race' (quoted in *ibid.*: 110).

By the time these views were being expressed, however, the ideology of nationalism was taking shape, a shape moulded by two forces at odds with the classical tradition. First, the French defined the nation as a *political*, not a *cultural* collectivity. The Abbé Sieyès posed the question: 'What is a Nation?', and answered: 'A body of associates living under *common* laws and represented by the same *legislative assembly*, etc.' (Sieyès, 1963: 58; his emphases). Second, the Germans turned away from the insights of reason to the appeal of emotion. Arndt wrote of the 'mysterious spirit of the nation, eternal like its nature and its climate' (quoted in Meinecke, 1970: 159 n.26), and the poet Schenkendorf formulated the advice that

> Only iron can rescue us,
> Only blood can redeem us.
> (Quoted in Kohn, 1961: 92)

Fuse these French and German features of the new nationalism and citizens become members of a nation to which they must feel an emotional attachment as the ultimate source of identity and the most righteous claimant on the individual's loyalty. Citizenship and nationhood are amalgamated and occupy the whole space; there is no room for world citizenship.

This outcome was not, it is true, immediately perceived. Let us take just two examples of men who strove to retain a cosmopolitan strand in their thinking while caught up in and expounding a nationalist policy. One is Robespierre who, in 1791, supported the policy of annexing the Papal enclaves of Avignon and the Venaissin on a nationalistic interpretation of the principle of self-determination; yet, eighteen months later argued (admittedly unsuccessfully) for the incorporation into the new Declaration of Rights an article stating that 'The men of all countries are brothers and the different peoples should help one another, according to their means, as if they were citizens of the same state' (quoted in Dann and Dinwiddy, 1988: 33). The other example is Fichte who, in his nationalist *Addresses to the German Nation*, explained that

> The noble-minded man's ... belief and his struggle to plant what is permanent, his conception in which he comprehends his own life as an eternal life, is the bond which unites first his own nation, and then, through his nation the whole human race, in a most intimate fashion with himself. (Fichte, 1968: 116)

Not without reason does one of his editors refer to his 'cosmo-nationalism' (*ibid.*: 187n.). Fichte was more significant than Robespierre in the attempt to prevent a fissure between nationhood and cosmopolitanism. He was perhaps the most renowned exponent of the German mystical belief in the interpenetration of the national and universal ideas. A century later, Meinecke strove to present this interpretation in succinct form. He wrote:

> The concept of the nation was raised to the sphere of eternity and religion. And through this, universally originated culture was made national in such a way that one could not and did not want to say where the universal ended and the national began. A bridge was thus built from the one to the other....
>
> First, the universal became national and the national political but in such a way that the universal note continued to sound for a long time. (Meinecke, 1970: 47–8)

But this note was systematically muffled by the blanketing ideology of nationalism.

Although the history of the nineteenth and twentieth centuries has shown just how powerfully embracing nationalism can be, the tradition of compatibility was maintained well into the nineteenth century by the singular, mystical mind of Guiseppe Mazzini. He believed that 'in labouring according to true principles for our Country we are labouring for Humanity; our country is the fulcrum of the lever which we have to wield for the common good' (Mazzini, 1961: 55). Furthermore, although not drawing upon Greek cosmopolitan thinking, he even so reflected their notion of God being part of this universal consciousness. He pictured the nations of the world setting up twin altars inscribed with the words 'Fatherland' and 'Humanity': 'And the incense of those altars shall ascend to heaven in two columns, which shall gradually approach each other until they unite on high, in God' (Mazzini, 1891: 133). But he was an anachronism; and we need to step speedily now into the twentieth century.

Despite the revival of plans for world government and the resurrection of the term 'world citizenship' during the half-century from about 1920 to 1970, no thought was given to rendering the three socio-political concepts of citizenship, nationhood and world citizenship as separate and compatible, as they had been in classical thinking. Nevertheless, all three were starting to undergo significant transformations by the end of the twentieth century. This process allowed the possibility of their renewed separate and compatible existences, developments which continue and enable us now to slip into the present tense.

Citizenship is ceasing to be a straightforward relationship between the individual and the nation-state. Dual or multiple nationality offers the possibility of holding citizenly status of more than one state in international law. In Europe, the formulation of citizenship of the EU by the Maastricht Treaty provides all citizens of member-states with citizenship in two tiers and, as more states join the Union, the number of individuals enjoying this double status will, naturally, increase. In any case, the state is now less able than hitherto to protect its own citizens – for instance, from the vagaries of the global financial markets and the greedy expansion of multinational companies. Thus, the implied contract between state and citizen weakens. Also, within states, the simple bond of citizenship is loosening because states are either becoming increasingly multicultural or their culturally heterogeneous populations are becoming increasingly conscious of their distinctiveness. Sole civic loyalty to the state is consequently diluted by citizens' allegiance to their ethnic or cultural group. In turn, the state comes to recognize the need to treat its citizens differentially, conceding group-rights to some: a violation of the principle that all citizens are equal.

So, the assertion that the political nation and the cultural nation are synonymous, upon which the nation-state and especially the ideology of nationalism have been constructed, is exposed as the myth that it has always been, although an exceedingly convincing one. Scots are a nation within the British state; the Inuit are a nation within the Canadian state. And constitutional adjustments in the form of devolution or federalism are required to accommodate the renaissance of the old reality that membership of a nation is a different identity from, if parallel to, citizenship of a state.

Meanwhile, forces are at work tending to the revivification of the concept of world citizenship. Understanding that the ecosystem of our planet – the only home that the human race has – is coming under intolerable strain is spreading apace. If citizenship entails a sense of responsibility, then acceptance of the duty to conserve the world's environment is an indication of the existence of a civic identity on a cosmopolitan scale. Moreover, the thrust of globalization – particularly of the global reach of finance, commerce and communications systems – is pushing in the same cosmopolitan direction, though, ironically, in two mutually opposing modes. In a positive sense, the more people who are caught up in the globalization process, the greater the number who feel themselves cosmopolitan in the Enlightenment meaning of the word. In the negative sense, however, insofar as this process has deleterious features, then individuals need to band together as world citizens to defend themselves and demand some control over these global trends and powers. And so there comes about the demand for accountability, to create new or develop established institutions for a form of global governance in which individuals can act as participating world citizens.

The state is losing its monopoly over the individual's sense of socio-political identity. The new classical age has arrived, replicating the classical patterns of the ancient and early modern eras, though with an important mutation. Nationhood is once again being confined to its true, cultural sphere. World citizenship is reawakening from the shadows into which it was cast two hundred years ago. However, citizenship today is evolving into a variegated status, very distinct from the unitary classical civic republican mode; but in this new formulation it is wrenching itself away from its unnatural adhesion to nationhood. The question therefore arises: how is the individual to manage his or her commitment to those multiple identities? The answer through the ages of classical tradition has been: concentrically.

Concentric Circles

Humans, being social animals who have devised various groupings to satisfy this need for togetherness (family, tribe, state), are faced with a quandary that springs from this very social inventiveness. Are the bonds of group commitment felt to be tighter in some relationships than others and are there moral guidelines to help in striving to accord priorities? The inclusion of world citizenship, whatever meaning we attach to the idea, adds an ultimate layer for consideration in attempting a resolution of this dilemma. With specific reference to the proposition that a cosmopolitan identity does and should exist, the issue has been discussed in two main ways. One is the particular argument about whether a world citizenship commitment should be allowed to vie with one's loyalty to the nation-state. This question has already provided some of the subject-matter for Chapter 1. The other way it has been approached is to envisage the individual as the centre of a series of ever-expanding circles of relationships. It is this image we now examine.

The image has, in fact, proved extremely durable. Its origin can be traced back to around 300 BC and features in many current discussions. Its earliest appearance (though not in precise geometrical terms) occurs in extracts from the work of Theophrastus, the philosopher who succeeded Aristotle as head of the Lyceum in 323. His argument proceeded as follows:

> We describe as naturally akin to each other those who are born of the same father and mother, and we further regard as kin those descended from the same ancestors, and moreover those who are fellow-citizens, because they are partners in a single country and society. . . . In my opinion there are two grounds for saying that there is kinship or a common relationship between Greek and Greek, and barbarian and barbarian, and indeed between all men: either because they spring from the same ancestors, or because they share the same upbringing and ways and the same stock. Hence we regard all men as kin and related to each other; and indeed for all animals the beginnings from which their bodies have developed are the same.

And for good measure, he includes the gods in this pattern of relationships by referring to the world as 'the common home of gods and men' (quoted in Baldry, 1965: 142–3). Three points arise from this extract. One is that Theophrastus makes no attempt to accord priorities for the individual's behaviour in these several kinship contexts. Another is that he includes gods and beasts. And the third is that, although today no divine circle is imagined when the concentric analogy is used, it is of interest to note that we are in fact coming full circle, in the temporal plane, to a recognition of animal kinship with man and the consequent argument that some at least should enjoy quasi-human rights. The tiny difference between human genetic make-up and other primates has led one legal authority, Steven Wise, to declare that:

> the ancient Great Wall that has for so long divided humans from every other animal is biased, irrational, unfair and unjust. . . . The decision to extend common law personhood to chimpanzees and bonobos will arise from a great common law case. (Wise, 2000: 270)

Similarly, the philosopher Peter Singer in his book *The Expanding Circle* has declared that:

> it is [as] arbitrary to restrict the principle of equal consideration of interests to our own species as it would be to restrict it to our own race. The only justifiable stopping place for the expansion of altruism is the point at which all whose welfare can be affected by our actions are included within the circle of altruism.
>
> The expansion of the moral circle should therefore be pushed out until it includes most animals. (Singer, 1981: 120)

True, neither Theophrastus nor Wise nor Singer uses the term 'citizen'. Theophrastus was not suggesting that animals should be allocated to the Athenian demes and attend the Assembly; nor is Singer suggesting that the Republicans or Democrats should recruit animals to their parties for civic activity. Even so, the term 'a quasi-citizenship position' has been used by a leading authority on modern state citizenship to describe growing animal rights (Turner, 1986: 99). Citizenship, has, it is true, a heavy moral content; but even the allocation of the status to humans at the global level has been seriously questioned, as we have seen in Chapter 1, so its attribution to other than humans is surely stretching the term too far; even though one can, perhaps, understand the temptation.

As we have already indicated, one of the main difficulties relating to the image of circles is how one should judge the priorities to be given to each. The notion has, in fact, been used in a great variety of ways. Some who have employed the analogy have made no attempt to place commitments in any order. Theophrastus avoided the issue. Cicero's contemporary Antiochus, one of the first to give a clear concentric picture, also avoided grading relationships by priorities, though he asserted that the happy life requires 'the good of friends for its own sake'. By 'friends' he meant, in order, a man's home, those in his locality, 'the peoples linked with him by the fellowship of mankind; or beings even of the universe, which is called heaven and earth', i.e. gods or angels (quoted in Baldry, 1965: 191). In the eighteenth century, Paine offered an analysis based on his belief of natural human adaptation, individuals behaving as social chameleons, thinking their identity according to context. Thus:

> all Europeans meeting in America, or any other quarter of the globe, are *countrymen*; for England, Holland, Germany, or Sweden, when compared with the whole, stand in the same places on the larger scale, which the division of street, town, and country do on the smaller ones; distinctions too limited for continental minds. (Paine, 1976: 85)

True, he does not mention here the level of cosmopolitan identity; none the less, because of his deep personal feeling of being a world citizen we can accept that he would not exclude this outermost circle. More recently, Singer has confronted the moral issue but has declared it a non-problem. He argues that there can be no sound *ethical* case for treating other individuals in whatever circle with anything but impartiality (Singer, 1981: 118–19).

Such a proposition, however, would seem to contradict the commonsense and observed expression of feelings: that the strongest attachments are felt for those closest. With one caveat, Cicero, citing Panaetius, presents this interpretation of the concentric model and, furthermore, suggests that this natural partiality is socially advantageous. He states as a general rule that 'the interests of society . . . and its common bonds will be best conserved, if kindness be shown to each individual in proportion to the closeness of his relationship' (Cicero, 1956: I, xvi, 50). He then examines the various degrees of closeness starting with 'the connection subsisting between all members of the human race'. Next 'is the closer [bond] of belonging to the same people, tribe, and tongue', though 'it is a still closer relation to be citizens of the same city-state'. 'But a still closer social union exists between kindred', within which category there are varying degrees of closeness (*ibid.*: I, xvi, 50–5). Having reached the innermost circle, Cicero appends two special categories, namely, friendship and love of country, and it is this latter bond that is the caveat referred to above and to which we shall return.

Cicero's basic pattern of kindness proportionate to closeness has been echoed in more graphic language by Henry Shue, who has criticized this common interpretation, as we shall see in Chapter 3. He describes the view thus:

An almost irresistibly natural-seeming image dominates much thinking about duties. We often see our duties from the point of view of a pebble dropped into a pond: I am a pebble and the world is the pond I have been dropped into. I am at the centre of a system of concentric circles that become fainter as they spread. ... My duties are exactly like the concentric ripples around the pebble; strongest at the centre and rapidly diminishing toward the periphery ... my duties to those on the periphery are going to diminish to nothing. (Shue, 1988: 691)

So much for world citizenship! A slightly different interpretation of giving preference to the circles closer to the individual has been given by twentieth-century papal thinking. In 1931, Pius XI expounded 'the principle of subsidiary function' in the encyclical *Quadragesimo Anno*, asserting that 'it is an injustice, a grave evil and a disturbance of right order for a larger and higher association to arrogate to itself functions which can be performed efficiently by smaller and lower societies' (Oakeshott, 1940: 58). This enunciation of the principle of subsidiarity, it is true, refers to government and stops short of the global dimension. Nevertheless, the implication is that individuals should be aware of the appropriateness of each level for different social and political functions; and in 1963 John XXIII issued his encyclical letter *Pacem in Terris*, in which he extended the principle to the global level (John XXIII, 1980: para. 140).

The exact reverse of this pattern of priorities was sketched by Epictetus, as follows: 'Consider who you are. To begin with, a Man. ... In addition to this you are a citizen of the world, and a part of it ... of primary importance.' He continues with his crucial statement: 'the whole is more sovereign than the part, and the state more sovereign than the citizen'. Then follow, in order, one's status as a son, a brother and then, if appropriate (and confusing the notion of relative distance), a city councillor (Epictetus, 1961: II, x, 1–10). The principle that 'the whole is more sovereign than the part' was reproduced epigrammatically in the eighteenth century by Montesquieu, who asserted:

If I know of anything advantageous to my family but not to my country, I should try to forget it. If I know of anything advantageous to my country which was prejudicial to Europe and to the human race, I should look upon it as a crime. (quoted in Schlereth, 1977: 191 n.2)

Diderot used this choice of priorities in abbreviated form in the article on *'cosmopolitain ou cosmopolite'* in the great *Encyclopédie* (see Heater, 1996: 72). We also hear the Epictetan viewpoint echoed in Mazzini's *The Duties of Man*, where he declares:

> Your first duties, first ... because without understanding these you can only imperfectly fulfil the rest — are to Humanity. You have duties as citizens, as sons, as husbands, as fathers ... but what makes these duties sacred and inviolable is the mission, the *duty*, which your nature as *men* imposes on you'. (Mazzini, 1961: 41)

One of the arguments in favour of believing that commitment should increase rather than decrease with distance is that this frame of mind ensures an *expansion* of virtuous thought and conduct. Perhaps the earliest example of this case is found in the work of the philosopher Hierocles of the Middle Stoa, a passage which is also significant as probably the earliest explicit and the clearest use of the concentric metaphor. He explains: 'In general each of us is as it were circumscribed by many circles, some smaller, others larger, some enclosing and others enclosed, depending on their differing and unequal relations to one another'. He then proceeds to list the circles in order. The first 'is the one which a person has drawn around his own mind as around a centre'. In the second 'are placed parents, siblings, wife and children'. The third circle is occupied by the nearer kin and the fourth by the more remote relatives. The fifth includes 'fellow-demesmen' (i.e. the local community). The sixth is composed of 'fellow-tribesmen'. The seventh, 'fellow-citizens', then 'people from towns nearby', then 'people of the same ethnic group'. Finally, 'The furthest and largest, which includes all the circles, is that of the whole human race.' Hierocles draws the conclusion from this pattern that 'it is for the person striving for the proper use of each thing to draw the circles somehow towards the centre and to make efforts to move people from the including circles into the included ones' (quoted in Annas, 1993: 267).

The concept of an all-embracing virtue found favour in the eighteenth century. The poet Alexander Pope used the pebble-in-the-pool analogy in *An Essay on Man* 250 years before Henry Shue:

> God loves from whole to parts: but human soul
> Must rise from individual to the whole.
> Self-love but serves the virtuous mind to wake,

As the small pebble stirs the peaceful lake;
The centre moved, a circle straight succeeds,
Another still, and still another spreads,
Friend, parent, neighbour first it will embrace,
His country next; and next all human race;
Wide and more wide, the o'erflowings of the mind
Take every creature in, of every kind;
Earth smiles around, with boundless bounty blest,
And Heaven beholds its image in his breast.
(Pope, 1733–4: IV, 361–72)

(And we may note in passing that Pope shares with Theophrastus and Singer the inclusion of 'every creature'.) Also, Edmund Burke justified his famous advocacy of an active civil society of 'little platoons' by placing them in an expanding context, explaining:

to be attached to the subdivision, to love the little platoon we belong to in society, is the first principle (the germ as it were) of public affections. It is the first link in the series by which we proceed towards a love to our country, and to mankind. (Burke, 1910: 44)

Durkheim too associated himself with this belief. Identifying family, nation and humanity as the three 'phases of our social and moral evolution, stages that prepare for, and build on one another', he concludes that 'Man is morally complete only when governed by the threefold force they exercise on him' (Durkheim, 1961: 74).

In our own day, Michael Walzer, denying that world citizenship exists in any real sense, nevertheless accepts the idea of concentric circles as a method of expanding an individual's morality. However, in so doing, he reverses Heirocles' recommendation:

My allegiances, like my relationships, start at the center. Hence we need to describe the mediations through which one reaches the outer circles, acknowledging the value of, but also passing through, the others. That is not so easy to do; it requires a concrete, sympathetic, engaged (but not absolutely engaged) account of the inner circles – and then an effort not so much to draw the outermost circle in as to open the inner ones out. ... We extend the sense of moral fellowship and neighborliness to new groups of people, and ultimately to all people. ... No doubt commitments and obligations are diminished as they are extended, but the extension is still valuable. (Nussbaum *et al.*, 1996: 126)

This passage probably reflects a widely acceptable modern interpretation of the concentric circles theme.

Walzer defined his position in response to Martha Nussbaum's commitment to a cosmopolitan position. Nussbaum particularly commends Heirocles' adjuration to draw the circles to the centre. However, in addition to the basic Stoic list of close-to-distant relationships, she suggests adding 'groupings based on ethnic, linguistic, historical, professional, gender, or sexual identities' (*ibid.*: 9). Of course, the circles enclosing these kinds of social categories cut across the traditional spatially defined categories so that, although she does not alert the reader to this, we arrive at a complex pattern rather in the form of a Venn diagram, a significant variation on the original formats.

This brings us to two other variations on the simple concentric design. The first is Cicero's caveat:

But when with the rational spirit you have surveyed the whole field, there is no social relation among them all more close, none more dear than that which links each one of us with our country. ... One native land embraces all our loves. (Cicero, 1956: I, xvii, 57)

It is scarcely surprising that he should have taken the individual's identity as citizen out of the spatial sequence; after all, the Stoics stood for a republican citizenship of conscientious civic virtue.

The third adaptation to the basic model is more subtle than either Nussbaum's or Cicero's variations. In the early twentieth century the English philosopher Henry Sidgwick, while as a general rule of thumb accepting the concentric pattern with the greater attachment to the nearer circles, nevertheless pointed out that demands on our loyalty and altruism vary with the circumstances. Consequently, he put forward the proposition 'that another's greater good is to be preferred to one's own lesser good' (Sidgwick, 1966: 246). A recent commentary on this proposition by Sissela Bok shows how this relates to the reaction of the world community to major disasters like an earthquake. However, while not using the term, Bok reminds us how quickly 'compassion fatigue' can set in and how quickly our feelings of responsibility and consideration retreat to the closer circle of 'family members and compatriots'. In particular, 'the

51

sheer magnitude and intensity of present suffering, challenge . . . all existing conceptions of human rights and duties and obligations' (Nussbaum *et al.*, 1996: 40–1).

Are we, therefore, to conclude that Cicero's argument for the overriding priority of duty to the republic and Henry Shue's characterization of the commonly held belief that the notional outermost circle is virtually non-existent together grievously undermine the very concept of world citizenship? Upholders of the ideal of bounded national citizenship would certainly celebrate the complete dissolution of that furthest ripple on Alexander Pope's lake. Yet that tremor on the water's surface can be neither denied nor ignored.

CHAPTER 3

Identity and Morality

The Issues of Identity and Morality

At the very heart of the dispute between the cosmopolitans and communitarians (see Chapter 1) are to be found opposing beliefs, interpretations and propositions concerning the moral relationships that link the three points of the triangle: individual, state and humankind. Communitarians (sometimes called 'patriots') hold that the individual is a moral being insofar as he or she is a member of a community, in particular a state, a proposition famously expounded by Aristotle: 'The man who is isolated . . . is no part of the polis, and must therefore be either a beast or a god' (Aristotle, 1948: 1253a). Hegel, in the nineteenth century, asserted that the state is the 'actuality of the ethical idea' and 'has supreme right against the individual, whose supreme duty is to be a member of the state' (quoted in Brown, 1992: 64); and, with the rise of nationalism, the nation was reckoned to perform this supreme ethical function. Consequently, according to this tradition of thinking, for the individual to reduce the state or nation to the mere convenience of providing safety and security is to lose the sense of community which alone renders the individual a moral being. And this is what cosmopolitans do. They assert that the individual's moral identity derives from his or her own conscience and from membership of the human race, not the state, and is defined by what, as we shall see in the third section of this chapter, Kant called 'the categorical imperative' of duty to one's fellow creatures. The protagonists in the current communitarian *v.* cosmopolitan contest tussle with each other over this fundamental issue, firmly seated on the shoulders of these two giants of German philosophy, Hegel and Kant.

A recognition of social identity, of which the moral sense of shared obligations is part, is both a powerfully magnetic force and an exceedingly complex phenomenon to explain. Leaving aside familial, local and tribal bonds, the forms of identity that have linked patriot and citizen to state and nation have been thought to be the most significant and the most important to be cultivated. An outline of this traditional kind of identity is necessary in order to assess whether and how an analogous sense of identity is feasible as a basis for world citizenship.

A fairly usual list gives a common set of attitudes, assumptions, dispositions and beliefs as the components of national identity; and since, in the modern world, nationhood and citizenship whether rightly or wrongly have for some time been almost universally conflated, we may accept this catalogue also as defining features of citizen identity (in the non-legal sense). Now, by displaying these common modes of thinking, citizens are looking both inwards and outwards, psychologically integrating with their fellow-citizens and differentiating themselves from those outside their civic/national group. But the process of integration has many elements. It involves the creation of and the holding on to a feeling of community, a moulded sense of solidarity with one's fellows and a willingness to share the tribulations as well as the benefits experienced by the community. This process of social bonding is assisted by the forces of socialization – of being educated to and growing up with an awareness of what all members of the community have in common, while the effectiveness of socialization is often helped by the existence of a common culture and language and common institutions. Furthermore, a conscious solidarity is essential for the efficient mobilization of the national or citizenly body to achieve common objectives. Embedded more deeply even than these ingredients of identity is the knowledge and experience of a common geography and a common history, a shared territory and tradition: both space and time create identity. Human beings, like so many other creatures, have evolved with a determined territorial sense, which in modern times has become focused upon the state and the nation: the recent practice of referring to the nation-state as the 'territorial state' is a most apt usage. Yet history makes a tighter bond than geography. Identity is forged out of shared experiences, memories and traditions. Moreover, memories of a collective past shape both present self-consciousness and hopes and ambitions for a future life together.

All these pieces that make up the psychological phenomenon we call identity have developed in human communities quite naturally in response to the need to escape from a life of isolation. Even so, the perceived negative danger of the bonds being loosened by the apathy, alienation and quarrelsomeness of members, and the positive desire to enhance the collective pride of the community, have been persuasive motives for devising means for artificially buttressing the processes of nature. Thus, history has been 'improved' by myth and the abstract concept of state made concrete by vivid symbols, so that identity becomes part invention.

This picture of political identity, it is often argued (and as is indicated at the start of this chapter), is a depiction of life in a state, a relationship that is not just the result of historical accidents – the very existence and notion of citizenship as a status and, especially, as a quality are dependent upon the state. Arguments that the state is the key element in the world's social-economic-political-moral system and that citizenship essentially derives from and is sustained by this system coalesce into a complex and formidable case against cosmopolitanism. Thinkers of the stature of Grotius and, *par excellence*, Hegel have argued that the state is either the source of moral rights or, even, of morality itself. Moreover, the assumption that 'in the international arena individuals are represented by states and that their "moral rights" are included in the pool of "moral rights" of states' is still widely accepted (Zolo, 1997: 65). States, therefore, are the only holders of legitimate power. It therefore follows, as Hegel was at pains to point out, that there can be no authority superior to the state: a world composed of a collectivity of autonomous states is ethically essential. Furthermore, the nation-state provides in the modern world the best possible combination of geographical reach and civic allegiance, in magnified mirror-image of Aristotle's concept of the ideal *polis*. How do these considerations concerning the signal importance of the state relate to the individual *qua* citizen? Hegelians, needless to say, consider that true, free citizenship outside the framework of the state is a nonsensical contradiction; the state makes citizens. A converse and less purist viewpoint is that citizens committed to the state – those possessed of civic virtue – are essential to the good health of the state. This is the very credo of the civic republican style of thinking about citizenship and, for different reasons, it is also true of the modern liberal democratic state.

Insistence that civic identity and morality are inexorably dependent on the citizen's relationship to the state can be reinforced by the observation that the spirit of nationhood is a powerful integrative force: a sense of nationhood, in other words, is deeply embedded in us. At its extreme, the German Romantic political thinkers taught that there was nothing more natural than membership of a nation. Moreover, citizenship and nationhood continue to be virtually synonymous in many states and certainly so in international law. The feeling of national identity thus melded with citizenship has accordingly now assumed the role of patriotism that partly and crucially defined citizenship in the republican tradition. Nor is patriotism itself, however it is infused into the individual's code of morality, by any means an obsolete virtue. As Charles Taylor has argued, in an age which sets great store by liberal democracy, states are even more reliant on patriotism than ever before because of the great stress today on negative liberty and individual rights. He explains:

> A citizen democracy can only work if most of its members are convinced that their political society is a common venture of considerable moment and believe it to be of such vital importance that they participate in the ways they must to keep it functioning as a democracy. (Nussbaum *et al.*, 1996: 120)

Political thinkers and commentators who find these arguments compelling are likely to have difficulty in accommodating the idea of a citizenly identity and morality that overarches the state to embrace the whole world. In truth, the case against a cosmopolitan identity and morality has been pursued to a greater depth than the retailing of these general principles would suggest. Thinkers of an Hegelian persuasion demonstrate, to their own satisfaction at least, that cosmopolitan identity and morality are neither, on the one hand, desirable nor, on the other, practicable or effectively existent.

To start with the undesirability. The case proceeds along the following lines. States need citizens and citizens need states; and that reciprocal need can be satisfied only if citizen and state are bonded together by deeply held and shared community values and heartfelt patriotism. Communitarian thinkers express the fear that the growth or cultivation of a cosmopolitan frame of mind would enfeeble this indispensable psychological underpinning of the state and leave the individual psychologically unrooted. A vague world-mindedness can be no substitute. In truth, so runs the argument, any attempt at such substitution would be actually dangerous – the individual would be left with a feeling of isolation at best or be tempted into selfish individualism at worst. Even Martha Nussbaum, a passionate advocate of world citizenship, has written of 'a sense of boundless loneliness' and the loss of the 'refuge' of having an idealized image of a nation [as] a surrogate parent (*ibid.*: 15). As one would expect, Burke had some particularly pungent words to say on the matter:

> To transfer humanity from its natural basis, our legitimate and home-bred connection – to lose all feeling for those who have grown up by our sides, in our eyes, the benefit of whose cares and labours we have partaken from our birth, and meretriciously to hunt abroad after foreign affections, is such a disarrangement of the whole system of our duties, that I do not know whether benevolence so displaced is not almost the same thing as destroyed, or what effect bigotry could have produced that is more fatal to society. (quoted in *ibid.*: 82)

Recently, Sissela Bok (*ibid.*: 39) and Michael McConnell (*ibid.*: 82) have taken Martha Nussbaum severely to task for asserting that national or ethnic identities are 'morally irrelevant' (*ibid.*: 5).

Some current trends have also given communitarians cause to be worried. Indeed, for all their emphasis on the importance, naturalness and persistence of local and traditional bonds, there can also be discovered a certain nervousness in their position: that because of the burgeoning of individualism, bureaucracy, the market economy and substantial demographic migrations, moral identity with state, nation and community is being loosened. Any advocacy of world citizenship which would further contribute to the dissolution of the vital communal adhesives must therefore be treated with the utmost concern.

This mood of anxiety ignores the possibility that world citizenship and patriotism can be held in simultaneous reconciled harmony by the development of a more generously capacious moral identity. Indeed, although some advocates of world citizenship judiciously avoid any polarization of the two modes of political self-identification, some writing in this field does justifiably draw the communitarian criticism that we are presented with an either/or choice. Yet this position, it can be argued, is both an unreal and a perilous antithesis. It is unreal because circumstances when individuals would be required to make a choice are often complex and are not sufficiently replicated to warrant the generalization that one's primary allegiance should always be to the moral community of all human beings. And it is perilous because the replacement of the strong bonds of community by the feeble bond of humanity could well lead to the collapse of all sense of socio-political morality.

But if the idea of world citizenship is too intangible to be desirable, and yet, as a proposed objective, is dangerous enough to threaten the morality that we have, based on the nation-state, would it not be desirable to replace state-grounded civic morality with an equally solid cosmopolitan morality made concrete by the construction of a world state? In fact, of course, the hazards of a world state are known, and no one suggests that present-day cosmopolitans would be anything but horrified at the prospect of a tyrannical world government. Indeed, their bitterest opponents can usually produce no more vicious condemnation of their consciously advocated goal than to label them 'naïve liberal do-gooders'. Nevertheless, some opponents do see a hint of a blinkered obsession in the cosmopolitan project that is quite realistically dangerous. By setting up an ideal of world citizenship, the implicit, even, indeed, explicit, message is that the subordinate loyalties to community, nation or state are of suspect moral value. This stance is not just injurious to these vital providers of moral identity and cohesion, as we have already seen the communitarians argue. It can also result in unfortunate attitudes to other individuals, such as contempt for those who cling to their traditional identities.

This undesirable feature of cosmopolitanism attracted the attention of two distinguished literary figures. Rousseau was famously antipathetic to the cosmopolitanism of his contemporary Enlightenment thinkers. In *Émile*, he declared: 'Distrust those cosmopolitans who search out remote duties in their books and neglect those that lie nearest. Such philosophers will love the Tartars to avoid loving their neighbour' (Rousseau, 1911: 7). Half a century later, in his *Up the Rhine: To Gerard Brooke*, the English poet Thomas Hood wrote, 'I don't set up for being a cosmo-polite, which to my mind, signifies being polite to every country except your own'.

The most common criticism relating to the undesirability of world citizenship is, however, the accusation that it cannot match the traditional forms of moral identity because it lacks their immediacy and emotional attraction. One can pile up the adjectives that have been deployed to state this case – empty, vague, abstract, arid, bloodless, colourless, thin – a legacy, perhaps, of the stern rationalist origins of cosmopolitan thought of the ancient Stoics. Benjamin Barber, criticizing Martha Nussbaum's vision of cosmopolitanism, expresses this concern lucidly:

> The idea of cosmopolitanism offers little or nothing for the human psyche to fasten on. By her own admission, it 'seems to have a hard time gripping the imagination.' Not just the imagination: the heart, the viscera, the vitals of the body that houses the brain in which Nussbaum would like us to dwell. . . .
>
> Like Ibsen's Pastor Brand, Nussbaum urges her parishioners up the harsh and lonely mountain to an abstract godhead they cannot see. (Nussbaum *et al.*, 1996: 33–4)

A common argument that straddles both forms of cosmopolitan denial – undesirable and impracticable – is the evident strength of traditional roots of identity and the feebleness of any comparable cosmopolitan identity that might seek to overlay them. The German historian Meinecke, for instance, writing about universal human values, asserted that they 'never are universal, for they always bring with them a clump of native soil from the national sphere that no individual can leave behind' (Meinecke, 1970: 20). More than that, both citizenship and democracy, it is widely recognized, require a degree of cultural homogeneity as a grounding for the contributions these political devices can make to social concord. Yet the very appeal and purpose of world citizenship today lie in the conviction that it would enhance global democracy and harmony. If, however, it can be demonstrated that the peoples of the world are lacking an effectively homogeneous culture, it follows that world citizenship is unrealistic. Long ago, St Augustine believed that linguistic differences were insuperable barriers to close human understanding:

> For if two men, each ignorant of the other's language, meet and are compelled . . . to remain together, then it is easier for dumb animals, even of different kinds, to associate together than for them, though both are human beings. (St Augustine, 1969: XIX, vii)

Today, the peoples of the world are culturally fragmented not only by language but by religion, nationality and ethnicity in myriad ways it would be wearisome to list.

The point we wish to make here is that cultural-social-political identity is a heritage – it takes time, often many generations, even centuries, to bed itself into the collective psyche of a community. This long process of maturation is not available to the advocate of world citizenship who wishes a transformation in the foreseeable future. In the words of Gertrude Himmelfarb, 'The "protean self", which aspires to create an identity *de novo*, is an individual without an identity' (Nussbaum *et al.*, 1996: 77). And Hilary Putnam adds:

> But in the absence of such concrete ways of life, forms of what Hegel called *Sittlichkeit*, the universal maxims of justice are virtually empty, just as in the absence of critical reason, inherited forms of *Sittlichkeit* degenerate into blind allegiance to authority. Tradition without reason is blind; reason without tradition is empty. (*ibid.*: 94)

So, we can join the links in this chain of reasoning: world citizenship as an identity has no rooted and felt cultural tradition; such a firmly embedded, shared cultural tradition is essential for any form of civic identity; bereft of this cultural tangible identity the notion of world citizenship is an empty idea, impossible of proper realization; and any attempt at realization in the absence of this foundation would produce institutions and laws shorn of ethical legitimacy. In down-to-earth terms, few people can bring themselves to think with any honesty and commitment that they are truly world citizens: there is little 'species consciousness' on a par with 'national consciousness'. If the great mass of the world's population do not think of themselves as world citizens, then world citizenship cannot be said to exist.

Now, if this criticism of the cosmopolitan idea is sound, it follows that the belief in the viability of world citizenship must be naïve. Even Richard Falk, a distinguished exponent of the need for more effective and just global governance, has added his criticism. The reason for voicing his concern stems from his judgement that the notion of world citizenship is utopian, oblivious of the most powerful and contrary trends in today's world. He does not mince his words:

> To project a visionary cosmopolitanism as an alternative to nationalist patriotism without addressing the subversive challenge of the market-driven globalism currently being promoted by transnational corporations and banks, as well as

currency dealers and casino capitalists, is to risk indulging a contemporary form of fuzzy innocence. A credible cosmopolitanism has to be combined with a critique of the ethically deficient globalism that is being enacted in a manner that minimizes the ethical and visionary content of conceiving of the world as a whole. . . .

Such a globalism has almost no affinity with the Stoic moral imagination. (*ibid.*: 57)

Yet, surely, the concept of human rights, enshrined in the Universal Declaration, which proclaims itself as 'a common standard of achievement for all peoples and all nations' (Preamble), is an indicator of the existence of a global ethic? Moreover, parallels with state citizenship rights are easily drawn. The legal/civil and political modes of citizenship – and the social, economic and environmental for that matter – are often discussed in terms of the civic rights that they carry with them. And many state constitutions are prefaced by or contain lists of such rights. The Universal Declaration of Human Rights and its supplementary covenants and regional adaptations are sometimes referred to as global counterparts of these national identifications of citizenly rights. If these rights are universally valid, then all may expect to enjoy them; all may thus be deemed to be world citizens. However, this syllogism, say the critics of cosmopolitanism, rests on an extremely shaky foundation. For the published so-called universal rights are, in reality, not universal; and they are not inalienable and natural, they are historical and arbitrary. No less an authority than Benedetto Croce succinctly asserted that point, as long ago as 1947 (UNESCO, 1949: 93–5). Also, this serious reservation has been reiterated by a number of scholars very recently (e.g. Zolo, 1997: 61, 117–21; Butler, Glazer, Himmelfarb and Putnam in Nussbaum *et al.*, 1996: 46, 51–2, 64, 75, 97).

The assumption that there can be an objective, universally and perennially accepted code of human rights is itself an historically and culturally determined belief. It is founded on the Stoic–Kantian tradition of a rationally discernible natural law: a Western tradition. To expect non-Western peoples to accept this tradition smacks of arrogance – 'neo-colonialism' is a word often used. 'What kind of cultural imposition is it,' Hilary Putnam asks, 'to claim that a Kantian may be found in every culture?' (Nussbaum *et al.*, 1996: 52). The Western bias in the concept of universal human rights is evident from the protests of many non-Western states both at the time of the drafting of the Universal Declaration and since. The ground for these concerns has been the stress in this liberal human rights tradition on the civil and political rights of individuals rather than the economic rights of communities and their socio-political cohesion and stability. We shall take three examples.

One is, tellingly, a comment on the conference held in 1993 to mark the forty-fifth anniversary of the Universal Declaration:

> At the UN World Conference in Vienna, the lipservice paid to human rights began to curl. From the strong men of Asia and the old men of Africa came a new and unsettling refrain: 'human rights' was an invention of Western liberalism which had little to offer countries whose values derived from tribal wisdom or other communal traditions, or which were poor and politically vulnerable. [They demanded that] human rights must ... accommodate 'the significance of national and regional peculiarities and various historical, cultural and religious backgrounds'. (Robertson, 1999: 64)

So much for the timeless universality of human rights as a justification for asserting the existence of a cosmopolitan ethic. The second example is specifically the foreignness of the Western concept of liberty. As one commentator has explained, Islamic culture is 'Profoundly marked ... by a religious sense of belonging to the community. The individual identifies with such a community not by claiming rights but by fulfilling duties, that is, scrupulously following collective rules of politico-religious behaviour' (Zolo, 1997: 119). The third example is taken from Africa. A comparison between the European Convention of Human Rights (couched, it goes without saying, in the Western mode) and the 1981 African Charter on Human and People's Rights is most instructive. The latter includes social and political duties as well as rights, leading one UK lawyer to judge that it 'might more honestly have been entitled the African Charter for Keeping Rulers in Power' (Robertson, 1999: 58). Indeed, charges of hypocrisy have been flung in both directions. However much justified these accusations might be, the point is, of course, that the difficulty of achieving universal agreement on a set of universal rights would seem to undermine the cosmopolites' claim that such a code of rights is contributory evidence of a world citizenship.

This questioning of the true universality of human rights as a feature of world citizenship can be interpreted as but one aspect of a general doubt that the world's peoples are as integrated as the supporters and advocates of the cosmopolitan concept would have us believe. This doubt is founded upon three main observations. One, to repeat, is the evidence that the nation-state remains a strong entity: it remains for the vast majority of people their 'community of fate', and even multinational companies rely on bases established in nation-states. Second, in so far as the weakening of the nation-state is discernible, this is because of sub-national strains, caused by increasing consciousness of regional cultural identities, more than any succumbing to supranational forces. And third, the homogenizing thrusts of globalization have been exaggerated (see, e.g., Hirst and Thompson, 1999: Ch. 9). The attacks on the desirability and plausibility or even the primitive existence of a cosmopolitan moral identity have been and are being delivered from a number of hostile positions: realism, communitarianism, nationalism, multiculturalism and post-modernism each fire their salvos of dubiety. How, then, have the cosmopolites established their position, defended it and launched their counterattack?

The Homogeneity of Humankind

The cosmopolitan case is a thorough one, in both content and tactics. In content, the argument that an individual can have an identity as a world citizen is based on the proposition that the human race has a considerable homogeneity that is observable in many regards; and that a moral responsibility for the planet and humankind as a whole is of an even higher order than, but certainly of an equivalent order to, one's moral responsibility to one's nation and fellow state-citizens. The cosmopolitans' tactics consist of both an attack on the communitarian case and a defence and advance of their own convictions. We shall proceed as follows. The present section will examine the perception that humankind is homogeneous; and the relationship of that perception will be connected to the issue of identity by shadowing the communitarians' arguments, providing these arguments with a cosmopolitan interpretation. Together with the next section, on global morality, the case emerges for accepting that a cosmopolitan identity and ethic are desirable and, to some degree, do exist. It is, moreover, worth noting that three kinds of cosmopolitan proofs of homogeneity can be detected as early as the Greeks: these are the arguments relating to religion, biology and human communication. (The first and second of these we shall illustrate here; the matter of communication will be more conveniently dealt with later.)

If the principles of identity are enshrined in the holding of common attitudes, assumptions, dispositions and beliefs, then from the Stoics onwards people have lived, and are living today, who have thought of themselves as citizens of the world – they have adopted this self-identity. Famously, men of the Enlightenment often styled themselves 'world citizens', and, for example, for over half a century now there has existed an International Registry of World Citizens containing the names of individuals from all parts of the globe. True, the precise attitudes, assumptions, dispositions and beliefs of all these world citizens – from Zeno and Marcus Aurelius to Thomas Paine and Peter Ustinov – will vary from age to age and, indeed, from individual to individual, in response to the intellectual, moral and political environments that have persuaded persons to adopt a cosmopolitan credo, and in accordance with the intensity of their cosmopolitan commitments. Even so, fluid as the set of attitudes and so forth might have been in the consciousness and consciences of those who have proclaimed themselves to be world citizens, and few in number as they might have been, it is clearly foolish and false to assert that such an identity cannot exist.

True, of the twin forces of integration and differentiation that knit together a community, the latter cannot exist – short, that is, of the discovery of intelligent extraterrestrial life: human beings have no other peoples to be different from. On the other hand, there are a number of persuasive integrative features of human life tending to forge a sense of common identity.

One of these, despite bitter doctrinal disputes, is religion. The ancient myths of creation posit a single origin of the human race, and the monotheistic religions posit a divine Creator. For instance, in Babylonian mythology Marduck killed another god, Kingu, and created man from a paste of dust and his blood. All humans are the creation of the gods, are the children of God; and, as Václav Havel has said, 'Somewhere in the primeval foundations of all the world's religions we find, basically, the same underlying moral imperatives' (United Nations, 2001). From a Christian point of view, Pope John XXIII stressed that:

> There is ... a unity in the human race deriving from the
> human nature that men have in common and which demands

that attention be given to the welfare of mankind as a whole: in other words to the universal common good. ... men today ... are becoming ever more conscious of belonging as living members to the whole family of mankind (John XXIII, 1980: paras 132, 145).

The notion of a human *family* is, of course, a powerful metaphor of identity.

It also has biological implications. As early as the sixth century BC, Greek travellers and map-makers were struck by the basic sameness of human beings wherever their journeys took them. In modern biological terminology, man was recognized, for all his cultural variations, as one species. What is more, modern research in genetics has amply confirmed the scientific basis of this ancient impressionistic evidence. This is what one British biologist has to say on this matter:

By comparison with other mammals ... man is a tedious beast. Although the world is divided by politics it is united by genes. ... The most remarkable thing about humankind is how uniform it is. ... Chimpanzees are three times more distinct one from the other than are men, with fifty times as much divergence among separate populations. (Jones, 1999: 337, 348)

In addition to the deep religious and biological foundations of human integration, two other forces have appeared very recently: these are the insistence that human rights should be universally recognized and the claimed homogenizing processes of globalization.

The very proclamation that all human beings are endowed with rights by virtue of being human is an assertion that, in principle and intention, these rights are of universal application and, therefore, that no subdivisions of the human race – by sex, class, ethnicity, state citizenship or any other category – can override or preclude the essential oneness of humankind in this regard. These rights, in the words of the Universal Declaration, belong to 'all members of the human *family*' (emphasis added). Moreover, some articles of the Declaration assert the irrelevance of state boundaries; Article 6, for example, states that 'Everyone has the right to recognition *everywhere* as a person before the law' (emphasis added; see also Articles 14.1, 19, 26.2). Nor has any state refused to recognize the Universal

Declaration. To mark its fortieth anniversary in 1988, the UN Secretary-General, Perez de Cuellar, delivered an address during which he commented that, 'since its adoption, over 100 countries have joined the United Nations, countries which could have called its universal applicability into question. That has not happened: none of these new States has ever challenged the Declaration' (Perez de Cuellar, 1989). (Naturally, the violation of rights in practice is another matter.)

Yet, as we have seen, the universality of rights in very principle has been denied. How can this denial itself be challenged by those who believe that recognition of human rights upholds the cosmopolitan case? The argument in this context is in essence part of the whole modern cosmopolitan philosophy, namely, that world citizenship entails the accommodation, not the obliteration, of other identities. In the words of Gerard Delanty, drawing upon the works of Jürgen Habermas, 'human rights can be seen as universal in the sense of discourses that are interpreted differently by the different historical cultures'. However, this implies that 'human rights are not pre-given natural rights but rather constructions' (Delanty, 2000: 77). David Beetham goes further and accuses of muddled thinking those who reject the concept of universal human rights because of cultural differences. 'Critics of human rights universalism,' he asserts, 'typically appeal to the equal respect due to other cultures, but it is difficult to see how such respect can be justified except in terms of the equal respect due to other people *qua* human' (Beetham, 1998: 60). Indeed, discussion about the ways in which particular cultural traditions can be most comfortably related to universally applicable human rights is a continuous practice. For instance, in 1998, Mary Robinson, the UN High Commissioner for Human Rights, reported:

> A few weeks ago I was glad to have the opportunity to bring together and listen to experts in Islamic Law discussing among themselves the theme 'Enriching the universality of human rights: Islamic perspectives on the Universal Declaration of Human Rights'. (Robinson, 1999: 2)

On the basis of these arguments there would therefore seem to be a strong *prima facie* case for equating the International Bill of Human Rights (i.e. the Universal Declaration and the two Covenants – see Chapter 4) with state Bills of Rights. Therefore, as a state Bill of

Rights treats the state citizenry as a unity, so the International Bill treats the world's citizenry as a unity.

A matter even more vexed by conflicting interpretations is the issue of globalization. Thankfully, we have no need to delve into the immense quantity of literature thrown up by this topic but rather just to indicate the ways in which this phenomenon – however old or new, shallow or deep, beneficent or malignant – can be perceived as contributing to the human integrative process. Bruce Mazlish is quite adamant that globalization is absolutely essential to a world citizenship identity: 'Any global identity,' he writes, 'will have to be based on the reality of globalization – an actual, lived experience', though he concedes that the 'dimensions [of this experience] and ways of forging identity are not clear' (Mazlish and Buultjens, 1993: 15).

The lack of clarity is doubtless due to the novelty of many of the features of globalization, notably speed of travel and electronic communications. So, just as a sense of nationhood took centuries to complement local and regional allegiances in the minds of the bulk of a state's population, so globalization is at first affecting the ways of thinking of a relatively small proportion of the world's population. Comment on this partial or gradualist tendency can be illustrated from two quite different sources. One is the view of an academic, Jan Aart Scholte, who has written, in the section of a book chapter entitled 'Homogenisation':

> Experiencing this world-scale convergence of symbols, actions, norms and social changes, people who have been pulled furthest into the maelstrom of globalisation (e.g. numerous managers, academics and artists) have often found territorially constructed distinctions of self and other to be increasingly artificial and unsatisfactory. (Scholte, 1996: 48–9)

The second source, in contrast, is a UK Ministry of Defence document entitled *The Future Strategic Context for Defence*. This contains the prediction that 'The idea of a transnational educated elite who identify more with their peers in other countries than with their compatriots may become more of a reality' (quoted in *Guardian*, 8 February 2001). At the present time, then, world citizens in a full sense are something of an elite. But that does not negate their title. In the traditional state context, the citizens of ancient Sparta and Renaissance Florence, for instance, were elites; they were citizens none the less. By integrating with people from other countries and cultures, an increasing proportion of the world's population are becoming world citizens even in their primary identity.

Does this therefore mean that world citizens can feel themselves to be attached to the whole planet as their territory, just as state citizens feel themselves attached to their nations? Since the 1970s planetary consciousness has indeed burgeoned, stimulated mainly by the fearful awareness of the frailty of Earth's ecosystem. A report published in 1972, dealing with the human environment, was entitled *Only One Earth: The Care and Maintenance of a Small Planet* (Ward and Dubos). The cover design was composed of a NASA photograph taken from a spacecraft of a tiny Earth set against the black vastness of space. To emphasize humankind's interdependent occupancy of this limited accommodation, the term 'spaceship Earth' was coined. However, this mechanical metaphor was misleading in the light of an increasing awareness of the interdependence of the totality of the planet's life-forms. The Gaia hypothesis, formulated by James Lovelock as the ultimate interpretation of this insight and named after the Greek goddess of the Earth, argues that the whole planet is a single living system. So, world citizenship has its form of geographical identity. Has it also an historical identity?

History is crucial, in particular because that discipline, as we have noted, has played such a key role in consolidating the identity of state and national citizenship. For history has traditionally been written and studied largely as a record of the past experiences and development of states and nations. By analogy, a world citizenship would need to be underpinned by a world, global or universal history. As with so many other features of cosmopolitan thinking, Kant is a salient figure in propounding the necessity of a world history, in his essay *Idea for a Universal History with a Cosmopolitan Purpose*. His aim was to indicate that historical laws could be uncovered on a par with those of physical science. These could be discerned by examining both what the whole of mankind has naturally in common and the urge for freedom. Furthermore, the historical development of these human characteristics has been the story of communal effort and needs to be completed by a political achievement. Reason '*could be fully developed only in the species, but not in the individual*' because communication of acquired understanding has been essential for such progress (Reiss, 1991: 42, emphasis in original). However, '*The greatest problem for the human species, the solution of which nature compels him to seek, is that of attaining a civil society which can administer justice universally' (ibid.*: 45, emphasis in original). Kant does not attempt even a summary of a Universal History, but believes that it *'must be regarded as possible and even as capable of furthering the purpose of nature itself (ibid.*: 52, emphasis in original).

The trouble about Kant's insights for modern historians is that his teleological approach smacks of the discredited 'Whig' history. Yet presentday historians face immense difficulties in attempting to construct any alternative universal history. These difficulties include, not least, the enormous quantity of potential material to be handled and the ways of devising methods for structuring narratives and analyses. But that is a large subject in its own right, for which there is no space here. From a range of different kinds of world history we may identify two main formulae which have recently been proposed for the construction of a comprehensible account. One aims to identify the current features of globalization and analyse their origins; the other aims to identify the common denominators of past human experience. An example of the second is provided by the doyen of world history, W. H. McNeill, who has written:

> Humanity entire possesses a commonality which historians may hope to understand just as firmly as they can comprehend what unites any lesser group. Instead of enhancing conflicts, as parochial historiography inevitably does, an intelligible world history might be expected to diminish the lethality of group encounters by cultivating a sense of individual identification with the triumphs and tribulations of humanity as a whole. (quoted in Mazlish and Buultjens, 1993: 55)

We have thus before us three models of a history written from a global perspective that could support a world citizen identity. One is an understanding of shared *past* experiences (McNeill; and reminiscent of Fichte's reference to nationhood being built upon a history of 'common deeds and suffering'). The second is an understanding of the historical sources of *present* universal conditions (the globalization school). And the third is an agenda for the *future* derived from the flow of historical trends (Kant). Each of these can contribute to a cosmopolitan identity. However, McNeill's has the advantage of being more objective, neither reading history forwards as Kant does, nor backwards as the globalization approach does. Also, it highlights the variations in different peoples' experiences of the universal in history and thus reinforces the lesson that the identity of world citizen is just one of a number of identities that individuals have and always have had throughout the ages of civilizations.

Sharing a common space and a common memory are basic requirements for the feeling of social cohesion that is such an important facet of citizenship. But a fully rounded civic community also needs a sense of justice, common institutions and cultural cohesion. Kant argued that the existence of a cosmopolitan law indicated that 'the peoples of the earth have ... entered in varying degrees into a universal community' (Reiss, 1991: 107). Hedley Bull, too, writing on cosmopolitan or world justice, states: 'These are ideas which seek to spell out what is right or good for the world as a whole, for an imagined *civitas maxima* or cosmopolitan society' (Bull, 1977: 84). In according this meaning to the term *civitas maxima*, Bull was expanding its cosmopolitan sense, to indicate a tighter sense of community, beyond the somewhat limited implications of its use by Christian Wolff, who popularized it some half-century before Kant. However, cosmopolitan law is properly the subject of Chapter 4, and the matter of global political institutions is the subject of Chapter 6. None the less, it is necessary to record here that citizenship requires institutions through which to operate, and in their absence a citizenly identity can barely be said to exist. Cosmopolitan citizenship, it is true, is not at all currently well provided with global institutions; indeed, one of the prime objectives of the cosmopolitan agenda is to improve this condition beyond the UN and NGOs that can be said only partly to contribute to this element of global community.

The emergence of some global styles of culture is already a more definite index of the existence of a cosmopolitan community than the institutional scene. Forms of entertainment, styles of art and clothing, modes of transport and communication of information have become increasingly homogenized. The evidence of the globalization of culture – even the use of ugly neologisms like 'homogenized' and 'globalization' – is all about us. The world citizen has, therefore, so much in common with his or her fellow world citizens, even though the quality of the global culture may not be able to match its pervasiveness. Anthony Smith, for example, is highly dismissive of the standards of this post-modern cosmopolitan culture, peppering his analysis with pejorative words such as 'pastiche', 'self-parodying', 'shapeless', 'artificial' (Smith,

1991: 157–8). On the other hand, as he concedes, this cosmopolitan culture is primitive because it is in its very early stages of development.

Much of the cosmopolitan culture derives from the extraordinary pace and diffusion of scientific discovery and technological invention. This relates to the Greek idea of the *logos*. The Stoic cosmopolitan idea was very dependent upon this Greek concept, of the universal capacity of man for reasoned speech in order to convey a message. Community requires communication. And the means of communication worldwide are available now to a degree unimaginable to the ancient Greeks. Intelligibility has been enhanced by the spread of English as a virtual *lingua franca*, and the constraints of time and space have to all intents and purposes been eliminated by the invention of the telephone, the radio, e-mail and the internet. The ether (to use an anachronistic term) is constantly alive with transmitted messages. Indeed, there is a connection here: the spread of English is being accelerated by its use as a common international computer language. Again, one may question the quality of this technologically driven communication-community. But there is no doubting that it exists and that it has come to stay. If the national flag is the symbol that confirms the state citizen's sense of identity, then the computer is becoming the symbol that confirms the world citizen's sense of identity. The symbols are also means of socialization and mobilization. The internet, as instrument as well as symbol, has been dramatically used to rally protesters worldwide against businesses and policies that are perceived as exploitative and pollutant. Both flag and computer can be abused, so the citizen and world citizen alike must balance a feeling of loyal identity with a moral sense of responsibility.

Cosmopolitan Morality

Any justification for a world citizenship stands or falls on the judgement whether or not it is preferable for individuals to live by the precepts of a code that can be defined as a global ethic. In essence, the case – heatedly contended by political theorists of the communitarian persuasion – is pursued along the following lines. An individual is a morally autonomous being who has a responsibility to treat other human beings, regardless of any particular other identity(ies), with consideration and respect.

71

Moreover, not only should all human action be undertaken with due regard to the effects on others, but those likely to be affected should have the facility of consultation about these actions. In addition, particularly in a world that is now so interdependent, state boundaries are losing their relevance because effects of human actions are so often unconfined by frontiers. It also follows that to define world citizenship by a catalogue of rights, such as the International Bill of Human Rights, must be a morally incomplete, even skewed, interpretation of that status: of greater import is the requirement that world citizens should be conscious of their duties, obligations and responsibilities. This paragraph is a summary amalgam of a number of contributions to the idea of cosmopolitan morality. Each of these components will be expounded in this section.

First is the proposition that the individual is a moral being. From the Stoics onwards there has existed a belief that human beings have an innate capacity to understand and/or have the capacity to learn what is a moral action, even though, because of human imperfection, it is rare to find an individual who has the will to lead an unblemished moral life. The cosmopolitan accepts this view, denying the alternative, namely, that moral understanding derives from living in society, especially a state (though the cosmopolitan may well concede that social structures are necessary to induce good behaviour in practice). Consequently, the individual's obligation to act morally towards others is not confined to his or her relations with fellow state citizens or compatriots: *all* humans are moral equals.

The connections that bind together morality, duty and cosmopolitanism can be discerned in and inferred from Kant's thinking (see, e.g., Archibugi, 1995: 445; Brown, 1992: 30–3; Hutchings and Dannreuther, 1999: 13–19; Reiss, 1991: 18–19). His starting point is what he called 'the categorical imperative'. This is a set of absolute, objective tests that define what is a moral action, basically distinguishing the pursuit of an interest or a desire, which is not moral, from the pursuit of duty, which is. Truly rational beings will pursue individual moral objectives or ends. The totality of individuals behaving in this manner Kant called 'a kingdom of ends'. However, as already indicated above, social, political and legal structures are necessary in order to enhance the possibility of moral action – indeed, the categorical imperative requires that individuals create such structures. Unhappily, however, the modern state's performance of this supportive function is dramatically impaired by constant war. Therefore, a cosmopolitan regime girded by a cosmopolitan law is necessary if the human race is to have any real chance of obeying the moral imperative.

This argument is grounded in the observation that the state is in practice inefficient in upholding the universal moral law. Another practical consideration relating to the behaviour of states derives from the current world condition of demographic mobility. Illegal immigrants, asylum seekers, refugees, temporary foreign workers and permanently settled aliens comprise a total world population of many millions who are residing in states of which they are not citizens. Is it just for them to be denied the civil, social and economic rights that are associated with state citizenship? What ethical principles should determine inclusion and exclusion? These people are in practice contributing or potentially will be contributing to the social and economic life of their countries of residence; moreover, as human beings they are bearers of universal rights. It can therefore be argued that a too sharp distinction between a state's treatment of its citizens and non-citizen peoples is immoral. Furthermore, the belief that the state has a special relationship with its citizens which no one else can share is being called into question by the growing realization that we all have multiple civic identities. In the UK, for example, a citizen of Glasgow might well think of him- or herself as a Glaswegian, a Scot, a Briton and a European. And, for good measure, is able to exercise the right to vote in each of these capacities. In terms of identity, though admittedly not of enfranchisement, this pyramidal structure may be topped by a consciousness of world citizenship. Consequently, the purist communitarian argument, based on the premise of a single citizenly identity, is at the very least obsolescent.

The cosmopolitan position, in contrast, starts with the assertion that all human beings are morally equal. In its fundamentalist version this belief becomes a principled rejection of the entrenched practice of states and state-citizens favouring compatriots over strangers. And this position is bolstered by the argument that states are arbitrary, artificial constructs, constantly being transmogrified over the years in both geographical extent and demographic composition: the political partition of the globe has been made for man's convenience, not organized upon the basis of any moral principle; worse, territories have as often as not been conquered, and the unequal distribution of the planet's natural resources among the peoples of the world is the result of happy or cruel chance, depending on one's allocation in the lottery. If the basis of political morality is consent, no states are ethically justified, because historically none was originally established on this basis, despite the myth (sic) of the social contract. Even the Mayflower Compact does not count – no native Americans were present in the cabin of the Pilgrim Fathers' ship when that document was agreed. The trouble is, philosophy and sociology are not at one on this matter since the ethic of cosmopolitanism clashes with the attraction of patriotism.

The cosmopolitan ethical questioning of the role of the state therefore needs to be taken further by suggesting that, as a political device, it has become a positive barrier to political morality. Particularly in its republican guise, state citizenship places great store by the civic virtue of patriotism. But is it really an unsullied virtue? During a dinner at the American naval base of Norfolk, Virginia, in 1816, a certain officer, Stephen Decatur, proposed a toast to 'Our country!', adding, famously, 'our country, right or wrong!' Is it a virtue, is it moral, to support one's country, knowing it to be harbouring attitudes or pursuing policies that are immoral? The ardent, unquestioning patriot of the Decatur stripe has so often not only condoned such habits but has himself grown into an aggressive nationalist and bigoted xenophobe – and called himself (usually 'him') a good citizen. The moral code of the world citizen deplores this kind of morality – a perverted morality in the cosmopolitan's book. A sense of cosmopolitan morality is therefore good both for its own sake and as a countervailing standard for testing and opposing the self-centred narrowness of a state morality that gives little or no thought to the moral rights of the foreigner. One of the aspects of world citizenship must therefore be for individuals to remind their governments and fellow-citizens that states have responsibilities as well as rights in a world setting.

So, too, do world citizens themselves. For over two centuries now insistent voices have demanded the listing and recognition of the *rights* of man/human *rights*. By the end of the twentieth century, however, a further demand was being heard, namely that these rights must, if they are to be morally justified in full, be balanced by a list of recognized universal human responsibilities. Article 29.1 of the Universal Declaration does indeed make a passing reference to the fact that 'Everyone has duties to the community in which the free and full development of his personality is possible'. A cosmopolitan reading of that sentence would construe 'community' as the 'world community', though hardly the interpretation the framers of the declaration intended. The task of drafting a list of duties or responsibilities for universal application has already been undertaken; but before outlining two notable examples we must investigate some of the very basic questions relating to the notion that world citizenship entails the acceptance and performance of duties.

In the first place, such duties can be justified on two main grounds. One is that the status of citizenship, especially in the civic republican mode, requires the citizen to have a sense of duty and to discharge that obligation at the state's behest. Because no world state exists to require world citizens to perform their duties, that is no reason why the moral requirement of citizenship should be ignored at the global level. The second justification is the accepted existence of human rights, the defence of which is both a matter of justice and of conscience. For rights cannot exist in a moral vacuum: if some individual or group is to enjoy rights, other individuals or groups must recognize their duty to refrain from abusing those rights or actively work to ensure the conditions for their enjoyment. No duties; no rights. Abstention from depriving individuals of rights is a negative form of duty; promoting rights is a positive form of duty.

However, Henry Shue has shown that the nature of duties is slightly more complicated than this simple bifurcation. His analysis has been summarized thus:

(i) duties to *avoid* depriving right-holding individuals of the content of the right,
(ii) duties to *protect* right-holders from being deprived of the right content, and
(iii) duties to *aid* deprived right-holders when avoidance and protection have failed. (Jones, 1999: 65)

Elsewhere (1988), Shue makes another distinction, namely, that between the (a) direct and (b) indirect performance of duties, the latter meaning assistance, or the exertion of pressure, to improve the institutional structures for the protection of rights. A simple example will show how these explanations relate to cosmopolitan duties. Article 5 of the Universal Declaration of Human Rights states: 'No one shall be subjected to torture ...' Using the above listings we can produce the following world citizen's duties: (i) not to torture anyone; (ii) to intervene to prevent a potential victim from being tortured; (iii) to effect the release of a prisoner being subjected to torture. Duties (ii) and (iii), the positive duties, can be discharged by either (a) directly working for Amnesty International, for instance, or (b) indirectly supporting Amnesty financially.

All civic rights – legal, political, social, economic and environmental, at global as much as at the state level – must imply concomitant duties, or the comprehensiveness and universality of rights are called into question. Accordingly, the following chapters will deal with each of these particular kinds of rights and duties. The reader will notice that the issue of cosmopolitan socio-economic duties has generated the greatest scholarly interest, for the matter of the responsibility of the rich to alleviate the sufferings of the poor is a highly visible issue yet presents a task enormous in scale and highly contentious in moral propriety. That question casts into sharp relief the most basic of all queries concerning the cosmopolitan ideal of responsibility: how far does or, rather, should the world citizen's duty reach in both geographical extent and depth of commitment?

The topic of how far duties should stretch brings us back to the metaphor of concentric circles, explained in Chapter 2. There we quoted Shue describing as the dominant view the conception of duties diminishing to nothing at the periphery. He challenges this assumption. He argues:

> What is wrong with the concentric image of duty is not that it has a center that is highlighted. What is wrong is the *progressive* character of the decline in priority as one reaches circles farther from the center [composed of one's intimates].
> ... Once the center has been left behind, however, I see insufficient reason to believe that one's positive duties to people in the next county, who are in fact strangers, are any greater than one's duties to people in the next continent ... a stranger is a stranger. (Shue, 1988: 692–3)

Relative distances are virtually meaningless today, Shue explains.

Our duties are thus potentially worldwide; we are world citizens. Nevertheless, no individual can be expected to guarantee the rights of six billion others. It is not a question of a slack conscience; it is literally impossible for one individual, be he even a hybrid of a Nietzschean superman and a Midas, to liberate all the chattel-slaves and bonded-workers or feed all the starving and malnourished. An

76

individual's resources of spare time, energy and money are minuscule in relation to the colossal scale of such problems. The world citizen's basic duty, therefore, is to channel what resources he or she can realistically contribute to supporting group (particularly NGO) activities protecting or advancing human rights. One urgent need is to ensure a worldwide acceptance of a Declaration of Human Responsibilities to match the Universal Declaration of Human Rights, a matter to which we now turn our attention.

In 1995, the distinguished Commission on Global Governance, in expounding their concept of a global civic ethic, expressed their unambiguous support for the concept of universal responsibilities. The key words are: 'all citizens, as individuals and as members of different private groups and associations, should accept the obligation to recognize and help protect the rights of others'; 'The tendency to emphasize rights while forgetting responsibilities has deleterious consequences'; and 'We therefore urge the international community to unite in support of a global ethic on common rights and shared responsibilities' (Commission on Global Governance, 1995: 56). Two years after the publication of this report, another group – this time, of former heads of state and government, and calling themselves the InterAction Council – produced a draft Declaration of Human Responsibilities. This document is prefaced by a lucid statement revealing the interconnectedness of rights, responsibilities and morality. It explains that:

> Rights relate more to freedom, obligations are associated with responsibility. Responsibility, as a moral quality, serves as a natural, voluntary check for freedom. . . . The more freedom we enjoy, the greater the responsibility we bear . . . [also], as we develop our sense of responsibility, we increase our internal freedom by fortifying our moral character. (InterAction Council, 1998: 1)

And, of course, as they record in the Declaration, the basic ethical principle is simplicity itself: 'What you do not wish to be done to yourself, do not do to others' (Article 4).

The two groups' lists of global/universal responsibilities do not exactly coincide, thus revealing the difficulty of constructing such documents. The Commission's 'consider the impact of their actions on the security and welfare of others' roughly equates with Articles 1–7 of the Council's sections on Fundamental Principles of Humanity and Non-Violence and Respect for Life; the Commission's 'contribute to the common good' approximates to the Council's Articles 9–11 on Justice and Solidarity; and the Commission's 'promote equity including gender equity' is covered by the Council's Articles 16 and 17 on Mutual Respect and Partnership. However, the Commission's 'protect the interests of future generations by pursuing sustainable development and safeguarding the global commons' is only briefly referred to in one sentence in the Council's Article 7; and the Commission's 'work to eliminate corruption' (sobering that it should appear as one of seven responsibilities) is indirectly alluded to in the Council's reference to 'integrity' in Article 8. The Commission's 'be active participants in governance' does not appear in the Council's Declaration, though, as we shall see below, the idea does feature in their Introductory Comment. However, the Commission's 'preserve humanity's cultural and intellectual heritage' has no parallel in the Council's document; nor does the Council's section on Truthfulness and Tolerance (Articles 12–15) have a parallel in the Commission's list.

Even without the detail of the draft Declaration, the reader will see that, taking the two documents together, with their slightly different emphases, the recommended human responsibilities would seem to be both sensible and comprehensive; furthermore, they were compiled by two independent groups, both of whom contained members from many different countries. In addition, they had support from a very rich range of advisers. For instance, Helmut Schmidt, co-chairman of the InterAction Council, has revealed that, 'it took about one decade of preparations and deliberations between political leaders, philosophical leaders, religious leaders of all the religions of the world, including Confucianism, all the ideologies, including Communism, to prepare the draft' (Schmidt, 1999: 5).

Both groups were evidently conscious of the need to relate ethics to institutional politics. We need to add this dimension of cosmopolitan morality to our survey. In order to be a good national citizen one needs to understand how to behave well towards one's state and towards one's fellow citizens. In addition, the state needs to provide opportunities, encouragement and discipline if good, rather than apathetic or bad, behaviour is to be demonstrated as widely as possible. So, too, for world citizens. Cosmopolitan political and legal frameworks are necessary, and they are in short supply. These are institutional topics dealt with in Chapters 6 and 4 respectively; at this juncture we are interested only in the need for a global civic ethic as a support for the required institutions. Kant understood this very clearly. In his *Foundations of the Metaphysics of Morals* he asserted that

> every rational being must act as if he, by his maxims [i.e. principles guiding actions], were at all times a legislative member in the universal realm of ends. The formal principle of these maxims is: So act as if your maxims should serve at the same time as the universal law (of all rational beings). (quoted in Hutchings and Dannreuther, 1999: 14)

Kimberley Hutchings comments that Kant's 'moral philosophy, premised on a recognition that we are all in some sense cosmopolitan by virtue of being human, places its principal emphasis on the imperative to construct the ethical cosmopolis', and points out Kant's 'stress on our active commitment to make the shadow cosmopolis of the rationally accessible moral law an actually legislated kingdom of ends' (*ibid.*: 13–14).

In simpler, more direct language the Commission on Global Governance declared that 'The quality of global governance will be determined by several factors. High among them is the broad acceptance of a global ethic to guide action within a global neighbourhood. . . . Global values must be the corner-stone of global governance' (Commission on Global Governance, 1995: 46–7). Notice the words 'legislative member' in the above quotation from Kant, 'active commitment' in Hutchings and Dannreuther, and 'action' in the excerpt from the Commission. Also, the InterAction Council makes the point pithily by stating that the objective of their document is 'to promote a move from the freedom of indifference to the freedom of involvement' (InterAction Council, 1998: 4).

But on what principle of political ethics should one argue the right and duty of involvement? A significant and helpful response to this question has been offered by the concept of 'discourse' or 'dialogic' ethics. This may be interpreted historically as the latest idea connecting communication with cosmopolitan political ethics. We have already had occasion to remark on the reliance of Stoic cosmopolitanism on the Greek notion of *logos*, incorporating, with moral overtones, the activity of communication. In the seventeenth century the Moravian theologian, educationist and cosmopolitan thinker Comenius wrote a multi-volume work recommending ways of improving 'human affairs'. In one volume, entitled *Panegersia*, he sketched out a scheme of political institutions to achieve this objective. The plan involved a global network of assemblies, through which matters of universal import would be debated. Comenius asserted that 'Because the matter is of common concern, no one should therefore be excluded from this consultation about human affairs, no one should be allowed to exclude himself' (quoted in Heater, 1996: 62). Whereas Comenius makes consultation on world issues equally a right and a duty, the modern cosmopolitan interpretation of the concept of the dialogic ethic lays rather more stress on the right not to be excluded from having a voice in policy decision-making when transnational interests are at stake. We must therefore investigate the basic idea of discourse ethics as expounded particularly by Jürgen Habermas, and its application to cosmopolitanism as expounded particularly by Andrew Linklater (1998).

The American educational psychologist Lawrence Kohlberg has indicated the stages of moral development from childhood onwards. The most advanced stage, not attained by all, can be said to be achieved when the person has learned to recognize that morality is more than obeying rules for their own sake, and that rules must be judged critically in order to act in a socially responsible manner. Habermas has built upon this insight to argue that the development of an appreciation that a universal moral code might be superior to group or state loyalties should be encouraged. The ultimate objective of this moral growth is a universal acceptance and implementation of what he calls 'discourse ethics', that is, the moral right of everyone who is or might be affected by a situation or policy to be engaged in a consultative process to discuss the moral implications of the issue. Linklater has provided a succinct explanation of the concept:

> Discourse ethics argues that norms cannot be valid unless they can command the consent of everyone whose interests stand to be affected by them. . . . It follows that a political community which has a commitment to discourse ethics will be deeply concerned about the damaging effects of its actions on outsiders. One of its central beliefs is that the validity of the principles on which it acts can only be determined through a dialogue which is in principle open to all human beings. (*ibid.*: 91)

Discourse ethics involves an empathetic search for moral agreement with due understanding and tolerance of all group and cultural perspectives, and the desire to enhance the right of all perspectives to be heard, considered and, ideally, embraced; in Linklater's words, 'to explore the possibility of an agreement about the principles of coexistence' (*ibid.*: 96).

The close relationship of discourse ethics to world citizenship is fairly clear. The concept provides for a set of arrangements based upon communication and collaboration, not domination or tight integration; it asks states to admit outsiders into their deliberative practices, but at the same time avoids overwhelming states with a threatening cosmopolitan system of governance. To quote Linklater again:

> National boundaries cannot be assumed to be so morally significant as to justify confining the right of access to unconstrained dialogue to members of the group. A dialogic community must therefore involve relevant outsiders in key decisions regarding the distribution of membership, citizenship and global responsibilities. Bonds between members have to be loosely formed to permit the evolution of wider communities of discourse which are in principle open to all others. (*ibid.*: 103).

Linklater is indeed convinced that dialogic ethics are of cardinal importance for world citizenship. He suggests, in fact, a reciprocal relationship of responsibilities. On the one hand, he asserts that 'the societies which contribute most to world citizenship will aim to ensure that the universal communication frameworks in which they take part reflect the vision of the dialogic community' (*ibid.*: 212); on the other hand, he claims: 'The primary function of cosmopolitan citizenship is to institutionalise the normative commitment to "limitless communication" through participation in diverse communities of discourse' (*ibid.*: 54–5).

We may add that, by stressing the *moral* weight of communication, the idea of discourse ethics reinforces the element of communication, which, as we have already noticed in this chapter, is a vital component of citizenly *identity*. Furthermore, a sense of world citizenship identity would be strengthened in the institutional sense in the event of consultative frameworks being created.

Nor are arrangements for transnational discourse justified only on the moral grounds of justice – they are also supported by democratic arguments that world citizens have a moral duty to press for deliberative assemblies beyond the confines of the nation-state. As

David Held has asserted: 'the establishment of a cosmopolitan community ... must become an obligation to build a transnational, common structure of political action which alone, ultimately, can support the politics of self-determination' (Held, 1995: 232; see also Chapter 6 below). But a widespread acceptance of the ethical principles underlying world citizenship is a distant prospect: the draft Universal Declaration of Human Responsibilities, for example, for all the thorough care that attended the lengthy process of its composition, has received scant interest or support – has even been met with considerable hostility. Have the schemes for creating the required institutions any better chance of implementation?

CHAPTER 4

Law and Civil Rights

International Law

It is a mark of citizenship that the possessor of that status should enjoy certain rights in law, crucially to be protected by the rule of law, and thus to be ensured of such freedoms as freedom of the person, of thought, belief and expression. These civil rights, where they exist by constitutional formulation and actual practice, are enshrined in and guarded by municipal, i.e. state, law. The questions to be addressed in this chapter are: whether it is desirable and/or feasible to replicate such rights at the global level in order to sustain a status of world citizenship; and whether they already exist in some measure in the form of the international human rights regime.

These questions, however, contain numerous component issues. First, there is the root matter of the interpretation of the source and legitimacy of law. The positivist view is that law is man-made, deriving from the actions and authority of the state. The alternative, natural law theory argues that law should derive from higher principles independent of contingent factors of time and space. Any overarching global law providing for a world citizenship would need to be grounded in and justified by an acceptance of the principle of natural law, especially in the absence of a world government. This, in turn, raises the question whether a three-tiered system of law is essential and possible – municipal, international and global. The idea of a third level was famously expounded by Kant in his triad of *ius civitatis, ius gentium* and *ius cosmopoliticum* (civil, international and cosmopolitan law). In the twentieth century, and into our new age, the idea of a global level of law has been found attractive by a number of writers, using different terms; for example, World Federalists advocate 'world law', Richard Falk (e.g. 1995) refers to a 'law of humanity' and David Held expounds the idea of a 'democratic cosmopolitan law' (e.g. 1995). We shall examine these concepts of a global law below. Before dealing with this matter, however, we need to investigate the relationship that does or might exist between world citizenship and international law.

Despite disagreements among students of jurisprudence regarding the precise relationship between international and municipal law, the established basic distinction is quite clear: municipal law is concerned with individuals; international law is concerned with states, who, in the eyes of international law, are legal 'persons'. Thus, it would seem to follow, municipal law provides state citizenship; but international law cannot provide world citizenship to individuals since such a concept is beyond its state-centric remit. The spheres of competence between these two forms of law are reasonably discrete and clear-cut. However, and certainly when one takes an historical perspective, the distinction between a notional naturalist cosmopolitan law and a positivist international law has not been as evident as Kant proposed.

In origin, in fact, law that regulated affairs between peoples and states was an amalgam of positivist and natural law. In order to handle the expanding contact between Rome and its citizens on the one hand and non-citizen foreign peoples on the other, Roman jurists evolved the *ius gentium* to supplement the *ius civile* (i.e. state-defined positivist codes). Initially, the *ius gentium* was a compilation that took cognizance of local codes, it then became influenced by Stoic cosmopolitan, natural law thinking and was accordingly considered as a law of universal application. Subsequently, when, in Europe in the seventeenth and eighteenth centuries, there was developed a modern international law (often called, as we have seen in Kant's classification, *ius gentium*), this new positivist system still bore signs of the natural law of the old *ius gentium* tradition. That great Victorian jurist Henry Maine, indeed, declared quite firmly that 'The grandest function of the law of nature was discharged in giving birth to modern international law' (quoted in Brierly, 1928: 17).

The classical writers on international law, while stressing the codes of conduct to which *states* should conform, nevertheless did indeed hold to certain *universalist* ideals. Vattel revealed this dualism most lucidly in his *Le Droit des Gens* (1758):

> Since the universal society of the human race is an institution of nature itself, that is, a necessary result of man's nature, all men of whatever condition are found to advance its interests and to fulfil its duties. No convention or special agreement can release them from the obligation. When, therefore, men unite in civil society and form a separate State or Nation, they may, indeed make particular agreements with others of the same State, but their duties towards the rest of the human race remain unchanged; but with this difference ... it devolves thenceforth upon that body, the State, and upon its rulers, to fulfil the duties of humanity to outsiders in all matters in which individuals are no longer at liberty to act. (quoted in Linklater, 1982: 81–2)

The early modern theorists were at pains to present three particular situations in which the cosmopolitan principle should be honoured. One was the duty of providing assistance; another was the right and duty of the state to engage in humanitarian intervention; a third was the individual's rights of residence and travel. Each of these principles may be briefly illustrated by quotations. 'On the basis of the *law of humanity, any one whatsoever is bound* ... to the extent of his power *to come to* [*the*] *aid of a second person* in an extreme necessity,' declared Pufendorf (quoted in Green, 1987: 159). Grotius asserted that 'Kings ... are burdened with a *general responsibility for human society*. ... The most wide-reaching cause for undertaking wars on behalf of others is *the mutual tie of kinship among men*, which of itself affords sufficient ground for rendering assistance' (quoted in *ibid.*: 158). The third cosmopolitan principle foreshadows Kant's *ius cosmopoliticum*, which is therefore not quite as original as some commentators imply. Vitoria asserted that:

> all men have the rights of residence and trade even in foreign lands. The right to reside somewhere on earth was considered such a basic natural right that the eighteenth-century writer of jurisprudence, Bynkershoek, contended that even an exiled criminal 'must dwell somewhere while he lives, *being a citizen of the world*'. (quoted in *ibid.*: 168)

85

All three of these cosmopolitan principles are, of course, very much alive today.

We might well conclude from this evidence that there is a *prima facie* case for believing that the cosmopolitan natural law mode of thinking could still inject into contemporary international law an element of sympathy for the principle of global citizenship.

Yet the Canadian academic lawyer L. C. Green, having analysed this literature, adamantly denies the validity of such an induction, on both historical and present-day evidence:

> The classicists clearly paid lip-service to sentiments favouring the brotherhood of man, but to a great extent these views were mere excuses to justify a prince's right to take over another's territory. ... Even when the ideas lacked any such ulterior motive, they were still limited by raisons d'état restricting concepts of international fraternity by selfish considerations, with national security overriding principle and idealism. (*ibid.*: 170)

He adds for good measure that, 'in customary international law ... [there is no] acknowledgment that something like world citizenship could exist in reality' (*ibid.*: 175). And he concludes that:

> Any suggestion that a world citizenship could exist side by side with existing nationalities remains artificial and any 'citizenship' so granted would be hollow in character. ... It must be recognized that if the Charter of the United Nations or the Universal Declaration of Human Rights had been proposed for adoption today, they would almost certainly have been rejected. What is true of these two manifestos is even more true of a world citizenship. (*ibid.*: 184)

Green's case is a mixture of historical evidence and pragmatic argument. A more radical rejection of any legal basis for world citizenship is presented by Stephen Neff. He makes three pertinent points. One is that 'positivism (at least in its "pure" form)' precludes any real kind of cosmopolitan citizenship because of its insistence 'that rules applicable to the conduct of individual persons must emanate exclusively from nation-states' (Neff, 1999: 112). Second, he even denies that natural law has given any support to the concept. The reason for making this judgement is the 'disjunction between law and government' in that tradition. (As we have seen in our summary of the position of the Roman Stoics in Chapter 1, commitment to the natural law and commitment to the state were to their minds two different sets of duties.) Neff continues:

> A direct consequence of this disjunction between natural law and government was that citizenship played hardly any role in natural-law thought. It could not, because citizenship was, quintessentially, a political concept. It meant – and, to lawyers, continues to mean – membership in a given *political* community. (*ibid.*: 107)

Neff's third point is even more trenchant: 'international law,' he asserts, 'has tended to move in the opposite direction from that of cosmopolitan citizenship. The thrust of legal reform efforts is not so much to promote a new idea of citizenship as to make the whole idea of citizenship irrelevant' (*ibid.*: 117).

International lawyers are concerned about the big global issues and try to use the tool of international law for the amelioration of problems and injustices; but the concept and status of citizenship are, in their eyes, not germane to this task. International law indeed defines citizenship in territorial terms: citizenship and nationality are synonymous. Moreover, it holds that, since the rights and duties of a citizen derive from municipal law, the individual is a citizen insofar as he or she is a member and has a genuine and effective link with a territorial state. This principle was consolidated by the judgement of the International Court of Justice in the Nottebohm case in 1955 (see Brownlie, 1990: 397–9, 407–20). Perhaps this is a semantic problem, an unwillingness to adapt or stretch the term 'citizenship' beyond its original use? This question will be taken up in the section on human rights below. Also, it is for us a matter of general concern, not just confined to the law, and relates back to part of the discussion in Chapter 1.

What is pertinent to the subject-matter of this chapter is the contrary evidence that some commentators have fastened onto, indicating a growth and increasing flexibility in international law. This development is seen to comprise several features. One British Professor of International Law, Christopher Greenwood, has stated that 'International law has evolved to the point where it no longer regards the way in which a state treats its own citizens as an internal matter' (*Guardian*, 28 March 1999). James Crawford and Susan Marks have commented: 'International law, with its enlarging normative scope, extending writ and growing institutionalization, exemplifies the phenomenon of globalization' (Crawford and Marks,

1998: 82). One result of these changes is the erosion of state sovereignty. Some go further and recognize that the greater flexibility of international law today is quite novel. Although, admittedly, not using the words 'world citizenship', Antonio Cassese writes of a post-1945 'new law' creating new standards of behaviour relating to human rights and what he calls 'world welfare conditions'. As a result, he avers, 'law has become less "realistic" and more "idealistic"' (Cassese, 1991: 273). This is a significant change for the development of a world citizenship. For it was the realism of post-Westphalian international law that has been a significant factor in inhibiting the incorporation of world citizenship into that legal system. Cassese's observation, together with Crawford and Marks's reference to 'enlarging normative scope', could therefore be interpreted to suggest that international law is again accepting natural law norms which it largely dispelled in the late eighteenth century (see also Bull, 1977: 148, 158). That being so, international law might be evolving a mode of thought less antipathetic to world citizenship than hitherto.

Crucial to such an adaptation would be the acceptance that the individual person can be a recognized actor in international law. And it can be argued that in the field of human rights this is in truth happening. The two clearest examples to support this contention are Article 28 of the 1948 Universal Declaration of Human Rights and the 1998 Rome Statute of the International Criminal Court (ICC). The former states unambiguously that 'everyone is entitled to a social and international order in which the rights and freedoms set forth in this Declaration can be fully realized'. And the Preamble to the latter includes the following clauses:

> Conscious that all peoples are united by common bonds, their cultures pieced together in a shared heritage, and concerned that this delicate mosaic may be shattered at any time. . . .
>
> Determined to put an end to impunity for the perpetrators of these crimes and thus to contribute to the prevention of such crimes.

Richard Falk describes human rights as a 'bridge' (Falk, 1995: 108) and declares that the 'law of humanity . . . is prefigured, and to some extent embodied, in the substance and theory of the international law of human rights' (*ibid.*: 163). What is of interest in this trend is not just that the aspiration for a future cosmopolitan law is creeping into a present reality, or that the individual is coming within the purview of international law, but that the individual in this legal context is seen as acting and receiving rights in his or her capacity as a member of a world community, a cosmopolis. Drawing the reader's attention to the ways in which the international law of human rights is even starting to influence judges in domestic cases, the Commission on Global Governance comment: 'We applaud this development, recognizing as it does the commonality of global identity' (Commission on Global Governance, 1995: 325). Even more forceful is the reference in the Rome Statute, already cited, 'that all peoples are united by common bonds'. A common global identity and common bonds make world citizens; these statements are made in instruments of international law; ergo, international law implicitly, even though still tentatively, recognizes world citizenship. The nature of the world citizenship contained in human rights law must therefore be investigated.

Human Rights

The topic of human rights is an area of international law that is fraught with controversy. To start with – and it is best to square up to this matter straight away – it could be argued that the subject is not the province of international law, but rather of ethics. For example, Geoffrey Robertson cites the 1912 edition of a well-used text on international law, which states that, if a state treated its citizens 'with such cruelty as would stagger humanity', intervention could be justified only by Christian charity, not international law (Robertson, 1999: 64).

But are not law and ethics near allied? Article 1 of the Universal Declaration of Human Rights asserts: 'All human beings are born free and equal in dignity and rights. They are endowed with reason and conscience and should act towards one another in a spirit of brotherhood.' These are moral philosophical propositions, yet form the foundation upon which the various covenants and conventions have been constructed and entered into international law. Thus, although the Universal Declaration of Human Rights (1948) does not have the force of law, the two subsequent 1966 International Covenants (on Economic, Social and Cultural Rights, and Civil and Political Rights) and the large number of special Conventions (e.g. on Genocide, on the Status of Refugees, on the Rights of the Child) do have recognized legal status. Indeed, the whole purpose of the post-1945 human rights endeavour is to have the instruments universally ratified and incorporated into international law.

However, this matter of classifying the nature of human rights pronouncements is by no means the only disputed feature surrounding the subject. There are other questions that are asked. Are human rights fully and truly universal or can they ever be so? (This is an issue of identity and has been more aptly discussed in Chapter 3.) What are human rights? What is the relationship between state citizenship and human rights? And – can human rights be construed as, potentially, the rights of world citizens? Even academics with a strong commitment to the cosmopolitan ideal offer differing answers to that last question, so important for our purpose of elucidating world citizenship rights. Two brief quotations are given to exemplify this lack of agreement:

> It is necessary to clarify that a theory of world citizenship is something completely different from a doctrine of natural rights. (Archibugi, 1995: 134)

> As to *content*, the agenda of the human rights covenants taken together provides much of what is required for the foundation of a global democratic citizenship. (Beetham, 1998: 66)

Why should the notions of human rights and world citizen rights be considered distinct? And how has this belief in distinctiveness arisen? After all, it may plausibly be claimed that present-day ideals of the rights (and duties) of citizenship, world citizenship and humanity all ultimately derive from the natural law mode of thought. During the century from about 1690 to about 1790 two key propositions laid the foundations for modern thinking in this sphere – that human rights are natural and that civil society is founded on a social contract. Locke was the pivotal figure because of his linkage of these two theories. In the *Second Treatise of Civil Government* he asserted:

> Man being born, as has been proved, with a title to perfect freedom and an uncontrolled enjoyment of all the rights and privileges of the law of nature, equally with any other man, or number of men in the world, hath by nature a power not only to preserve his property, that is, his life, liberty, and estate, against the injuries and attempts of other men, but to judge of and punish the breaches of that law in others ... But ... there,

and there only is political society, where every one of the members hath quitted this natural power, resigned it up into the hands of the community in all cases that exclude him not from appealing for protection to the law established by it. (Locke, 1962: s. 87)

A century later, the French Constitution, which came into effect in 1791, overtly distinguished between the 'rights of man and the citizen' (the Declaration of Rights) and, as an alternative formulation, between 'natural and civil rights' (Title I); though, in truth, what characterized each in this bifurcation of rights was anything but clear.

Yet there persists an assumption that there is a difference between human and citizenship rights. Two means of differentiation may be identified. One is that human rights are given by nature, and cannot legitimately be abused, indeed should be positively *protected* by the state; whereas citizenship rights are given by the state, and, because of that derivation, the state is at liberty to *withdraw* them. Second, human rights predate the creation of political society; they exist for all and for all time (even though the precise list is subject to adaptation), whereas citizenship rights are specific to the state that has accorded them. Alan Gewirth goes further, according absolute primacy to human rights. He contends that:

> Human rights are of supreme importance, and are central to all other moral considerations, because they are the rights of every human being to the necessary conditions of human action, i.e., those conditions that must be fulfilled if human action is to be possible either at all or with general chances of success in achieving the purposes for which humans act. Because they are such rights, they must be respected by every human being, and the primary justification of governments is that they serve to secure these rights. (Gewirth, 1982: 3)

This is surely tantamount to saying that states must ensure the right of individuals to act as human beings, an empowerment that furnishes them, via citizenship rights of the state, with the rights of world citizenship.

Yet, those who stress a strong distinctiveness between citizenship and human rights will tend to deny that human rights can be equated, even approximately, with world citizenship rights. We

91

must start by remembering that citizenship involves duties as well as rights. Moreover, in its Stoic origins the concept of world citizenship required duties – it did not offer rights; world citizenship was a commitment to a moral code devoid of any institutional structure for its implementation. In contrast, the *sine qua non* of rights is that there must be machinery to ensure their enjoyment and defend them against abridgement or blatant violation. This function – equally for national citizenship rights and human rights – is performed by the state. That the framers of the Universal Declaration of Human Rights intended the signatory states to play this role is evident from the text: the Preamble declares that 'Member *States* have pledged themselves to achieve ... the promotion of universal respect for and observance of human rights'; and Article 8 asserts that 'Everyone has the right to an effective remedy by the competent *national* tribunals for acts violating the fundamental rights granted him by the *constitution* and the *law*' (emphases added).

Citizenship rights are accorded and ensured by the state, the citizens having political rights to participate in the task of guardianship. The regime of universal human rights is not equipped with any equivalent world political system; to be blunt, it is parasitic on nation-states for its implementation, so we have the paradox that legal world citizenship can be approached only through the state system that denies world citizenship. It follows, therefore, that the relationship of individuals to human rights cannot be that of world citizens because the necessary political institutions to act in this way do not exist. As the nature of the rights clearly indicates, the relationship involves individuals as *humans*, not citizens. If the lists of universal human rights that exist in the several international documents are to assume the status of world citizenship rights, then political institutions must be created with powers formally to confer the rights and to monitor and enforce their observance.

Let us pursue this argument hostile to the cosmopolitan case a little further. If individuals do lodge complaints against their own states, they are behaving in only the most shadowy manner as citizens. For example, even if the UN Commission of Human Rights were an efficient watchdog (which it is not), individuals appealing to that body about their states' transgressions of their rights, it can be argued, are claiming justice as *human beings* because their rights as *citizens* are being abused.

But there is an even more fundamental justification for insisting on the key role of the state: it is that the protection of human rights can effectively be undertaken only by individual states acting as sovereign powers. This condition has two components.

In the case of liberal democracies, David Miller believes that, because of differing local circumstances, 'citizenship is better served by constitutional reform within those states than by the creation of transnational bodies, whose likely effect is to dilute the quality of citizenship by applying uniform criteria in fields where uniformity is neither necessary nor appropriate' (Miller, 1999: 75). In the more difficult case of the persistent and often horrific abuse of human rights by autocratic, even genocidal, regimes, again, in practice, the best response is that taken by individual states, even if acting sometimes in concert. Writing of humanitarian intervention, Nathan Glazer has written:

> All these commitments to others' claims and rights involve costs, in money and lives, and these costs are not assessed against the world, but against the citizens and soldiers of a specific country, the only entity that can lay taxes and require soldiers to obey orders. It is hard to see, practically, how to move beyond a situation in which the primary power to grant and sustain rights rests with constituted states. (Nussbaum *et al*, 1996: 62–3)

This is a task for regional powers. In taking their positions, notice, Miller and Glazer use the words 'appropriate', 'reality' and 'practically': they are questioning both desirability and feasibility of world citizenship as a feature of human rights protection.

Any suggestion that the recognition of a set of universal human rights is evidence of some form of world citizenship is rejected. But there are opposite, supportive arguments. Some of these are conceded grudgingly; others are expressed with a deeper conviction.

One form of the tentative or partial equation of human rights with world citizenship is to suggest that only some rights can be accepted as bearing this synonymity. It is, in fact, common to cluster rights into different groups, or generations (as explained below). Thus, Geoffrey Robertson refers to 'the notion of a *third* generation of rights, belonging to citizens of the world, to peace and development and a clean environment' (Robertson, 1999: 12). More common is the acceptance that a code of human rights is necessary as a protection for citizens against their own states. David Miller, a prominent opponent of the idea that world citizenship can or should exist, nevertheless admits that, 'If a state has acted unjustly, and it is possible to put the injustice right by invoking transnational or international law, that is all to the good.' But, he insists, 'only a minimal kind of citizenship is involved when this occurs' (Miller, 1999: 74).

If, however, we wish to construct a more whole-hearted case for a close kinship between human rights and world citizenship, we need to demonstrate that both the global and citizenly features co-exist in the post-1945 human rights regime.

For all the reservations concerning the true universality of human rights (see Chapter 3), there can be little doubt that the great number of conventions and covenants that now comprise the UN and regional human rights codes are intended to be of universal application. Moreover, just as the standards set by these documents aim at universal protection, so, as David Beetham claims, the threats to these rights are universal problems. He explains that:

> The increasing evidence of global interdependence (consequences of population growth, environmental degradation, pressures for migration, 'social dumping', etc.) indicates that the costs of human rights denials are increasingly exported, not just experienced by their immediate victims. Such interdependencies combine with the processes of global shrinking and the internationalization of the media to expand our definition of the stranger who merits our concern. (Beetham, 1998: 61)

The question as to whether it is justifiable to use the word 'citizenship' is more complex and needs to be assessed in relation to the creation of the human rights regime, the content of the rights proclaimed and their implementation. One of the most cogent arguments embraces all three of these aspects: it is that the growth of the system has involved world citizenship in recognizable forms in a two-way process. Some individuals have behaved as world citizens in establishing and monitoring the human rights concept and structure, while all have yardsticks by which to measure the protection they should expect to enjoy, in principle, as world citizens, irrespective of their status as citizens of nation-states.

The very existence of catalogues of human rights is due to the campaigning from the beginning of the Second World War of individuals who were utterly convinced of the desperate need for an improved world order. Of these, the dedicated believer in world government, H. G. Wells, was by far the most successful campaigner, particularly through the publication of his *The Rights of Man: or What Are We Fighting For?*, issued as a Penguin Special in 1940 and subsequently translated into thirty languages. More recently, NGOs have been influential in shaping a number of human rights documents. Beetham cites, among other examples, the success of the women's movement in achieving the incorporation of anti-discrimination clauses in the two basic International Covenants, and in influencing the texts of the Convention on the Elimination of All Forms of Discrimination against Women and the Declaration on Violence against Women (see *ibid.*: 63). These may be taken as instances of individuals working on vital documents as world citizens for the sake of other world citizens. Participation and legal protection are both marks of citizenship.

The range of rights protected by the covenants and conventions is by now extremely comprehensive, but it is not part of our purpose to examine them. What is of interest is to ask whether we can discern any features of comparability with defined rights of national citizenship. Analysts of rights both in academic discussions on the nature of (state) citizenship and in international law have fallen into the habit of using the image of 'generations'. In the case of state citizenship the most usual classification is to place civil and political rights in the first generation, social and economic in the second and, as the most juvenile, environmental rights into the third generation. International law, in turn, speaks of civil and political rights as first generation, economic, social and cultural as second, and the right to food, to a decent environment, to development and to peace as the third generation. The correspondence is very close. So, just as state citizens' rights are enshrined in articles of constitutions or attached bills of rights, the key UN documents, the two legally binding Covenants, may be interpreted as performing the same role for the rights of world citizens.

In this chapter we are mainly concerned with civil rights – the others being the subjects of Chapters 5 and 6. All the accepted civil rights such as the rule of law and basic freedoms are clearly listed in Part III (Articles 6–27) of the International Covenant on Civil and Political Rights. Moreover, each state party to the covenant undertakes 'To ensure that any person whose rights and freedoms as herein recognized are violated shall have an effective remedy' (Article 3(a)).

Whether a person's civil rights are infringed is relatively easy to determine: political censorship, banning of meetings, torture and summary executions either do or do not take place. However, there is a notable difference between state citizenship rights and human rights. In the case of the former, executive and judicial branches of government exist with the authority, responsibility and power to implement and monitor the observance of all civic rights, whereas the institutions and methods for performing these roles barely exist at the transnational level. For this reason, it is often concluded that the equation of human rights and world citizenship is fallacious.

Yet the distinction is by no means absolute. The UN has established an International Court of Justice, a Human Rights Committee and a Human Rights Commission and, although they remain dormant, were they allowed to rouse themselves, they could perform some of the necessary transnational functions for protecting basic rights. Even so, supranational monitoring and exertion of pressure can be and are being undertaken in the informal realm of the mass media, popular opinion and, particularly, NGOs. Commenting on the growth of this form of supervision, David Beetham gives his opinion that 'the human rights regime is increasingly taking on the character of an independent jurisdiction' (Beetham, 1998: 62). Those engaging in these tasks, again, can be said to be behaving and treating others as world citizens.

In one respect, progress is being made in constructing formal institutions and procedures to defend human beings' rights: this is the prosecution and punishment of those who criminally transgress the code of human rights by being guilty of committing crimes against humanity. Arraignment of such individuals is becoming a key feature of the international rule of law. Consequently, just as all state citizens are required to obey the domestic law and none may be exempted from punishment if they break it, so, by analogy, all human beings *qua* world citizens are now required to obey international law and can be expected to suffer retribution for any criminal acts they may perform. True, only a tiny proportion of those guilty of torture, murder and genocide during the past two horrendous generations have been brought to justice. Nevertheless, a start has been made. We need to take note of the main milestones. After the Second World War, a Charter was drawn up to guide the proceedings in the prosecution of Nazi war criminals in Nuremberg and these 'Nuremberg principles', as they are called, have in turn guided subsequent treatment of those believed to have committed crimes against humanity. For example, the Charter stated categorically: 'That international law imposes duties and liabilities upon states has long been recognised. ... The very essence of the Charter is that individuals have duties which transcend national obligations' (quoted in Maser, 1979: 268).

Nuremberg was an *ad hoc* tribunal. So, too, are the Hague and Arusha tribunals for the trial of those indicted for human rights crimes in the former Yugoslavia and Rwanda respectively. However, the Statute of Rome, drafted in 1998, creates the possibility (when the required minimum number of states ratify it) of a permanent International Criminal Court. The ideal sought for in establishing these courts is that all states would agree to deny asylum to any person indicted of such crimes and, where appropriate, to assist in their arrest. The whole world is the field of jurisdiction of these courts.

In addition to these institutional developments, two particular judicial decisions recently handed down deserve special notice. One is the judgment of the Hague tribunal in 2001, finding three Bosnian Serbs guilty of mass rape and sexual enslavement. This was an historic ruling: the first time that these actions have been categorized as serious crimes against humanity, and a vindication for women's rights organizations who have argued that definitions of human rights have been biased in a number of ways towards male interests. The second particular decision was the arrest in Britain in 1998 of General Pinochet, the former Chilean President, who was widely believed to have been responsible for the torture and 'disappearances' of political opponents. True, he was allowed to return to his homeland (where he was subsequently put on trial). None the less, his original arrest was, in the opinion of one human rights lawyer, 'momentous'. The reason for this assessment is that Pinochet believed his status as a former head of state and as a citizen of a sovereign state gave him immunity from arrest in another country. This assumption was shown to be mistaken, and 'the *Pinochet Case* became the first and paradigm test of international human rights law' (Robertson, 1999: 347, 348).

The idea of world citizenship is implicit in the whole human rights documentation and structure. Admittedly, only a very small number of individuals are active in this sphere, mainly through the work of NGOs like Amnesty International. But their numbers and effectiveness are growing. In the words of Beetham:

there is a strong cosmopolitan elite in both the formal and informal sectors committed to the greater effectiveness of the human rights regime. A distinctive feature of this elite is its ability to forge links with popular struggles at the most local level anywhere in the world. (Beetham, 1998: 68)

These people are the vanguard or, to use the distinction drawn in the Introduction to this book, they are the active world citizens. This mode of differentiation is particularly apposite here, for the mass of humankind can be thought of as the passive world citizens – the passive recipients of human rights and the passive bearers of the obligation not to deny these rights to others. One way in which the body of active world citizens could be enlarged is to increase the opportunities for individuals to use the law in order to enhance the level of enjoyment of human rights throughout the world; that is, by the creation of a system of supranational jurisprudence.

Cosmopolitan Law

A clear concept of cosmopolitan law can be found in the thought of the Greek philosopher Heraclitus, *c.* 500 BC. Starting with the understanding of *logos* as a capacious word with a meaning beyond its basic concept of reasoned speech, he argued (as H. C. Baldry has explained) along the following lines: 'Because the *Logos* is "common", thought also is common to all; and the universality of the *Logos* lies behind all human laws or customs (*nomoi*)' (Baldry, 1965: 26). In Heraclitus' own words: 'all human laws are nourished by one law, the divine law' (quoted in *ibid.*: 27).

Modern discussion of the concept of world or cosmopolitan law may be said to start with Kant, and in a rather more concrete way than in the philosophy of Heraclitus. Even so, it is possible to hear an echo of the Heraclitan idea in his work. The *logos* is more highly developed in the minds of the philosophers, who can therefore discern the universal law with greater clarity than others. Similarly, Kant declares that:

The legislative authority of a state ... [should] seek instruction from *subjects* (the philosophers) regarding the principles on which it should act in its relations with other states. ... And no special formal agreement among the states is necessary ... for the agreement already lies in the obligations imposed by universal human reason in its capacity as a moral legislator. (Reiss, 1991: 115)

Admittedly, this passage is of interest only in revealing in general Kant's mode of thinking, though important none the less; it does not relate directly to his concept of cosmopolitan law (*ius cosmopoliticum*), to which we must now turn our attention.

For all the slenderness of his presentation of a *ius cosmopoliticum*, it has provided a source of considerable interpretive disagreement (see, e.g., Archibugi, 1992: 312) and a significant intellectual under-pinning for current discussions, particularly the notion of cosmopolitan democracy. Kant expounded the concept in both *Perpetual Peace* and *The Metaphysics of Morals* (see Reiss, 1991: 98–9n., 105–8, 172–3). (A linguistic note before summarizing Kant's ideas: he uses the Latin word *ius* and the German word *Recht*; translation is difficult because the meaning incorporates both law and justice; and there is the further complication that the translation cited here renders it as 'right' – an unfamiliar use of the word. So, except in quotations, 'law' will be used here.)

As explained in the first section of this chapter, Kant depicts law as existing in three forms – civil, international and cosmopolitan law. In the process of expounding this novel, third form, he gives two different interpretations – a confined and a wide sense. The sub-section in *Perpetual Peace* devoted to the topic states: '*Cosmopolitan Right shall be limited to Conditions of Universal Hospitality*' (*ibid.*: 106). He explains: 'hospitality means the right of a stranger not to be treated with hostility when he arrives on someone else's territory' (p. 107). Even this limited right is restricted, though in making his proviso Kant gives his basic reason for the existence of the right, which has wide potential: 'The stranger,' he declares, '... may only claim a *right of resort*, for all men are entitled to present themselves in the society of others by virtue of their right to communal possession of the earth's surface' (p. 107). (In contrast, what in his view is an 'appalling' distortion of this principle is the conquest by Europeans of other lands for commercial gain.)

Now, this 'communal possession' – or utilization, for it is not accompanied by any international legal legitimation – leads to the possibility of the several nations of the earth being able to engage in reciprocal understanding and action, indeed having the right to do so.

> This right [argues Kant], in so far as it affords the prospect
> that all nations may unite for the purpose of creating certain

universal laws to regulate the intercourse they may have with one another, may be termed *cosmopolitan* (*ius cosmopoliticum*). (*ibid.*: 172)

In this passage in *The Metaphysics of Morals* Kant has clearly moved from the very constricted meaning of cosmopolitan law quoted above from *Perpetual Peace*. Yet even within the space of this essay on peace he gives another, broader definition, saying that the essence of cosmopolitan law lies in the following condition: 'in so far as individuals and states, co-existing in an external relationship of mutual influences, may be regarded as citizens of a universal state of mankind' (*ibid.*: 98–9n.). Moreover, he expands on this point when he suggests a kind of cosmopolitan law which embraces a recognizable world citizenship. He writes:

> The peoples of the earth have thus entered in varying degrees into a universal community, and it has developed to the point where a violation of rights in *one* part of the world is felt *everywhere*. The idea of a cosmopolitan right is therefore not fantastic and overstrained; it is a necessary complement to the unwritten code of political and international right, transforming it into a universal right of humanity. (*ibid.*: 107–8)

Some commentators have insisted that Kant's cosmopolitan law needs to be set in the context of his moral philosophy, his tripartite classification of law and his image of a global confederation (see, e.g., Archibugi, 1995; Brown, 1992: 28–41, Reiss, 1991: 21–4); and that Kant's meaning can be, indeed has been, misconstrued if these connections are not made. His vision is indeed holistic. Man is endowed with reason and moral sense, encapsulated in his ideas of the categorical imperative and the universal kingdom of ends (see Chapter 3 above.) Practical moral reason underpins the three forms of law, but only states incorporating and honouring these are likely to contribute to a peaceful confederal world. The crucial connection in Kant's thinking between ethics on the one hand and law on the other is his concept of universal right. He explained: 'Every action which by itself or by its maxim enables the freedom of every individual's will to coexist with the freedom of everyone else in accordance with a universal law is *right*' (Reiss, 1991: 133). Reiss comments: 'The universal principle of right is only an application of the universal principle of morality, as laid down in the Categorical

Imperative, to the sphere of law, and thus also the sphere of politics' (*ibid.*: 23).

But, naturally, our interest is to understand how this pattern of thinking specifically relates to world citizenship. The connection is clearly expounded by Daniele Archibugi. He identifies two main ways in which Kant's coherent thinking implies a conception of world citizenship. One concerns his understanding of the universal implications of the violation of rights. Archibugi explains:

> Although cosmopolitan rights ultimately perform a function similar to the one which natural law attributed to natural rights, their theoretical foundation is entirely different and much more solid insofar as citizens of the world are at once possessors of these rights and the ones who, in the final analysis, are called upon to make them apply. This is the meaning we must attribute to the assertion that, 'a violation of rights in *one* part of the world is felt *everywhere*'. . . . As soon as he assumes the role of a citizen of the world, the citizen is called upon to use his reason to assess if and when the rights of his fellows are violated. (Archibugi, 1995: 449)

Archibugi's other important insight is his perceived connections between Kant's triad of laws, his objective of peace and world citizenship. He explains that Kant defines cosmopolitan law as:

> 'a necessary complement to the unwritten code of public and inernational right, transforming it into a universal right of humanity', and, at the same time, as a necessary prerequisite for 'advancing towards perpetual peace' . . . that is, to found peace on respect of individuals as citizens of the world. (*ibid.*: 447)

We must not forget, indeed, that Kant's central political purpose was to encourage a confederation of republican states for the purpose of preserving peace (see Chapter 6 below). Only such politically liberal states would be likely to collaborate in this way; and, what is more, only citizens living in such a political culture could be expected positively to support this ideal. Consequently, citizens enjoying the benefits of Kant's concept of *ius civile* are likely also to think in cosmopolitan terms. Kant, in fact, emphasized just how felicitous this connection could be when he wrote, 'To consider oneself, according to internal civil law, as an associate member of a cosmopolitan society is the most sublime idea a man can have of his destination. One cannot think of it without enthusiasm' (quoted in Hassner, 1998: 285–6).

Kant was no believer in the virtues of democracy; nevertheless, his introduction into political thinking of the notion of cosmopolitan law has inspired the exponents of cosmopolitan democracy, notably David Held, with the idea of a cosmopolitan democratic law. Starting from the basis of his work on the theory of democracy and becoming conscious of and concerned about the 'democratic deficit' (to use the European Union term) at the global level, Held and like-minded scholars have developed the concept of cosmopolitan democracy. This complex proposal is presented with great thoroughness in Held's *Democracy and the Global Order: From the Modern State to Cosmopolitan Democracy* (see also Archibugi and Held, 1995; Archibugi, Held and Köhler, 1998; Kymlicka and Straehle, 1999). As in Kant's work, there are a number of interconnected strands in the tightly knit programme. Accordingly, we need to set the legal aspects in context here, as well as revealing the debt to Kant, but postpone a survey of the political features to Chapter 6.

Held starts with the basic premise that a juridico-political system should ensure the individual's autonomy, by which he means, 'the capacity of humans to reason self-consciously, to be self-reflective and to be self-determining' (Held, 1995: 151). This condition requires the existence of 'democratic public law' for ensuring rights and regulating public institutions. However, since an individual's autonomy can be threatened by events beyond his or her own state, democratic public law must also be extended beyond the confines of the state by the development of 'cosmopolitan democratic law'. In choosing the term 'cosmopolitan', Held explicitly acknowledges the origin of the concept in Kant's thinking (*ibid.*: 227).

However, the relationship between Held's and Kant's cosmopolitan law goes deeper than the mere choice of a word. Just as Kant's *ius civile* and *ius cosmopoliticum* have a necessary co-existence, so do Held's democratic public law and cosmopolitan democratic law. Furthermore, Held argues, with the evolution of cosmopolitan democracy,

> the principles of individual democratic states and societies could come to coincide with those of cosmopolitan democratic law. As a consequence, the rights and responsibilities of people *qua* national citizens and *qua* subjects of cosmopolitan law could coincide, and democratic citizenship could take on, in

principle, a truly universal status. In these circumstances, it could be said, adapting Kant, that the individuals who composed the states and societies whose constitutions were formed in accordance with cosmopolitan law might be regarded as citizens, not just of their national communities or regions, but of a universal system of 'cosmo-political' governance. (*ibid.*: 232–3)

Even Kant's limited notion of cosmopolitan law as the principle of universal hospitality has, according to Held, wider implications that underpin the latter's concept of cosmopolitan democratic law. For, universal hospitality must involve, in Held's opinion, 'both the enjoyment of autonomy and respect for the necessary constraints on autonomy'. This means 'mutual acknowledgement of, and respect for, the equal rights of others'. Therefore, no matter where an individual lives in the world, all must be able to participate, agree and consent. From this line of argument Held concludes that 'The condition of universal hospitality, or, as I would rather put it, of cosmopolitan orientation, is a cosmopolitan democratic public law' (*ibid.*: 228–9).

As Kant realized, of course, a cosmopolitan law requires institutional structures to generate and protect the universal code. These, in turn, must erode, to some extent, established seats of sovereignty. Whereas Kant envisaged a centripetal solution of *states* coming together for the crucial purpose of perpetual peace, Held envisages a centrifugal solution of the dispersal of *sovereignty* for the crucial purpose of universalizing democracy (see Chapter 6 below).

The agenda for a cosmopolitan law conceived under Kantian influence has not been the only approach to a supranational law that would codify and institutionalize the rights and obligations of world citizenship. The shock of the Second World War gave an urgent impulse to the conviction that what was generally referred to as 'world law' was essential if the peoples of the planet could have any hope of a civilized life with peace and human rights assured. From the time of the First World War, in truth, a multitude of plans for a world federal government were drafted, particularly in the USA, with the object of securing global peace. Then, in 1947, there took place at Montreux the inaugural conference of the World Movement for Federal World Government (subsequently more conveniently renamed the World Federalist Movement). The Montreux Declaration reveals the attitude of world federalists to world law in that era:

'The human race will cease to exist unless a world government capable of enforcing world law is established by peaceful means', ran the assertion, bleakly reflecting the current fear of a nuclear holocaust (quoted in Nathan and Norden, 1960: 421). A similar plea for effective world law as a means to peace was voiced by two American lawyers, Grenville Clark and Louis B. Sohn, who entitled their major work on the subject, *World Peace Through World Law*. Clark explained their understanding of the meaning of world 'law':

> Law which would be uniformly applicable to all nations and all individuals in the world and which would definitely forbid violence or the threat of it as a means for dealing with international disputes. This world law must also be law in the true sense of law which is capable of enforcement, as distinguished from a mere set of exhortations or injunctions which it is desirable to observe but for the enforcement of which there is no effective machinery. (Clark and Sohn, 1958: xi)

Enforcement, needless to say, was and is the rub. Accordingly, fully convinced world federalists and advocates of a mighty strengthening of the UN, like Clark and Sohn, have argued for a robust institutional setting for world law: an elected world legislature, courts of law and equity and an executive world police force. Belief in the necessity for such a structure persists down to our own day, especially among world federalists in the USA. One such advocate for world law makes the issue quite explicit:

> the question of whether it would be desirable to establish a federal world government ... is basically the question of whether it would be desirable for the world community to move from reliance on international law to reliance on world law. (Glossop, 1993: 48)

Now, although the prospect of nuclear war petrified those in the post-1945 years who hoped that world law might mitigate that threat, defence of human rights was also a motivating force in their thinking and became increasingly so with the abatement of the early Cold War terror of a nuclear Armageddon. Some world federalists, indeed, shifted their focus from world government for peace to world law for human rights (see, e.g., Roberts, 1993).

A rather different approach has been sketched out by Richard Falk in his concept of 'the law of humanity' (see Falk, 1995). Although accepting that such a code is 'mainly in the dreaming (or purely aspirational) phase' (*ibid.*: 167), he nevertheless recognizes signs of waking reality in the evolving human rights regime, especially under pressure from global civil society. Yet we are in practice far from creating a fully effective law of humanity which would treat 'each person on earth as a sacred subject' (*ibid.*: 172), despite the fact that progress towards this goal is necessary, and for two reasons. One is the slow pace of adaptation of international, inter-state law to recognize the individual as a subject of that system. The other, more importantly, is the danger, as Falk sees it, of the powerful forces of globalization. He suggests that 'the law implications of globalization-from-above would tend to supplant inter-state law with a species of global law, but one at odds in most respects with "the law of humanity"' (*ibid.*: 170). The growth of the latter law will be dependent on globalization-from-below, in other words, on the activities of individuals working as world citizens.

The development of a fully fledged cosmopolitan law, world law or law of humanity is, in any case, also an intrinsic requirement for the development of a fully fledged world citizenship. The rights of world citizenship cannot be secure without an entrenched system of cosmopolitan law, and the obligations of world citizenship cannot be exacted without an effective system of global monitoring. Furthermore, to reiterate the globalization-from-below concept, the likelihood that cosmopolitan law will be established is exceedingly remote without individuals acting as world citizens by exerting pressure on nation-states and the established institutions of global governance in order to bring about the necessary changes. But, by the exertion of pressure, individuals are and will be behaving as world citizens in the political rather than juridical sense – the subject of Chapter 6.

CHAPTER 5

Social, Economic and Environmental Citizenship

Social and Economic Rights: Evolution

When the rights of man and the rights of the citizen were being classically proclaimed in the countries on the rim of the North Atlantic in the century very roughly from 1690 to 1790, they were defined almost entirely in civil and political terms, the famous exception being Locke's inclusion of property in his tripartite classification. The French Declaration of Rights of 1789 and the American Bill of Rights clearly focus on the civil and political spheres (though the French document does include the Lockean property). However, during the nineteenth century, the idea gained ground that there should be social and economic rights to complement – even, perhaps, take priority over – civil and political rights. Thus, when the Leninist constitution came into effect in the new Soviet Union in 1918, it was prefaced by the already drafted Declaration of Rights of the Toiling and Exploited People, described by E. H. Carr as 'the announcement of a social and economic policy' (Carr, 1966: 151).

Now, this addition to the catalogue of rights not only extended their scope, it introduced a new dimension. Civil and political rights were defined and fought for in order to *protect* citizens from oppression by the state; social and economic rights were defined and fought for in order to ensure that the state *provided* such entitlements as a reasonable standard of living, welfare and education. Moreover, just as the Bolsheviks established a case and an institutional framework for socio-economic rights based on a Marxist-socialist model at the end of the First World War, so British governments and the social theorist T. H. Marshall provided a social democratic/liberal version in the concluding years of the Second World War and its aftermath.

The late 1940s were in fact years of vital importance for the consolidation of the notions of social and economic rights in the definitions of both citizenship and human rights. In 1949 Marshall delivered a series of lectures in Cambridge, later published under the title *Citizenship and Social Class*. Impressed by the welfare state reforms of the time, he argued that these added the social coping-stone to the rights of citizenship in the UK, the civil and political components having been put in place in earlier centuries. The essence of citizenship is equality – equal access to civil and political rights – but class divisions, poverty and lack of education prevent effective access to these rights. Provision by the state of unemployment benefits, old-age pensions, health care and education rectify this condition; and, given as *entitlements*, free of the disparaging stigma of charity, they are, like the right to trial by jury and the suffrage, the dignified marks of citizenship. Marshall's insistence that social rights are as integral a part of the status of citizen as the traditional civil and political rights has become widely accepted.

The year before Marshall's lectures, the United Nations proclaimed the Universal Declaration of Human Rights. It is noteworthy that the task of drafting this document had been remitted to the UN Economic and Social Council and that UNESCO conducted an enquiry into the theoretical problems attendant upon the framing of such a declaration. The chairman of the UNESCO committee, E. H. Carr, stated unequivocally 'that any declaration of rights which would be felt to have any validity today must include social and economic as well as political rights' (UNESCO, 1949: 22). Furthermore, in striving to define universally acceptable principles of *human* rights, at least some members of the UNESCO committee were alert to the implication that what they were analysing was a feature of world citizenship. Thus, their final summary report declared:

These rights must no longer be confined to the few. They are claims which all men and women may legitimately make, in their search, not only to fulfil themselves at their best, of becoming in the highest sense *citizens* of the various communities to which they belong and of *the world community*. (*ibid.*: 260; emphases added)

Thus it can be said that, by the middle of the twentieth century, no definition of state citizenship or human rights and consequently of world citizenship could be considered complete without the full acceptance of the principle of social and economic rights.

The Universal Declaration of Human Rights in fact does reflect this new concern for social and economic rights. It states the fundamental principle that:

> Everyone, as a member of society, has the right to social security and is entitled to realization, through national effort and international co-operation and in accordance with the organization and resources of each State, of the economic, social and cultural rights indispensable for his dignity and the free development of his personality. (Article 22)

Articles 23–27 expand on this general proposition, dealing with the topics of work, standard of living, education and cultural life.

Because the Declaration had, and indeed has, no legal standing, the idea was mooted that the principles should be incorporated into an international treaty. However, agreement to such a proposal not only hit up against the solid barrier of state sovereignty, it also had to navigate the ideological chasm of the Cold War. The Western, US-dominated stance was to stress civil and political rights; the Communist, Soviet-dominated stance was to stress social and economic rights. There was nothing for it but to draft two documents, the Covenants on Civil and Political Rights and on Economic, Social and Cultural Rights, which, even so, did not see the light of day until 1966 and did not come into legal force (with the minimum number of states ratifying them) until ten years later. The controversial issue of the distinctiveness of the two sets of rights is to be examined in the next section of this chapter. Here we are concerned with just the simple list of economic, social and cultural matters as presented in the Covenant devised to protect this category of rights. Harking back to President Roosevelt's 1941 'four freedoms', the Universal Declaration referred to 'freedom from fear and want'. This formula was picked up in the Covenant, which insists that 'The ideal of free human beings enjoying freedom from fear and want can only be achieved if conditions are created whereby everyone may enjoy his economic, social and cultural rights, as well as his civil and political rights' (Preamble).

The whole thrust of the Covenant is towards the obligation of the signatory states to ensure to their best ability that their citizens enjoy the level of well-being indicated in the document. The predominant image is of individuals as citizens of states and as passive recipients of these rights. One can therefore argue that the Covenant has no bearing on world citizenship. Yet it does have relevance, and for two reasons. One is that the Covenant is a universal standard, a checklist of the economic, social and cultural rights everyone ought to be able to enjoy – and note the deliberate use of the word 'everyone' in the excerpt from the Preamble just quoted. It is a statement of a welfare 'floor', and an assertion that the quality of life of no member of 'the human family' (to cite the Preamble again) should be allowed to fall below this level. Just as the Beveridge Report, referring to the need to attack the five giants of Want, Disease, Ignorance, Squalor and Idleness, laid the foundations for the welfare state for British citizens, so the International Covenant on Economic, Social and Cultural Rights may be thought of as a founding document for what is sometimes referred to as 'welfare internationalism' for world citizens.

Nor is the role of the individual presented as entirely passive: this is our second reason for suggesting that the Covenant does contribute to the concept of world citizenship. For the Preamble explains that 'The individual, having duties to other individuals and to the community to which he belongs, is under a responsibility to strive for the promotion and observance of the rights recognized in the present Covenant.' Maybe the drafters of the Covenant meant by 'other individuals' co-citizens of the state and by 'community' any level of society not transcending the state. And yet, by reference back to the first paragraph of the document, both forms of duty could – perhaps should – be interpreted in a cosmopolitan sense, namely, reading 'individuals' as 'members of the human family' and 'the community' as the 'human family' itself.

What, however, of the practice? If putative world citizens are to be assured of welfare support analogous to that provided by states to their citizens, then the global system should approximate to state systems. These may be characterized by three features. Taxes are paid by citizens to provide the public services; the state ensures that its citizens have these services available to them; and citizens help their co-citizens by working in the service and caring professions or by doing community work. To use the jargon, the first two features are expressions of 'vertical' social citizenship; the third, of 'horizontal' social citizenship. The question is, whether the global community is or is not capable of offering a comparable pattern of welfare provision so that one can speak with honesty about a world social and economic citizenship.

It goes without saying that there is no world state to which world citizens pay taxes in return for services. However, the UN Specialized Agencies exist for this work. Indeed, the League of Nations which came before the United Nations was committed to the principle of social and economic assistance. Article 23 of the League Covenant pledged member states to 'endeavour to secure and maintain fair and humane conditions of labour for men, women and children, both in their own countries and *in all countries to which their commercial and industrial relations extend*' (emphasis added); and 'to endeavour to take steps in matters of international concern for the prevention and control of disease'. In pursuit of the first of these objectives, the League created the International Labour Organization (ILO), which continues in existence as a UN Specialized Agency. The Specialized Agency regime, in fact, covers all economic, social and cultural matters, the evidence for which exists in the exhaustive use of the alphabet in so many abbreviations and acronyms, e.g. the United Nations Educational, Social and Cultural Organization (UNESCO) for education and culture, the United Nations Children's Fund (UNICEF) for children's welfare, the World Health Organization (WHO) for health, the United Nations Development Programme (UNDP) for economic development. The funding for the activities of these bodies comes from the UN member states: virtually every state in the world. Nor must we forget economic and financial assistance provided direct by the more affluent states to the impoverished. These payments are therefore a kind of global income tax paid indirectly by citizens via their states for these cosmopolitan purposes.

There is evidence of a closer parallel to national welfare state arrangements when we examine the third feature of social citizenship, that is, the activities linking citizens to citizens. Clearly, those individuals administering the Agencies and working in the field as doctors, nurses, teachers, agronomists and so forth are working for the global community in exactly the same way as are their national counterparts in their states. However, the most striking example of social world citizenship is the work undertaken by members of NGOs and individual citizens' initiatives. Just as one may talk of the good active citizen at the state level, so one may surely name as virtuous world citizens people working for bodies like Médecins sans Frontières (MSF), Red Cross, Oxfam and the Jubilee 2000 project. Also, in a less prominent way, members of the public who contribute the essential funds to organizations of this kind are behaving as world citizens too.

Let us take MSF and Jubilee 2000 as two very different examples. In a leaflet, MSF has described its activities thus:

> Our work takes us to over 80 countries worldwide where casualties of war, disaster and epidemic look to us to provide assistance. Each year about 2,500 doctors, nurses, logistics specialists and engineers of all nationalities leave on field assignments. .... We also campaign locally and internationally for greater respect for humanitarian law and the right of civilians to impartial humanitarian assistance. (n.d.)

Jubilee 2000 was a scheme run by a handful of enthusiasts in London to exert pressure for the cancellation of unpayable international debts accrued in the poverty-stricken countries. Within four years, 24 million signatures in support were received and nearly a hundred countries set up 'Jubilee coalitions'. The following comments add to the inescapable judgement that this was a most remarkable enterprise:

> It was an extraordinary coalition of groups ranging from aid agencies and churches to the British Medical Association, the music industry and the Mothers' Union. This formula was replicated in each country forming an enormous civil network which commanded considerable respect at the World Bank and the International Monetary Fund. (Madeleine Bunting, *Guardian*, 28 December 2000)

> It has turned a complex subject into a mainstream campaign issue and in the process has educated thousands of activists. ... The result has been the first bold experiment in creating a global political culture. (*Guardian*, 30 December 2000)

For 'global political culture' read 'sense of world citizenship'.

Not, however, that the struggles against want, disease, ignorance, squalor and idleness are making more than the slowest progress. There are, of course, manifold problems including, notably,

111

precisely defining adequate levels of welfare, availability of financial and human resources for the raising of standards, and the ineffectual enforcement of the terms of the International Covenant. Two comments relating to these difficulties must suffice here before examining in the next section the issues of definition and justification that lie at the heart of implementing effective world social citizenship. First, the UN Committee on Economic, Social and Cultural Rights has attempted to define 'an absolute minimum entitlement, in the absence of which a state party is to be considered in violation of its obligations' (quoted in Beetham, 1998: 62). The second comment concerns the lack of international legal machinery and political will to ensure that these obligations are met. These deficiencies need to be filled by two complementary developments: that wealthy countries supply the necessary supplementary funds and that the governments of the indigent states accept some erosion of their state sovereignty occasioned by the stringent monitoring of the use of those funds. Geoffrey Robertson has called for the creation of a 'quasi-legal system' to ensure that in these ways all the world's people can enjoy the entitlements listed in Articles 22–27 of the International Covenant (see Robertson, 1999: 149, also 146–7).

This kind of argument involves an alignment of socio-economic rights with the legally definable and enforceable civil and political rights. But are the two broad categories of rights, treated in two distinct international covenants, really sufficiently alike to be handled in the same way? For the nature of social and economic rights is an issue of some contention.

Social and Economic Rights: Essence

Analyses of and assertions about the social and economic rights of the state citizen have provoked considerable scholarly and political disagreement. At the global level, the literature on the cognate issues that it is necessary to review, in order to contemplate the essence of the world citizen's social and economic rights and their justification, forms a rich body of epistemological, moral and pragmatic arguments (see Jones, 1999). The nature and meaning of rights, justice, equality and humanitarianism in the socio-economic sense and their relationship to citizenship of the world become drawn into our examination of the topic. So too does the question of the appropriateness of the domestic analogy; that is, whether the principles which may be considered sufficiently cogent to justify the creation and maintenance of a welfare state for citizens of a territorial state are compelling enough to warrant a similar system for individuals in their status as world citizens. We must first of all be clear about what is meant by distributive justice and understand the argument about the domestic analogy.

The use of the term 'justice' in a socio-economic sense must not, of course, be confused with justice in a judicial sense. Justice as a social principle implies the provision of basic needs for life and the distribution of goods beyond the minimum entitlement in a just manner. But what is just? Aristotle worried round this problem (see, e.g., Aristotle, 1948: 1282b–1283a). He argued that justice resides in equality, but that equality should be construed as proportionate equality, that is, treating people on their merits, relating distribution *to* them by society to contribution *by* them to society. Whereas Aristotle started from the principle of equality, in our own day, John Rawls has started from the reality of inequality, arguing that 'Social and economic inequalities are to be arranged so that they are . . . to the greatest benefit of the least advantaged' (Rawls, 1971: 302). Lower rates of taxation for those on low incomes is an example of this principle.

Now, equality is a characteristic of citizenship – Aristotle, for instance, writes of 'the natural equality of citizens' (Aristotle, 1948: 1261b). And the welfare state form of distributive justice, supported by Rawls's 'difference principle', as he calls it, is a system to mitigate the injustice of a 'second-class citizenship'. Furthermore, we have already seen in the first section of this chapter how Marshall argued that social rights are essential to the status of citizenship. So, if distributive justice is an integral feature of state citizenship, it must also surely be a feature of a parallel world citizenship. Yet, as will be shown, this extension of the principle is not readily accepted.

Indeed, Onora O'Neill has stated, 'The discussion of international distributive justice is both new and messy' (O'Neill, 1991: 276). It is new because disparities in peoples' living standards are widening, facts concerning the gap are broadcast by the increasingly pervasive news media, and it is now technically and administratively more feasible than formerly to tackle this injustice. Between 1960 and 1997, the disparity in income between the richest 20 per cent of the world's population and the poorest 20 per cent rose from a multiple of 30 to 74. The injustice is blatant. And the discussion is messy because the search for principles of redistribution, hard enough to define at all, is bedevilled by doctrinal splits across the political spectrum and the difficulty of devising institutional structures to achieve agreement in practice.

The simplest and most powerful argument against the very notion of global distributive justice is the belief that the domestic analogy is totally false. Hobbes presented this case in its most unambiguous manner. In a state of nature, he asserted, 'The notions of Right and Wrong, Justice and Injustice have there no place. Where there is no Power, there is no Law: where no Law, no Injustice.' And the same principles 'that dictateth to men that have no Civil Government ... dictateth the same to Common-wealths' (Hobbes, 1914, ch. 13: 66; ch. 30: 189). Since states have between them no equivalent of the civil compact that exists among civilized men, they continue to relate to each other in the equivalent of a state of nature. In rather different language, Rawls has used the contractarian argument to draw the same conclusion. Society, he argues, is a 'co-operative venture for mutual advantage' (Rawls, 1971: 4), but by equating a society with the territorial state and also by assuming that a state is a socially self-sufficient unit, Rawls denies any global analogy that would posit a cosmopolitan social justice akin to that enjoyed by citizens of a state. State welfare systems, or distributive justice, can both exist and be justified because there is a sense of community, a give-and-take ethos, a general will (to use Rousseau's term) or, in short (and *pace* Margaret Thatcher), a society; in Rawls's alternative term 'a fair system of co-operation' (quoted in Beitz, 1999: 277), which involves proper legal and social structures. These requirements, according to Rawls, do not exist at the global level: there is no 'world community' in this truly cohesive sense. Therefore, there can be no cosmopolitan social justice, no global welfare state. The implications are clear: it would be an impertinence, an injustice indeed, to require as a matter of duty (as opposed to voluntary charity) that the world's wealthy contribute to the improvement of the condition of the world's poverty-stricken; consequently, social world citizenship cannot legitimately exist.

A most cogent response to these negative arguments has been deployed by Charles Beitz. He denies the fallacy of the domestic analogy. He sees a different planetary picture, one of considerable social interaction, of economic interdependence, of poverty perpetuated by unjust global structures that cry out, in all justice, for regulation. He trenchantly asserts that the Hobbesian 'conception of international relations as a state of nature is empirically inaccurate and theoretically misleading'. It is inaccurate because the world is rapidly becoming an interconnected community analogous to domestic society, and it is misleading because the moral scepticism of the argument cannot be self-contained and therefore leads to 'a more general scepticism about all morality' (Beitz, 1979: 179). Furthermore, because the interdependent world economic system tends to favour the rich countries over the poor, 'confining principles of social justice to domestic societies has the effect of taxing poor nations so that others may benefit from living in "just" regimes' (*ibid.*: 149–5). By extension, therefore, human beings are rapidly becoming members of a world society and may be considered, accordingly, as world citizens; the moral argument against global distributive justice – the denial of a more just distribution of the world's benefits among all peoples – is undermined; and a world citizenship containing social and economic rights is both a plausible and a just idea.

These basic points explained, we are now in a position to examine numerous detailed controversial matters relating to the concept of global social and economic rights.

It is useful to make a distinction between the prevailing view of limited international responsibility in the face of desperate poverty in many countries of the world on the one hand, and the cosmopolitan view that this arrangement is systematically unfair on the other. Beitz has used the term 'social liberalism' to describe an influential kind of the former thinking, and explains its viewpoint: 'The international responsibility is to encourage the flourishing of *societies*, not individuals. ... The equality to which it aspires at the global level is a political equality of (just and decent) peoples organized as states; it is not in any sense an equality of persons' (Beitz, 1999: 280). Moreover, the collection and publication of statistics, notably by UN agencies, reinforces this stance: poverty, or underdevelopment, to use the euphemism, is gauged by the position of states in the gross national product (GNP) or human development index (HDI) tables. (The HDI includes figures for literacy and life expectancy, as well as income.)

But it is individuals, as world citizens, suffering shortfalls in social and economic rights who should be counted and considered – that is the alternative, cosmopolitan position. The difference may be summarized in the following manner. The conventional position is that *states* have a *responsibility* to channel *aid* to poor *countries*; the cosmopolitan position is that the *world community* has an *obligation* to meet the social and economic *entitlements* of poor *individuals*. The two schools of thought are thus at variance on four counts. How do the cosmopolitan thinkers justify their case?

To oversimplify, we may identify four basic arguments. The first, to repeat, is the contention that a world society is rapidly evolving and that if distributive justice is valid at the state level, by the same criteria it must be valid at the global level. Second, and following this proposition, moral responsibility, duty rather, of the advantaged to share their advantages with the disadvantaged cannot be considered to be bounded by the frontiers of the territorial state. Third, and with specific focus on economics, the impoverished are often doomed to that condition because of geographical chance: harshness of climate and paucity of natural resources condition standards of living. Yet, conversely, one may question the right of the more naturally favoured countries to exploit merely for themselves those of the planet's resources that, arbitrarily, are located in those fortunate lands. 'If one shares the view,' Beitz argues, 'that individuals are entitled to benefit equally from the world's resources, then the right conclusion is that resource inequalities should be compensated for' (*ibid.*: 286). And fourth, in global as well as domestic conditions, poverty goes hand-in-hand with powerlessness. Because the impoverished, for no fault of their own, are in want of the political strength to rectify their disadvantage themselves, there rests upon the global community of world citizens the obligation to effect a redistribution of the planet's resources. These four arguments can, in fact, be derived from a variety of basic positions – for example: that all individuals are possessed of human rights; that all human beings are morally equal and consequently all have a right to a reasonable standard of living; and, the utilitarian case, that resource redistribution would extend the level of happiness and induce a greater tendency to peace in the world – which are cosmopolitan goals in any case.

Not, however, that the cosmopolitan argument is proof against criticism, particularly queries deriving from some very untidy loose ends. Here, we shall do little more than pose them as questions – and leave them as ends untied. Let us start by asking: how far along the route to social and economic interdependence and integration does the world need to travel in order to be rated as a moral community analogous to a social-welfare nation-state? If, or when, that required sense of community has been achieved, how far does resource redistribution have to be taken, that is, how much wealth would the rich be required to surrender? Carried to extremes, this process would lead to a world citizenship of extraordinary self-sacrifice for the quondam privileged akin to the austere code of the ancient Spartiates. Even a much more realistic objective would be difficult to impose: so, who is to persuade the relatively rich to effect even modest transfers of wealth? And what institutions would be needed to exert this persuasion and administer the redistribution in an efficient – and just – manner?

An optimistic response to this sheaf of questions may be offered along the lines that a wide range of aid agencies already channels multilateral assistance to the least economically developed countries. However, this is to confuse humanitarian charity with citizenly entitlement, assistance with justice. Both may be reckoned as considerate actions. But the humanitarian motive is a task of tackling poverty as first aid so that, once the patient has been treated, the responsibility has been discharged; whereas the citizenly motive is to treat poverty as a malfunctioning of the global body politic and to ensure a sustained cure. We can pursue the distinction. The liberal view of international aid is that it should be used to ensure stable societies. In Rawls's words, 'once the duty of assistance is satisfied and all peoples have *a working liberal or decent government*, there is no reason to narrow the gap between rich and poor' (Rawls, 1999: 114; emphasis added). In contrast, Beitz defines the cosmopolitan view: 'that the basic institutions of society, at both the global and sectional levels, should be justified in ways consistent with [the] fundamental commitment' that individuals are 'entitled to equal concern on a global scale' (Beitz, 1999: 296).

Beneath this divergence of opinion lies an even more fundamental issue, namely, whether socio-economic rights can correctly be categorized as rights at all; because if they are not, then talk of world citizens' entitlements and distributive justice loses its force. In the domestic setting even, the assumptions, policies and lines of argument of the 1940s and 1950s stressing social and economic rights have subsequently been challenged.

There is no doubt that social and economic rights are different in kind from civil and political rights; the former are vague, the latter precise. To state that all citizens have a right to at least a minimum standard of living, for example, raises numerous difficulties concerning the definition, quantification and guarantee of that right. These difficulties derive mainly from limitation of resources, at either the state or the world level. To take the latter case: the exiguous funds that are available to the world community for transnational use are required for peace-keeping operations, responding to man-made crises such as the effects of war and coping with natural disasters, as well as paying for the strategy of raising the living standards of those in the most desperately straitened circumstances. Even in the arena of development programmes, the multitudinous varieties of claims for education, health, infrastructure, agriculture and industry force the setting of priorities that require Solomonic wisdom if anything but the roughest of justice is to be meted out. And if these so-called rights can be neither precisely measured nor precisely delivered, is it not a perversion of language and politically misleading to use the term 'rights' at all? Should we not more accurately and truthfully speak of aspirations or goals for raising people to an adequate citizenly standard in the socio-economic sense?

The reader will readily observe that the case for denying socio-economic standards the status of rights rests on a clear-cut differentiation between the nature of these standards and those referred to as civil and political rights. The former, declared Maurice Cranston, 'belong to a different logical category' (quoted in Donnelly, 1985: 90). However, this attempted bifurcation has been strenuously challenged, both by exponents of the nature of state citizenship and by the commentators on human rights. The reasoning is that the most fundamental right is liberty, that the purpose of liberty is freedom to act, and that the freedom to act is seriously impaired in a condition of grinding poverty. Civil and political rights are not separate from economic and social rights; on the contrary, the two pairs are symbiotic. Such an interpretation was confirmed by the World Conference on Human Rights, convened by the UN in Vienna in 1993. The consequent statement described civil, political, economic, social and cultural rights as 'universal, indivisible, and interdependent and interrelated'. As Alan Gewirth had stated a decade earlier:

> The relief of starvation as a human right ... is closely connected with the civil liberties so highly prized in the Western constitutional democracies as human rights. There may, indeed, be political dictatorships which promote an equitable distribution of food and hence secure one human right at the expense of another. [But] the relief of starvation is

a political as well as a technical problem, and the moral guidance of both sorts of problem require that the freedom of the recipients be protected equally with their well-being, and this for the sake of well-being itself. (Gewirth, 1982: 215–16)

It may be that morally and logically the social and economic rights of world citizens are on a par with civil and political rights, but that does not mean that they are easily matched in practice. We have already noticed in the first section of this chapter that, as the concept of rights developed in the nineteenth century, liberal and socialist emphases diverged, stressing freedom and welfare respectively. Moreover, the ability of world citizens to reconcile these two values today is no easy matter because of the spread of capitalism and industrialization. In his study of the evolution of citizenship in Britain, Marshall famously and exaggeratedly asserted that capitalism and citizenship had been 'at war'. Is that perhaps true on the world stage now? In recent years, anti-capitalist demonstrations, notably against the *laissez-faire* policy of the World Trade Organization (WTO) and the perceived evils of economic globalization, have been organized, for example in Seattle, Prague and Genoa, to assert, in effect, that the freedom of the few to make money is harming the welfare of the many. And not just in social and economic senses but, as will be explained in the next section, this kind of freedom is also damaging the environment.

However, an attempt to relate citizenship as freedom with citizenship as welfare becomes easier if we remember a third facet of citizenship, namely, duty. If citizens have duties not just to their state, but to their fellow citizens, then, *pari passu*, world citizens have duties towards their fellow world citizens; and in no sphere is the need to call that duty into play greater than in the matter of relieving hunger. The grounds for asserting this form of obligation are controversial. Briefly, it can be argued either that rights are meaningless unless citizens or institutions are willing and able to perform their duties to ensure that these rights are in fact enjoyed, or that, as human beings, we have by our very moral nature a requirement to meet our obligations irrespective of the existence of rights. Be that as it may, we still need criteria for determining the limits of the demands on our sense of duty in the context of distributive justice. As rights in this sphere are not precisely measurable, nor either are duties. This is merely to reiterate the vexed question raised earlier of the level of self-sacrifice that citizenly duty can justly demand.

If there are so many difficulties, both theoretical and practical, must we conclude that socio-economic world citizenship is, in effect, virtually an impossibility? The *realpolitik* answer is in the affirmative. The issue of wealth redistribution in order to raise the standard of living of the most indigent to a reasonable level is economically possible; what is not readily available is the political will to bring it about. Moreover, the political stumbling blocks are universal, as doubts about and resistance to more than the most minimal programmes of overseas aid indicate. One American commentator pulls no punches in expressing his judgement:

> Aid is ... *inherently* bad, bad to the bone and utterly beyond reform. As a welfare dole to buy the repulsive loyalty of whining, idle and malevolent governments ... it is possibly the most formidable obstacle to the productive endeavours of the poor. (quoted in Brown, 1992: 163)

Or, to put the view more temperately, the institutional restructuring of the world's financial, economic and political systems to achieve even an approximation of a world socio-economic citizenship would be a daunting operation.

Moreover, it can be further argued that a fundamental problem lies at the very heart of the concept of a 'global welfare state'. The thinking proceeds along these lines. The extension of the concept of state citizenship into the social and economic spheres has involved the stretching of the feeling of community commitment beyond the relatively straightforward civil and political relationships of state and citizen into more complex and controversial arenas. This process of extension requires the acceptance by the whole community, both rich and poor, that a welfare state has benefits for all; and presupposes that in the mutual give-and-take, even the rich recognize that they or their descendants might need the health, education and pension provisions of the system. Even at the state level, the neo-liberal ideology of the 1980s severely weakened this social philosophy. How much more difficult is it, therefore, to build a global welfare state in conditions of an incomparably much more loosely knit world community in which the impoverished countries and peoples would appear to have nothing to offer to any reciprocal programme.

Inadequacy of redistributive structures and of individuals' sense of obligation are, of course, separate issues; indeed, a distinction is often made between the moral and institutional aspects of the distributive justice question. The first aspect relates to the subject-matter of Chapter 3, the second, to Chapter 6. Even so, the two approaches to the problem are related. If one accepts that a task ought to be undertaken, this implies a moral responsibility to bring about that improvement – to change 'ought' to 'is'. But there can be no moral responsibility if the operation is impossible – 'ought' therefore implies practicability. In the case of distributive justice, if a cosmopolitan sense of moral obligation to improve the lot of the world's poor cannot be translated into effective action within the framework of present institutions, then those institutions must be reformed, supplemented or replaced. In truth, current development institutions (e.g. World Bank, United Nations Development Programme) are based upon the principle and policy of aid, not justice. However, the relationship between the moral and the institutional is in danger of being an inert circle: justice is required; the institutions do not deliver justice; institutional reform is impossible; therefore no moral obligation (beyond aid) can be said to exist.

Yet the circle might be broken and movement started by the combination of a determined effort at institutional reform and an expansion of the cosmopolitan mode of thinking. Both forms of momentum depend on stimulating individuals to what would be for many unfamiliar styles of action and thought. For new institutions cannot be imposed by any kind of universal *diktat*; they must be created and sustained by popular will and participation. To cite David Held:

> Determinate principles of social justice follow [the establish-ment of a cosmopolitan order]: the *modus operandi* of the production, distribution and the exploitation of resources must be conducive to, and compatible with, the democratic process and a common structure of political action. (Held, 1995: 271)

There is also the matter of how we live our everyday lives. A fundamental ethical principle is that our behaviour should be governed by the realization that both what we do and what we fail to do affects others. Thus, when possible, we should buy goods under a fair-trading label rather than an alternative. Also, instead of thinking in the inert circle of impossibility of institutional restructuring, to think in the cosmopolitan concentric mode (see

Chapter 2), imagining the outermost circle as populated by billions of individuals, not scores of countries. By the growth of numbers who think in this cosmopolitan way, perhaps they might gel into a critical mass sufficient to effect the transformation of world economic and development institutions into bodies committed to distributive justice. This kind of global consciousness is rather more evident in the form of environmental pressure-group activity of those concerned about the condition of the planet – a model, perhaps, for world citizens concerned about the economically unjust condition of the planet's human inhabitants.

Environmental Citizenship

Humankind has three basic needs: food and water; resources for industrial production; and fuel for industrial production, for using the products of industry and for warmth and light. The inexorable rise in the world's human population and the spread of industrialization are depleting mineral resources and biological species and polluting the land, water and sky of our geosystem. Thus do the world citizenship rights to a reasonable standard of living connect with the problem and duty of environmental protection. All this is commonly known; and, because it is commonly known, many people worry about the condition of the planet's environment and its deterioration, think about the rights and responsibilities of individuals in relation to the Earth's ecosystem, and support and participate in organizations bent on reducing the pace of, even reversing, the processes of planetary degradation. Moreover, because the minds and consciences of individuals have become engaged with these problems of global extent, we may properly speak of environmental citizenship as an aspect of world citizenship alongside the civil, political, social and economic facets. However, in some respects environmental citizenship has features that distinguish it from the components of Marshall's three bundles. In particular, where Marshall could refer quite coherently to rights while playing down concomitant obligations, the issue of responsibilities towards the planet's environment is so central to the nature of environmental citizenship that it must be given greater salience than the identification of rights.

World environmental citizenship may be briefly defined as: the right to live in a non-harmful environment and to have that environment protected; the responsibility to refrain from harming others by actions that excessively deplete resources or pollute the environment and, when possible, participate in schemes for positive conservation and cleansing; and the understanding that the most deleterious effects of environmental degradation can rarely be contained within the boundaries of the state where the depleting or polluting processes originate.

The concept of environmental citizenship, at both state and world levels, is, in fact, a recent insight. Yet no other facet of world citizenship epitomizes that notion more readily today than the environmental aspect. If the belief that all humankind is governed by a natural law was the chief characteristic of Stoic world citizenship, then the conviction that all humankind has environmental rights and responsibilities has become the chief characteristic of current world citizenship – or, to express the point in another way, it is concern about the biosphere that brings most people who think of themselves as world citizens to that frame of mind. And yet, we should not overstress the difference between the Stoic *kosmopolitēs* and the modern, ecologically conscious world citizen, for both have drawn their cosmopolitan mode of thought from an awareness of Nature and of man as part of, and not distinct from or dominant over, Nature.

Not that global consciousness is necessarily disinterested, as this blunt warning indicates:

> 'the natural resource' most threatened with pollution, most exposed to degradation, most liable to irreversible damage is not this or that species, not this or that plant or biome or habitat, not even the free airs or the great oceans. It is man himself. (Ward and Dubos, 1972: 295)

Written for the United Nations Conference on the Human Environment, held in Stockholm in 1972, the report, *Only One Earth*, from which this quotation is taken, set the mood of global environmental consciousness. This mood had a number of effects: it produced Green movements and political parties; there followed the report of the World Commission on Environment and Development (the Brundtland Report) entitled *Our Common Future*, published in 1987; and the United Nations Conference on Environment and Development was convened in Rio in 1992. One commentator explained the impact of this burgeoning interest and concern in these words:

> Green politics has set the relationship of the individual and society in a dramatic new light. The green outlook is marked by a striking renewal of collectivism, universalism and social purpose: the individual is seen in the context of global identity, the human species; the ecology of the planet is given a primary status which informs all policy issues; interdependence and sustainability set the terms for individual and social choice; and finally, the future of the planet is a fate shared by all and is therefore the overriding focus for common purpose and action. (Steward, 1991: 65)

Ecological or environmental citizenship entered the political vocabulary (see, e.g., van Steenbergen, 1994: esp. 142; Jelin, 2000: 48–9).

By thinking ecologically, the world citizen places Nature at the centre of his or her agenda. The citizen in the national sense has an identity, a set of rights and a range of duties in relation to the state, recognizing that the state has the right to the citizen's loyalty. Environmental world citizenship requires a similar responsibility on the part of the individual towards Nature: Nature has rights, the one of commanding importance being the right not to be despoiled by humans. Humankind is part of Nature; and, just as in an Aristotelean sense it is inconceivable that a good citizen should harm the *polis* of which he or she is a natural part, so the good world citizen cannot contemplate damaging or destroying the planetary environment of which he or she is a natural part. Furthermore, before and as part of Nature, all human beings are equal: all world citizens are therefore equal just as all state citizens are equal in their communities.

But because environmental citizenship involves citizens placing the needs of Nature as a priority over the needs of their national societies, and because it 'has set the relationship of the individual and society in a dramatic new light', it has raised issues concerning the manner in which environmentalism can be accommodated into the overall pattern of the status of world citizenship.

First, the very primacy of Nature in the concept of environmental citizenship raises an absolutely fundamental question: can concern about global ecology be truly graced with the style of 'citizenship'? Citizenship is an identity and status that brings the individual into relationships with other individuals and, quintessentially, with humanly devised institutions. By introducing Nature into the concept, it can be argued, a non-human, non-institutional 'agent' (to use the sociological term) becomes part of the formula. One may suggest with some validity that Nature is an alien intrusion into the very notion of citizenship and cripples its meaning beyond recognition. At the very least, the addition of Nature to the pattern of relationships strains the elasticity of the citizenly concept.

Second, environmental citizenship highlights the tension between freedom on the one hand and competing ideals on the other. The liberal style of state citizenship has tended to stress the citizen's right to benefit from a capitalist economy, a right that can so easily conflict with the taxation demands of a welfare state, necessary to satisfy the social rights of citizenship. The parallel with capitalist exploitation versus ecological conservation in the context of environmental citizenship is clear. A particularly dramatic clash of interest occurred in 2001 on the subject of carbon emissions. It is widely accepted that by far the severest threat to the planet's ecosystem is global warming, with its climatic change and attendant storms and floods. A major contribution to this phenomenon is the 'greenhouse effect' of gases rising into the atmosphere. Therefore, in 1997 world leaders met at Kyoto in Japan to agree targets to restrain these outputs, particularly of carbon dioxide, which is produced, among other means, by the burning of fossil fuels, notably petrol and oil. In 2001 George W. Bush, the US President, announced that his country, which accounts for a quarter of all the world's emissions of that gas, would not abide by the Kyoto Protocol. 'We will not do anything that harms our economy, because first things first are the people who live in America,' he declared. Nor would he do anything to harm the oil industry of Texas, his own state, cynics added. Bush was acting to defend the economic freedom of US citizens in preference to the environmental rights of world citizens.

The incident is illustrative of two separate clashes of priorities, the one an amusing irony, the other the most excruciating question facing humankind. The irony lies in the self-image of the businessmen who, constantly airborne in polluting airliners and uprooted from their nation-states in pursuit of environmentally destructive wealth creation, can think of themselves as elite citizens of the world (see, e.g., Falk, 1994: 134–5). The sombre point has been made by Ralf Dahrendorf. The question arises, he says, about 'how we can curb unfettered expansion without violating other entitlements of citizenship. Can we survive freedom? For those who share my own belief that freedom matters above all – even above survival – the alternative is literally vital' (Dahrendorf, 1994: 18)

Nothing is more imperative for the world citizen, therefore, than to attempt the formulation of policies and lifestyles that can bring freedom and sustainable development into some kind of consensual concord. For this solution to the rapidly impending crisis is essential not just for our own well-being, survival even, but for future generations. Citizenly virtue involves consideration and responsibility for fellow-citizens and, though it is rarely mentioned, that obligation is not confined to the citizens co-existent with ourselves. Burke famously expressed this idea in his *Reflections on the Revolution in France*, where he explained that:

> Society ... is a partnership.... As the ends of such a partnership cannot be obtained in many generations, it becomes a partnership not only between those who are living, but between those who are living, those who are dead, and those who are to be born. (Burke, 1910: 93)

In addition, there is no doubt that he had the widest context in mind when he expressed this thought, for he went on to talk about 'the great primaeval contract of eternal society, linking the lower with the higher natures, connecting the visible and the invisible world' (*ibid.*). And in the following year, 1791, in his *Appeal from the New to the Old Whigs*, he wrote:

> We have obligations to mankind at large, which ... arise from the relation of man to man, and the relation of man to God ... out of [which] arise moral duties, which as we are able perfectly to comprehend we are bound indispensably to perform'. (Burke, 1962: 96–7)

Taken together, these quotations offer a pertinent message for those of us contemplating world environmental citizenship over two centuries later.

The key concept, which was devised by the Commission chaired by Gro Harlem Brundtland, is sustainable development, which they defined as 'development that meets the needs of the present without compromising the ability of future generations to meet their own needs' (World Commission on Environment and Development, 1987: 43). It is an agenda which seeks to bring into balance the three desiderata: freedom, forbearance and future. Each of us as world citizens, in all the myriad environments in which collectively we live, and with all the unjust differentials in standards of living, should be aware of the need to achieve this balance and to recognize our rights and responsibilities.

Our environmental rights as world citizens have been succinctly stated at the beginning of this section. But can these rights be delivered in practice? Dahrendorf is soberly hesitant, pondering,

> I am not sure whether we can stipulate an entitlement for all of us as world citizens to a liveable habitat, and thus to actions which sustain it, but something of this kind may well belong on the agenda of citizenship. (Dahrendorf, 1994: 18)

How, then, should the world citizen behave in order to contribute to a tempering of Dahrendorf's pessimism?

That individuals acting as world citizens are vital to any hope of reducing the stresses on the Earth's ecosystem is widely recognized. In commending the principle of sustainable development, Brundtland wrote in the Foreword to the report of her Commission:

> Unless we are able to translate our words into a language that can reach the minds and hearts of people young and old, we shall not be able to undertake the extensive social changes needed to correct the course of development ... we appeal to citizens' groups, to non-governmental organizations, to educational institutions, and to the scientific community. ... They will play a crucial part in putting the world onto sustainable development paths, in laying the groundwork for Our Common Future. (World Commission on Environment and Development, 1987: xiv)

And, with greater concision, the Rio Declaration gives as its foremost objective the establishment of 'a new and equitable global partnership through the creation of new levels of cooperation among states, key sectors of societies and *people*' (quoted in Held, 1995: 106, emphasis added).

How then, more specifically, can the world environmental citizen contribute? Bart van Steenbergen has distinguished between global citizens who wish to *control* or *manage* the planet in a more beneficent way and those who wish to exercise planetary *care*, the latter being the more altruistic (van Steenbergen, 1994: 149–50). One might feel this distinction somewhat artificial, for responsibility is the key requirement, however it is discharged. In terms

127

everyone will recognize, Fred Steward has observed that 'Personal responsibility for the consequences of one's actions has become a prominent theme on matters ranging from recycling newspapers to the purchase of fur coats' (Steward, 1991: 66). World civic responsibility must therefore incorporate a willingness on the part of the privileged to forgo the enjoyment of some of those privileges, well beyond Steward's relatively trivial examples, for the sake of improving the condition both of their most disadvantaged co-world citizens and of the planet as a unitary ecological system. A reduction in electricity and petrol consumption might save some vulnerable islands of the Indian and Pacific Oceans from inundation as global warming results in an inexorable rise of sea waters.

So, from responsibility to the duty of participation. For the environmentally aware world citizen the word has two meanings. One is that humans should participate with Nature in order to sustain the diversity and fruitfulness of the planet, not behave in an aggressively greedy manner towards its mineral and biological riches. Second, of course, participation means personal engagement in activities in order to curb man's destructiveness. Campaigns by bodies such as Greenpeace and Friends of the Earth (FOE) are organized by an elite of world citizens, the deeply committed. However, all human beings have a role to play. As FOE explains, one of its three methods (the others are campaigning and supplying information and ideas) is 'citizen action' at local and national levels to exert leverage on government, industry and financial institutions. Sadly, most of this activity is perforce directed against established institutions and businesses to reform their practices. Ideally, however, citizen action should take place in association with rather than against governments and businesses; and one of the pleasing achievements of environmental pressure groups is that they are occasionally able to work in this way.

The task, it goes without saying, is of an awesome scale, and the analysis of the particular motivations and compositions of environmental movements has, in fact, shown a great variety of responses, from the communication of scientific data to radical direct action, for example (see Jelin, 2000: 50). Even so, if, as politicians are wont to believe, politics is the art of the possible and the environmentalists' agendas seem impossible, then fatalistic despair can easily supervene. Yet, as Richard Falk has argued, that is the point of environmentalist militancy. The world citizen must be inspired by the conviction that it is important to make 'the impossible' happen by dedicated action that is motivated by what is desirable, and not discouraged by calculations of what seems likely. Encouraging appropriate activity can alter the horizons of what seems possible to leaders and to the mainstream public. Such a shift helps provide hope, which is needed, especially when the prospects of success seem poor. (Falk, 1994: 132)

CHAPTER 6

Political Citizenship

Problems

How to transform a human being into a world citizen in a true sense
by furnishing the individual with a reasonable set of political
functions is the kernel of the cosmopolitan problem. For the very
purpose of the citizenly status is political: in the republican
tradition the citizen has the duty to contribute to the good running
of the state; in the liberal tradition the citizen is required to make
the government accountable for its actions. True, many historical
examples can be produced – from the Roman Empire to the French
Republic – where political participation in practice was so minimal
as to seem to belie these principles. But they do not negate the
validity of the basic models; rather, they show that throughout
history many citizens have been denied or chosen not to use the
opportunity to act as fully fledged citizens. It is the constitutional
availability of political rights and the expectation of the
performance of duties that makes for citizenship in the proper and
fullest sense of the term.

There is, in addition, a deeper, ethical case for stressing the
political component of citizenship. It is that citizenship treats all
who enjoy that status as moral equals and, if that be so, there is no
justification for excluding any from access to the political process.
This argument can, moreover, be extended to the cosmopolitan level
for, if all humans are moral equals (*pace* Stoic elitism), then none
should be denied the opportunity to participate in political matters

that span the whole world. In the words of Andrew Linklater, 'the logic of moral equality ... is best realized through democratic processes which bring insiders and outsiders together as transnational citizens with equal rights' (Linklater, 1998: 126). The problem, of course, is how to give this logic institutional reality.

Since political participation requires a state for the citizen to participate in, and if the status of world citizen should faithfully mirror that of the state citizen, it would appear to follow that world citizenship has not existed and cannot exist in the absence of a world state. There are four possible responses to this proposition. One is to reject the need for such an exact correspondence between state and world citizenship. Second, is to seek to construct a world state. Third, is to reject world citizenship because a world state is neither desirable nor practicable. Fourth, is to devise compromise solutions. This chapter is essentially an examination of the fourth option. But initially a few words are necessary about the other two.

First, the matter of correspondence. The whole of the distinguished Stoic tradition, of course, dispenses with the notion of a politically constructed world state of which the individual would be a citizen: to adapt the French mathematician's comment about God – they had no need of that hypothesis. However, to confine the concept of world citizenship just to a moral code – vitally important as the ethical strand in world citizenship most assuredly is – is really not acceptable in the twenty-first century AD, for two reasons, one semantic, the other pragmatic.

Citizenship is a concept and a status, both of which are central to present-day social and political life and to the academic analysis of that life. And the word 'citizenship' in both lay and academic discourse has an intrinsic political content. To exclude the political facet is to damage the integrity of the word; not overtly to admit to the exclusion, so that a political content might by analogy be merely assumed, is to encourage unreal expectations of what world citizenship can achieve. By all means promote world-mindedness, a global conscience, but let not the word 'citizenship' be attached to it – that is confusing, even dishonest. We have already cited Michael Walzer's view along these lines in Chapter 1. The pragmatic case against a less stringent definition of world citizenship is, in essence, the existence of what in European Union parlance is referred to as 'the democratic deficit' in the present-day pattern of world governance. Decisions are being made with increasing frequency by institutions that have transnational power and influence. Most obviously, the United Nations and its Specialized Agencies have global remits and spend large sums of money derived indirectly from national taxes, yet are not answerable for their policies and actions to the people of the world thus affected. In an age which boasts of the spread of democracy to many states hitherto oppressed by authoritarian regimes, the lack of democratic structures – in other words, effective political citizenship – at the supranational level might readily be thought to be anomalous. So much for the argument that a political component to world citizenship akin to state citizenship is unnecessary.

The second option is to create a world state with representative institutions. Perhaps the earliest example is *Bases Constitutionnelles de la République de Genre Humain* drafted by Anacharchis Cloots in 1793 (see Heater, 1996: 78–81). This was to be a French Republic writ large. In the twentieth century much time and ingenuity were expended, especially by Americans, in producing draft constitutions for a United States of the World – often thought of as just a bigger version of the United States of America (see *ibid.*: 103–13, 166–70). These differed from earlier, pre-democratic plans, from Dante's *De Monarchia* onwards, in that the need for citizenly participation had to be built into the blueprints in order to satisfy modern liberal expectations. However, difficult problems arise: for example, a just numerical apportionment of global constituencies would today result in China and India alone providing a third of the world's electorate, not to mention the problems of ensuring free and efficient selection of candidates and management of elections. The sheer undesirability and impracticability of forging a world federation have reduced the convinced advocates to a tiny fringe minority.

This brings us to the third option, namely, to reject world citizenship because a world state is politically neither desirable nor practicable. This case has two facets, namely, defence of the sovereign state and assault on the notion of a world government. Dilution of civic commitment because of the citizens' belief that their prime allegiance should be not to the state but to the community of humankind as a whole would have a debilitating effect upon the state, the continuing strength of which is, according to communitarian thinking, to be so preciously preserved. Tolerance and freedom require stable, democratic states; and they are in danger of decaying if they lose the positive and alert support of their citizenry. And in so far as individuals need to be involved in spheres beyond the confines of their states, they can in any case, if they are citizens of democratically responsive polities, act indirectly by exerting pressure on their respective governments. 'Nation-states,' Paul Hirst and Grahame Thompson have argued, '... are pivots between international agencies and subnational activities because they provide legitimacy as the exclusive voice of a territorially bounded population' (Hirst and Thompson, 1999: 276). The function of citizens in an age of globalization is therefore not to seek to act on the global stage themselves, but to assist their states to represent their opinions and interests for them. 'Such representation,' to cite Hirst and Thompson again, 'is very indirect, but it is the closest to democracy and accountability that international governance is likely to get' (*ibid.*).

Agreed, most contemporary proponents of world citizenship are not advocates of world government. But those hostile to the cosmopolitan case are not altogether satisfied with this denial, and for three reasons. One is that the very concept of citizenship presupposes a state: a state is necessary to give the citizen rights and, in turn, receive the duties and allegiance involved in the civic status, an issue to which we shall return. The second, a similar reason, is that the quality of citizenship is one of freedom and equality, attributes which can be provided only by a state. And third, even if it is conceded that world citizenship is a valid concept – albeit of a much less precise type than state citizenship – once it is widely recognized, the tendency will be to accord it greater institutional precision; the logical end of this process would be a world state. Yet a world state is highly undesirable. Kant, for all his cosmopolitan sympathies, was quite adamant in warning against such a dystopia: 'laws progressively lose their impact as the government increases its range,' he declared, 'and a soulless despotism, after crushing the germs of goodness, will finally lapse into anarchy ... universal despotism ... saps all men's energies and ends in the graveyard of freedom' (Reiss, 1991: 113–14). At the beginning of the twenty-first century it is even easier to imagine this bleak scenario than it was two centuries ago. For since Kant's day we have been made keenly aware of the evils of Nazi and Leninist-Stalinist universalist pretensions; in the latter ideology, a unified world society was clearly envisaged in its creed.

Compromise solutions have nevertheless been commended and proposals have emerged. This is our fourth option. The details of the current scene will be presented in the second and third sections of this chapter, but before coming to these it will be helpful to sketch in the historical background.

A survey of the historical record throws up three main difficulties in the search for a cosmopolitan system short of the concentration of power in a world state. The first concerns the devising of a nice balance between central and local/regional power: the history of the USA in the mid-nineteenth century is sufficient warning of the difficulties attendant upon this constitutional issue. The problem relates to world citizenship in the following way. If an amalgamation of states is weak, in the form of a league or confederation, then the supranational citizenship of that union will itself be scarcely worth the paper upon which that constitutional document is written. One can argue, for example, that the status of citizenship of the European Union, partly as defined by the Maastricht Treaty and still further in its practical application, is a pretty feeble interpretation of supranational citizenship. On the other hand, strengthen the central government in order to strengthen the supranational/world level of citizenship and one runs into the danger of creating an over-whelming world state: even plans to integrate the EU more tightly are facing doubts and difficulties. The domestic analogy is clear: state citizenship has, historically, subordinated the citizenship of the province, city or township to an extremely minor role; would national citizenship succumb in its turn?

The second difficulty relates to the style of government of the putative member-states of such a union. Advocates of a transnational confederation since the late eighteenth century have generally been of the opinion that only states with a liberal political culture would agree to even this minimal reduction in their absolute sovereignty: autocratic governments are autocratic. Three examples may help to confirm this observation.

The first comes from Kant. He envisaged the possibility of a *foedus pacificum*, a confederation committed to peace among its members, as developing by agreement among states with 'republican' constitutions because in those states the citizens would be able to exert sufficient pressure against war (see, e.g., *ibid.*: 90, 100, 104). Implicit in Kant's vision is a kind of world citizenship in the initiation of the eirenic confederation: he declared that 'distress must force men to form ... a lawful *federation* under a commonly accepted *international right*' (*ibid.*: 90; and by 'federation' we should understand *con*federation, and by 'right', law).

For our second example of the recognition that a loose union of states is conceivable only by agreement among liberal polities, we move forward nearly one-and-a-half centuries to Clarence Streit's *Union Now*, a work incomparably less erudite and of only passing interest, yet which commanded widespread attention in the USA and UK when it was published in 1939. He advocated a union of fifteen democratic states of the Atlantic region and British Dominions with a common, Union citizenship and a Union legislature.

Our third example is the present-day European Union, which, for membership, requires adherence to political liberalism. The signatories of the Maastricht Treaty confirmed 'their attachment to the principles of liberty, democracy and respect for human rights and fundamental freedoms and of the rule of law'. (Because of this ideal, Turkey's poor human rights record has impaired her prospects for membership.) The Maastricht Treaty not only confirms the EU's liberal principles, it also established the formal status of citizenship of the Union. In political terms this confers the right to petition the European Parliament, to stand as a candidate and vote in local elections and in elections to the European Parliament, wherever the citizen resides (Articles 8b1, 8b2, 8d).

In addition to the belief in each of these three projects that member-states should adhere to a homogeneity of liberal political culture, there was also contained the prospect of an expansion of membership from a founding nucleus. Kant established this pattern. At his most optimistic he declared:

> It can be shown that this idea of *federalism*, extending gradually to encompass all states ... is practicable and has objective reality. For if by good fortune one powerful and enlightened nation can form a republic ... this will provide a focal point for federal association among other states ... and the whole will gradually spread further and further by a series of alliances of this kind. (*ibid.*: 104)

Streit wrote of 'the nucleus method' as a start of a process of 'growth to universality' (Streit, 1939: 126–7). And the EU is a living example of an incremental system. Starting in the 1950s with six members, by the end of the century it not only numbered fifteen states, but entertained the prospect of even doubling that number.

However, the pertinence of these three illustrations of compromise solutions to the concept and status of a world political citizenship is limited. Expansion from the nucleus to cover the whole world has been widely recognized as an unrealistic fantasy.

This is our third identified difficulty. Kant, in his heart, recognized that such a federation would be impossibly unwieldy (see, e.g., Reiss, 1991: 171) and restricted his concept in its proper sense to a legal, not a political right (see Chapter 4 above). Streit was more starry-eyed, pinning his hopes on the pressure of public opinion in non-member, including autocratic, states to accelerate the process of expansion. Even so, in 1939 there were only a third of the number of sovereign states in the world as there are today. At the same time as Streit was writing and campaigning, the idea of a European union was being formulated by enthusiasts for the device of federalism. Some held that the creation of a limited, European body should be but a way-station to a world federation. One British Professor of International Law wrote in 1940: 'A post-war federation of Europe will be merely a step towards world democracy' (quoted in Mayne and Pinder, 1990: 4). However, the real founding fathers of the EU – the likes of Monnet, Spaak and Schuman – had their eyes firmly focused on Europe. Thus, in so far as these compromise solutions were realistic, they bought their realism at the price of the loss of true cosmopolitan coverage. Homogeneity and viability were, in all probability, incompatible with universality.

Yet, for all the barriers to an easy solution, there is a growing body of opinion urging that something needs to be attempted. Economic and technological globalization 'from the top' must be balanced by political globalization 'from the bottom'. The issue has been pungently expressed by George Monbiot, who has written, 'As nation states cede their decision-making capacities to international bodies, the world is coming to be governed not by its citizens but by institutions manoeuvring to exploit a dearth of global account-ability.' Citing as examples WTO, OECD and 'an exclusive club of chief executives called the Transatlantic Business Dialogue', he complains that 'None of us can vote to change these institutions. Our representatives are excluded from their deliberations. They are running the world without mandate' (*Guardian*, 22 June 2000).

Nevertheless, changes are occurring of a political kind: a modicum of world political citizenship is being conceded or seized.

Political Quasi-World Citizenship

For all its limitations, citizenship of the EU is the best example we have of a constitutionally established supranational political citizenship. Yet, of course, it is not and has no pretensions of becoming global in geographical scope. What we must therefore now examine is the existence of two kinds of what might be termed features of quasi-world citizenship with full global reach or, to use an architectural metaphor, the footings upon which might, just possibly, arise a recognizably world citizenship structure. These two features are the assertions in international law of the individual's right to a state political citizenship and the evidence of worldwide political activity which has earned the name of a global civil society.

Three UN documents recognize the right of human beings to political rights within their states, thus giving the universal imprimatur of international law to state political citizenship. These documents are: the Universal Declaration of Human Rights, the International Covenant on Civil and Political Rights and the Optional Protocol to the Covenant. By the end of the twentieth century, 144 states had ratified the Covenant and ninety-five the Protocol. As we have seen in Chapter 4, the stress in these documents is on civil more than political rights. However, Article 25 of the Covenant, echoing Article 21 of the Declaration, but having the extra force of being a treaty, lists the rights as follows:

(a) To take part in the conduct of public affairs, directly or through representatives;
(b) To vote and to be elected at genuine periodic elections which shall be by universal and equal suffrage and shall be held by secret ballot, guaranteeing the free expression of the will of the electors;
(c) To have access, on general terms of equality, to public service in his country.

The Protocol gives individuals the right to inform the Human Rights Committee, established under the terms of the Covenant, of any violations of rights enshrined in the Covenant. It has to be said, though, that the system thus constructed has been virtually useless in practice. The importance, particularly of the Covenant, lies rather in the unambiguous statement in international law that all human beings, in whatever country they live, have the right to a politically active life should they wish to exercise it. Moreover, the potential for development from these agreed principles is even greater: we have already quoted, for example, David Beetham's firm belief that the human rights covenants provide a foundation for democratic world citizenship (Beetham, 1998: 66; see p. 90 above).

If the UN has established standards of universal political rights, it has been left largely to local and international NGOs to monitor the infringement of these rights by tyrannical state governments. Indeed, Richard Falk has said that 'the historical potency of the international law of human rights is predominantly a consequence of its implementation through the agency of civil society' (Falk, 1995: 163). By virtue of their involvement in this work, members of these bodies may be said to be acting as members of a global civil society. Two queries nevertheless arise. One is to question how far, even at the state level, participation in civil society activities can be regarded as citizenly activity; the other is to question whether a global civil society can be said to exist.

Michael Walzer, to take an example of a recent commentator, has argued that membership of civil society is distinct from membership of a state, only the latter being proper citizenship. Two succinct statements make the point: 'civil society incorporates many of the associations and identities that we value outside of, prior to, or in the shadow of state and citizenship' (Walzer, 1995b: 1); and 'citizenship has a certain practical pre-eminence among all our actual and possible memberships' (Walzer, 1995a: 170). In other words, *qua* trade unionists, for example, activists are not behaving as citizens. In any case, and to cite Walzer again, for all its commitments and ambitions, 'civil society requires political agency. And the state is an indispensable agent' (*ibid.*: 170). It follows that, even if members of an NGO exert pressure upon a state government, it could be said that they are legitimately and effectively acting because of their rights and power as citizens, not as members of civil society.

The negative case against equating civil society and citizenship is even stronger in the global context, precisely because the only effective channel for inducing change is through *state* governments. Moreover, this dependency can sometimes weaken an NGO's claimed disinterestedness upon which its transnational legitimacy rests – it becomes a 'GONGO', a government-controlled NGO! So, the existence of a global civil society – of numerous NGOs, even INGOs (international NGOs with multinational memberships) – does not necessarily provide evidence of an embryonic world citizenship. There is yet a further denial, namely, that the kind of sense of national belonging which characterizes civil society at the state level is lacking at the global level. The thousands of NGOs and INGOs that exist pursue very different, often conflicting agendas;

there is no sense of community among them all (see, e.g., Miller, 1999: 78).

On the other hand, there are plenty of observers of the world scene who are convinced that a global or transnational civil society does exist at least in a formative stage, and that a consciousness of world citizenship is growing and being nurtured by and through this activity. *The Guardian*, for instance, has declared that 'the world already has a "civil society" and it publishes in peer-reviewed journals' (*The Guardian*: 5 December 2000). At the same time, sociologists especially are re-examining and debating the relationship between civil society, the state and citizenship, some drawing the conclusion that, at the state level, citizenship and civil society are indeed interdependent concepts. In the Aristotelean and communitarian traditions, citizenship includes a sense of community; civil society is an institutional expression of communal feeling; and the distinction between the legal-political arena of citizenship and the socio-economic arena of civil society is being eroded.

The increase in the number of NGOs and INGOs and consequently the number of individuals acting on the world stage, particularly during the last quarter of the twentieth century, is incontrovertible. For example, the number of INGOs increased from 176 in 1909 to 4,624 in 1989, to 5,472 in 1996. Not only have numbers risen, but so has their influence. Members of these multifarious bodies (some often called new social movements (NSMs)) collect and disseminate specialist data, mobilize support and exert pressure. Some of these bodies – high-profile ones such as Amnesty International and Greenpeace – are constantly at work. But at the turn of the twentieth century three new styles of activity became common. These were: the attendance of members of relevant organizations at UN-sponsored international conferences; the self-conscious pronouncement that global civil society *does* exist; and the mobilization of protest meetings in parallel with conferences convened by what we might term the global 'establishment'.

Already, in 1972, groups descended uninvited on the UN-convened Stockholm Conference on the Human Environment and, by this dramatic action, secured considerable publicity in the news media. The real breakthrough occurred in 1992 on the occasion of the Conference on Environment and Development in Rio, when 1,400 NGOs were officially invited; however, more importantly, thousands of others sent representatives to a parallel Global Forum. It is notable that the bodies participating in this manner are sometimes referred to as civil society organizations (CSOs). The significance of this development has been summarized by Martin Köhler:

> The practical and detailed knowledge of CSOs has made these forums a valuable resource for government actors. Vice versa, CSOs have managed to gain far-reaching influence over agendas and outcomes of official conferences, so that it is now accepted UN policy to grant CSOs access to intergovernmental 'preparatory committees' and follow-up working groups. (Köhler, 1998: 232)

This kind of gathering connected to UN events reached its climax at the turn of the twentieth century when the UN called a Millennium Summit of World Leaders in New York in 2000. Over a thousand civil society organizations held a simultaneous United Nations Millennium Forum, which concluded with a clarion call for greater transnational accountability, effected, in part, by 'a vibrant civil society', and for the creation of a Global Civil Society Forum to meet at regular intervals.

A year prior to this mass gathering, a conference was held in The Hague to mark the centenary of the 1899 Hague Peace Conference. The conference was convened by four INGOs – the International Association of Lawyers Against Nuclear Arms, the International Peace Bureau, International Physicians for the Prevention of Nuclear War and the World Federalist Movement. Nearly 10,000 people and 1,000 organizations from over 100 countries attended. They produced *The Hague Agenda for Peace and Justice in the 21st Century*, described as 'a citizens' agenda'. 'This will entail,' the document declared, 'a fundamentally new approach, building on the recent model of New Diplomacy in which citizen advocates, progressive governments and international organizations have worked together for common goals.' Note the term 'citizen advocates', a name equivalent to Falk's 'citizen pilgrims' (see below). *The Hague Agenda* lists an impressive catalogue of recent achievements of global civil society, drawing the lesson that 'these campaigns have generated unity and cohesion and demonstrate what can be done when people are listened to instead of talked at' (the text is available from World Goodwill, Suite 54, 3 Whitehall Court, London SW1A 2EF).

The third recent development has been the organization of civil society protest meetings to coincide with official conventions on topics to which many individuals and bodies object. The world capitalist system has been a favourite target. In 1999, the World Trade Organization (WTO) conference was abandoned because of the vociferousness of the demonstrations. The following year, the International Monetary Fund (IMF) and the International Bank for Reconstruction and Development (IBRD; part of the World Bank Group) held their meetings in Prague, bringing forth in turn a congregation of protesters, who not only demonstrated but held informative discussion sessions. Katherine Viner reported:

> Every 'affinity group' – NGO or group of friends – sent a spokesperson to meetings to make decisions and work out strategy. It sounds impossible to contain, and it was laborious, but it worked and consensus was found. It felt like proper democracy in a way that the ballot box does not. (*Guardian*, 29 September 2000)

Much criticism was levelled at the disruption caused by activities such as these. On the other hand, the *Guardian* leader-writer argued:

> the protest movement has played a role in shifting the thinking of the international institutions – it has raised the profile of debt relief and poverty reduction – while embarking on a mass education campaign. The seminars in the streets of Prague on the details of the global financial architecture such as structural adjustment programmes and capital liberalisation, are a healthy contribution to global democracy. (*Guardian*, 29 September 2000)

Two questions arise from this new pattern of activity. One is how to explain the proliferation and strengthening of these organizations; the other is how to assess the potential of this development for the evolution of a world citizenship. The judgement that the beginnings of what can legitimately be foreseen as a global civil society is an historically noteworthy development is encapsulated in the assertion of the Commission on Global Governance that we are witnessing a 'global associational revolution' (Commission on Global Governance, 1995: 253). All revolutions have complex origins, and this one is no exception. First has been the remarkable, almost simultaneous, arousal of interest in and concern about numerous single-issue problems of global scope: human rights, including women's rights, threats to the planet's ecosystem, proliferation of local wars, the deleterious effects of what is sometimes termed 'turbo capitalism', to name the most obvious and pressing. Yet, for all the particularity of these movements, they all have come to share certain features, namely, a recognition that the problems are caused by transnational forces and that nation-states have decreasing effectiveness in ameliorating the worrying conditions – indeed, are sometimes in league with the forces of threat or even the very causes of the emerging crises. This common understanding among many members of global civil society organizations has led to a consciousness that getting to grips with the world's grossest forms of threats, injustice and violence is seriously hindered by the obsolescence of the Westphalian state-centric political system. The confluence of all these factors may be interpreted as producing a growing force that can, at least potentially, lead to a marked transformation in the world's political structure, engineered by world citizens and involving a consolidation of that status.

These observations have now led us to our second question, that is, how to assess the importance of the burgeoning global civil society for world citizenship. Again, there are several components to our answer. In the first place, the proliferation of NGOs with global agendas should be viewed in the broad context of the recent phenomena of 'identity politics' and 'new social movements'. The age of firm class and national identities is fast receding. Increasingly, individuals are conscious not just of other forms of identity but also of the need to proclaim and secure rights for those particular groupings. Moreover, when these new recognized identities are unconfined to states, the movements make global connections. The issue of women's rights is an especially notable example. Feminist movements in a number of Western countries became 'globalized' by the UN's naming of 1975 as the International Year of Women. Four UN conferences were held from 1975 to 1995 to identify and alleviate the subordinate conditions under which women suffer the world over. However, for our purposes, it was the fourth conference, held in Beijing, that was most significant, for it was marked by a weighty presence of representatives from many women's organizations.

The second reason why the rise of a global civil society is important for world citizenship is that, starting perhaps from a local or national concern, members of NGOs have become increasingly aware of the limitations of thinking about their causes in such a parochial way. Then, having comprehended the global extent of their interests, some have come to appreciate the need to press for changes in decision-making and accountability processes to achieve their own ends and to understand that many other interest groups require the same kind of transformation in the style of world governance.

True, only a minority perhaps have the flexibility of imagination to make the mental leap from discontent with the present to a more acceptable hypothetical future; this is the third item in our answer. Leadership is a natural and required aspect of all political activity, so leaders should be expected and welcomed in the evolution of world citizenship. Indeed, the Commission on Global Governance has placed great stress on leadership. It explains:

> Whatever the dimensions of global governance, however renewed and enlarged the machinery, whatever values give it content, the quality of global governance depends ultimately on leadership. . . . By leadership we do not mean only people at the highest . . . levels. We mean enlightenment at every level. (*ibid.*: 353, 355)

They list a multitude of examples such as the professions, scientists, teachers, religious bodies. Richard Falk has coined the term 'citizen pilgrim' to describe these people, who might perhaps be more appositely described as 'vanguard world citizens' (see also Chapter 1). Falk defines his 'citizen pilgrims' as those with

> A commitment to an imagined human community of the future that embodies non-violence, social justice, ecological balance, and participatory democracy in all arenas of policy and decision, and embodies these perspectives in current modes of feeling, thought, and action. The citizen pilgrim prefigures humane governance in both imaginative and political modes of being. (Falk, 1995: 95)

Part of Falk's vision is that democracy must be more deeply and widely embedded, a process for which the activities of global civil society and 'citizen pilgrims' are essential. This is the fourth reason why the development of global civil society is important for world citizenship. A person is only a part-citizen without opportunities for political participation; democracy is a device to maximize these opportunities. This proposition must be valid for world citizenship as much as state citizenship. At present such opportunities are effectively limited to membership of CSOs. However, considerable thought is being given to ways in which more avenues for political participation in global governance might be opened.

Proposed Developments

Thus far in our exposition, anyone who pretends to the status of world citizenship would appear to have precious little scope to exercise the political rights that should be the key part of that role. Drawing the parallel with state citizenship, a world citizen should be able at the global level to vote, stand for election to public office and exercise freedom of speech and action with the reasonable expectation, in a politically just cause, of effecting some beneficial change. Currently, these rights are by no means fully available. The conundrum is how to replicate these political rights of the state citizen on the cosmopolitan plane, short of creating a world state. Two by no means mutually incompatible, strategies present themselves. One is to create an institutional structure of connected tiers with representational arrangements as a means of introducing a democratic element into the system of global governance that already exists. The other is to establish, either by itself or, more feasibly, in association with a tiered structure, a democratically elected supranational institution (or institutions) with some effective authority and power, but well short of a supranational government.

If world citizenship is to exist realistically in the political meaning of the term, the erection of these constitutional structures would need to take account of five requirements. These are: the reform of established institutions, in particular, the UN family of organizations; the devising of completely new institutions, particularly at the sub-national and sub-continental regional levels; facilities for NGOs/CSOs to slot into the new constitutional geometry; the encouragement of individuals to think and behave as citizens with multiple sets of political rights; and the recognition in international law of the necessary and complex form of multiple citizenship as a confirmation of the several levels of political rights. A few comments to expand on each of these points will be apposite immediately before examining two particular initiatives, namely, the elaboration of the concept of cosmopolitan democracy and the agenda of the movement, Charter 99.

If the UN is to be used to enhance world political citizenship, one condition is the resolution of the often-cited contradiction in its very founding document. The Charter opens with the ringing declaration, 'We the peoples of the United Nations determined . . .'. Yet Article 2.1 refers to 'the sovereign equality of all its Members', the members of the UN being the sovereign states of the world, not the peoples of the world. Nor has the history of the UN at work provided much evidence of a balance between the interests and influence of 'the peoples' and the 'Members'. Members' interests have remained paramount, and the cause of world citizenship requires the rectification of this imbalance. This is but an example of the basic problem of dual subject status in constitutional theory, that is, the relationship between territorial and population representation. The matter has aroused very considerable concern and generated a number of proposals for the reform of the UN to ensure some modicum of popular participation. On the other hand, it has also attracted the derision of some political analysts who believe that radical reform of the UN is impossible; and if reform is a precondition for world citizenship, ergo, that must be impossible too.

The idea that the UN would offer the most fertile ground on which an effective world political citizenship would be likely to flourish derives from the coalescence of two propositions: that, as we have noted, the intention of the founding fathers who inserted the formula 'we the peoples' has been contravened; and that reform of the UN as an existing institution is far less impractical than any plan to create a parallel world body *de novo* (compare Zolo (1997) and Archibugi, Held and Köhler (1998)). With fluctuating intensity of interest, discontent with the undemocratic and statist character of the UN has been aired for decades. For example, Grenville Clark and Louis B. Sohn published their *World Peace Through World Law* in 1958 (see p. 104 above), proffering a detailed revised Charter for the UN. This included a new Article 4, introducing the status of citizen of the United Nations. They explained: 'The reason for this feature is that the revised Charter would not only grant certain rights and privileges to individuals, but would also impose definite obligations on individuals' (Clark and Sohn, 1958: 15). Furthermore, Articles 9 and 10 required representatives to the General Assembly to be directly elected and to be provided with certain legislative powers (*ibid.*: 19–31).

However, interest flagged until the 1980s. A number of factors contributed to the revival that happened especially in the 1990s.

One was the example of the European Community/Union. In 1979, the European Parliament made the transition from being an assembly of national parliamentarians to a directly elected chamber; and in 1993 the Maastricht Treaty created the status of citizen of the Union. Could the UN be guided along similar lines? Second, the apparent triumph of democracy as a result of the collapse of Communism in central and eastern Europe and of a number of military dictatorships in Africa and Latin America gave hope of support from national governments for the 'internationalization' of democracy. Third, the UN's fiftieth birthday and the imminence of a new millennium, in 1995 and 2000 respectively, were taken as opportunities to canvass support for the democratization of the UN.

Two main proposals for the reform of the UN pertinent to our survey here emanated from this renewed enthusiasm. One was to press for the creation of a second assembly alongside the General Assembly: the second was for the regularization of consultations with NGOs.

Individual citizen initiatives created INFUSA (the International Network for a UN Second Assembly), and this body combined with the World Citizens' Assembly to convene a series of meetings from 1989 under the acronym CAMDUN (Campaign for a More Democratic United Nations). Many individuals acting alone also produced blueprints for transmuting the UN into a bicameral institution (see Barnaby, 1991). The generally agreed strategy follows these lines. A gradualist approach is most likely to be more successful than sudden radical institutional reform. Conveniently, Article 22 of the Charter makes provision for the establishment by the General Assembly of 'subsidiary organs'. Thus a plan for an assembly created under this rubric with merely a consultative function and composed of members drawn from state parliaments (shades of the early European parliament) would attract less hostility than a scheme for a directly elected assembly with real powers. However, once established, this UN Parliamentary Assembly could form itself into a constituent body to draft a constitution for such a People's (or World Citizens') Assembly.

Not, one may suggest, that even this Fabian approach has more than a slender chance of gaining approval for implementation. (And this assessment is made despite the advocacy of Brian Urquhart, a former UN Assistant Secretary-General.) There is little evidence that member-states would countenance such an arrangement, even in its most modest form. Resistance would be especially obstinate from the USA where the Right harbours considerable doubt about the utility of the UN at all. In addition, there are practical difficulties relating to the cost, administration and electoral provisions of a fully fledged People's Assembly (though *ad hoc* UN People's Assemblies were convened in various locations from 1995, when the first such gathering took place in San Francisco).

Less complexity and financial outlay would attend the construction of regional representative institutions of a transnational but sub-global geographical span. This is the second of our suggested requirements for the existence of a realistic political world citizenship. The advocates of this objective favour regional assemblies for two reasons. The basic point is that they would provide a stage in the building of a pyramidal structure topped by a cosmopolitan representative body such as the proposed UN People's Assembly. The second reason is their interpretation of the European Parliament as a pioneering model for other sub-continental (or continental) regions to copy.

The third requirement is the need to form clear and permanent institutional arrangements so that the organizations of the nascent global civil society may be able to present the views, recommendations and pleas of their members to a supranational body, i.e. a reformed UN, with the expectation that they be seriously considered. It must be said that this avenue for enhancing political world citizenship has a greater likelihood of being pursued than the more ambitious project of a directly elected People's Assembly. There are three main indicators for this positive judgement. The Report of the distinguished Commission on Global Governance recommended the convening of an annual Forum of Civil Society of representatives from 300 to 600 CSOs, underpinned by regional consultations. The Forum would advise the General Assembly and would 'strengthen the capacity of civil society to influence the governments of member-states of the UN on issues on the Assembly's agenda'. The Report firmly states: 'We attach much importance to this proposal' (Commission on Global Governance, 1995: 260, 258). Five years later, the Secretary-General's Millennial Report included in his list of recommendations for the renewing of the United Nations the provision of greater opportunities for NGOs to contribute to the Organization's work. Nor were the NGOs themselves slow to take advantage of the millennium gatherings in New York, in particular the Secretary-General's invitation for a Millennium Civil Society Forum to draw up proposals for the

147

reform of the UN (already referred to in the second section of this chapter). Five regional meetings were organized throughout the world to forward ideas to the Forum, which was attended by representatives from over 100 countries.

The involvement of large numbers in making contributions to the Millennium Forum was evidence that people are increasingly thinking of themselves as citizens in a multiple sense – this is our fourth requirement. The nation-state can no longer sustain its role as the be-all and end-all of political citizenship: power and influence are both drifting upwards to supranational institutions and organizations and seeping downwards to regional authorities and bodies. As a consequence, opportunities are growing for individuals to participate at various levels; moreover, people need to be made aware not just of these opportunities, but also of their interconnections. Let us take two examples. First, David Brower, the founder of Friends of the Earth, coined the slogan, 'think globally, act locally'. Second, the EU has formally adopted the principle of subsidiarity which, strictly interpreted, requires decisions to be taken at the lowest practical level in a pyramidal political structure. Citizenship as political participation is now therefore a much more flexible concept and status than hitherto and, in so far as it can be considered (albeit controversially) as no longer the monopoly of the nation-state, then world citizenship can the more easily be accommodated in the political pattern.

Even so, and the fifth requirement, multiple citizenship will remain little more than an interpretation or conscious understanding unless and until international law catches up with and formally gives recognition to these developments. True, dual citizenship and the 'layered' citizenship of federal states (and, *sui generis*, of the EU) have such recognition; nevertheless, as we have seen in Chapter 4, citizenship as nationality still lies at the heart of the legal interpretation of the status. The status of world citizen remains to be codified and political activity by virtue of the status remains to be given the imprimatur of the law.

The presentation of these desiderata as a list inevitably gives an impression of a fragmented, *ad hoc* handling of the matter. And maybe that is a true reflection of the only realistic way of promoting political world citizenship. Yet, there is a feeling that a more coherent approach might be possible, indeed might be the only way of achieving the political rights of a world citizenship worthy of being so described. After all, despite his reservations, as we have recorded above, Kant hankered after something more than his conception of a cosmopolitan law or confederation of republican states would offer. In his *Idea for a Universal History*, for instance, he foresees the emergence of 'a great political body of the future, without precedence in the past'. He continues:

> And this encourages the hope that, after many revolutions, with all their transforming effects the highest purpose of nature, a universal *cosmopolitan existence*, will at last be realised as the matrix within which all the original capacities of the human race will develop. (Reiss, 1991: 51)

The intellectual distinction of Kant and his willingness to think in the long term have perhaps encouraged the proponents of the notion of cosmopolitan democracy (a little over 200 years after Kant's *Universal History*) to develop their own proposals – with the stress on democracy, obligatory for any credible political thinking in this sphere at the beginning of the twenty-first century. Because the agenda of the advocates of cosmopolitan democracy is so thoroughly all-embracing, as explained in Chapter 4, the reader is asked to understand the survey of the political facets here in that broader context.

The political content of the cosmopolitan democracy project is clear from this summary of its nature, where the authors explain that it

> attempts to specify the principles and the institutional arrangements for making accountable those sites and forms of power which presently operate beyond the scope of democratic control ... It argues that in the millennium ahead each citizen of a state will have to learn to become a 'cosmopolitan citizen' as well: that is, a person capable of mediating between national traditions, communities of fate and alternative forms of life. ... In addition, the cosmopolitan project contends that, if many contemporary forms of power are to become accountable and if many of the complex issues that affect us all – locally, nationally, regionally and globally – are to be democratically regulated, people will have to have access to, and membership in, *diverse* political communities. (Held *et al.*, 1999: 449)

Beyond this succinct explanation lies a thorough working through of the justifications, bases and recommended institutions for the realization of cosmopolitan democracy. The starting point is what David Held has called 'the principle of autonomy'. He explains:

> *persons should enjoy equal rights and, accordingly, equal obligations in the specification of the political framework which generates and limits the opportunities available to them; that is, they should be free and equal in the determination of the conditions of their own lives, so long as they do not deploy this framework to negate the rights of others.* (Held, 1995: 147, emphasis in original; see also 71, 149–51)

Herein lies the essence of citizenship, a status enjoyed intrinsically by all in a democratic polity. But, in the world today, are citizens able to enjoy autonomy?

The problem is that national citizen and state alike are affected in multifarious ways by decisions made and actions taken by other states, agencies and organizations across the globe, and, as a consequence, the citizen's autonomous control of his or her life via the state is seriously eroded. The repair and extension of citizenly autonomy, argue Held and other advocates of cosmopolitan democracy, require the rethinking of democratic theory and the restructuring of the world's pattern of institutions along democratic lines. Democracy should permeate the world's economic and political systems so that individuals can act as world citizens and hold accountable those transnational institutions and agencies that affect their lives. Indeed, the role of the world citizen is two-fold: to work for the achievement of cosmopolitan democracy, and to participate in the reformed system as it comes into being. The parallel with the evolution of democratic citizenship at the state level is evident, as Daniele Archibugi shows:

> What is needed now is the participation of new political subjects. According to the cosmopolitan project, they should be world citizens, provided with the institutional channels to take part and assume duties *vis-à-vis* the global destiny. If citizens had not been capable of assuming this responsibility directly, democracy would never have enjoyed such great success in so many countries. It is no vain hope, therefore, to believe that in time the citizens of the world will take upon themselves the responsibility of managing this small planet of theirs democratically. (Archibugi, Held and Köhler, 1998: 223–4)

Note the modifying phrase, 'in time'. The proponents of cosmopolitan democracy have no illusions about the magnitude of the task they are commending; but they deny any charge of simple-minded utopianism by depicting the possibility of the building of their kind of edifice upon the limited transnational structures that already exist and of the task being spread over a considerable span of time – short of an unforeseen revolutionary event.

It is quite evident that global or transnational problems exist and that responses have been made by the creation of international organizations to supplement the all too inadequate powers (including will-power) of nation-states to cope. Some random examples: the Bretton Woods institutions (IBRD and IMF) to deal with economic underdevelopment; the UN Environment Programme (UNEP) to deal with environmental degradation; the North Atlantic Treaty Organization (NATO) to deal with northern hemisphere security problems; Amnesty International to deal with infringements of human rights. Organizations such as these have been devised in order to guard against the further deterioration of the problems and perils the world already faces. But, to adapt Juvenal, who is to monitor the decisions and actions of these guardians? Patchwork global governance exists, but is lacking a strong thread of democracy to bind it into a system of recognized legitimacy.

What, in political terms, would a cosmopolitan democratic pattern look like? The key feature is multiplicity: multiple institutions of multiple kinds at multiple levels, involving individuals acting through multiple citizenships. The world would be organized into a network of local, national, regional and global bodies providing for democratic participation, including the use of referendums, and operating in accordance with the principle of subsidiarity. Thus, at the truly global level, a reformed, democratically accountable UN would deal with the issues of truly global extent. World citizenship would burgeon by the proliferation of levels and kinds of citizenships. David Held has expressed this putative outcome thus:

These mechanisms would help contribute ... to the preservation of the ideal of a rightful share in the process of governance, even in contexts where dispute settlement and problem resolution would inevitably be at some considerable distance from local groups and assemblies. (Held, 1995: 273)

As a result, 'citizenship would be extended, in principle, to membership in all cross-cutting political communities, from the local to the global' (*ibid.*: 272).

The political scientists who have devised the concept of cosmopolitan democracy and those of like mind are sometimes dubbed 'transformationalists'. In the Marxian tradition they are philosophers who wish not just to interpret the world, but to change it, though they reject the interpretation of the 'hyperglobalists' who foresee the trend of globalization as involving the complete collapse of the nation-state. However, if the world is to be politically transformed, world citizens must organize themselves to render world citizenship more realistic and effective. This is the purpose of a movement, named after the year of its foundation, Charter 99. Its full descriptive title is: 'A Charter for Global Democracy – Our call for international accountability, equality, justice, sustainable development and democracy'. The initiators of the movement declared in their Charter document:

> The first aim is to make the already existing processes of world administration and governance accountable. We want to know what decisions are being taken and why. We want the decision takers to know they are answerable to the public in every country which feels the breath of international bodies.

In 2001, Charter 99 launched its Global Accountability Index project. By investigating the relative openness of the work of transnational institutions, the scheme is designed to identify the key criteria by which an organization can be rated democratic and accountable, to discover good practice and to devise proposals for the reform of those organizations that score low in the enquiry.

Charter 99 was launched in Britain and by the end of 2000 claimed supporters in 120 countries, including the heads of over ninety NGOs. This is, on a smaller scale, very reminiscent of the creation of the World Citizens' Registry after the Second World War (see Heater, 1996: 171–2). But are such movements any more than the converted preaching to the converted? Better, perhaps, to pose the question in a more helpful way. We need to ask: will the number of individuals considering themselves to be world citizens increase to a substantial number only if institutions are first created to encourage this attitude of mind and propensity to world citizenly action? Or, conversely, will more institutional opportunities for global participation be created only as responses to the pressure of the body of self-regarding world citizens reaching a critical mass? If the answer to this latter alternative – that people create institutions – is a more weighty affirmative than the former, then the role of education through the mass media and schools takes on a special significance.

CHAPTER 7

Competence and Education

Requirements and Impediments

A person is neither born with citizenly qualities nor grows to be a perfect exemplar of citizenship. For, although as a legal status citizenship has a clear-cut definition – one is or is not a citizen of a particular state – no such precision can be given to citizenship as a mode of behaviour: knowledge and understanding must be acquired, skills must be developed, and a wish and a will to perform the role must be felt. In short, to become a citizen in the true sense requires competence and competence is acquired through a process of education. Yet, however excellent the educational process and however apt and keen the pupil-citizen might be, few can be expected to mature into anything but an approximation to the ideal citizen, even if such a model could be conceived. The questions consequently arise: What are the kinds of competence a citizen needs? Are there special elements required by the world citizen? And what difficulties impede the development of a person as a world citizen?

The starting-point in this learning process is an awakening to the fact that one is or can be a citizen of the world, being brought to an awareness that one's condition as a human being has a meaning beyond mere biological existence and familial, local and national relationships, and can be, even should be, consciously related to a universal ethic. This expansion of awareness cannot, needless to say, be experienced in a state of ignorance. The mind of the world citizen must be furnished with information about the Earth's peoples, countries, cultures and the interconnectedness of the several elements of both human living and the planet's ecosphere. Yet knowledge is inert if the significance and implications of that knowledge are not appreciated and understood. Martha Nussbaum has referred to a crucial feature of this form of the learning process as the cultivation of the 'narrative imagination', that is, 'the ability to think what it might be like to be in the shoes of a person different from oneself'. She explains that 'understanding the world from the point of view of the other is essential to any responsible act of judgment' (Nussbaum, 1997a: 10–11; see also Chapter 3 above). To be a world citizen is to understand that there are myriad differences in ways of living and thinking throughout the world, yet different does not necessarily imply good or bad and, in particular, that the familiar is not necessarily the better. It is also to understand the effect of one's own way of life and one's own country's policies on the world and its peoples.

Partly in order to understand and partly in order to act as a world citizen, the individual needs both intellectual and practical skills. Truly to lay claim to the title of 'world citizen' the individual needs to master such intellectual skills as critically judging the coverage of world issues by the news media, and such practical skills as lobbying politicians about, or campaigning to mitigate the severity of, a global problem.

Listed briefly, these requirements might not appear too difficult of achievement. Yet one has only to ask oneself what proportion of one's acquaintances – let alone of one's country, let alone, even more, of the whole population of the world – could measure up to merely the minimum standard of these criteria to realize how simplistic and complacent a judgement of this kind would be. There are, in truth, formidable obstacles to even a minute percentage of the world's population being or becoming effective world citizens by the test of this listed definition. The impediments to a substantial number of people being world citizens in anything but the weakest meaning of the term may be viewed in two categories. One relates to the difficulties of being in the fullest sense a citizen *tout court*, these difficulties being germane also to world citizenship. The other concerns the additional difficulties that must be taken into account when one incorporates the global dimension into the tally.

Initially, we shall take the basic problems. Even in developed countries with full educational provision and wide access to the several news media, ignorance and apathy most aptly describe the condition of popular attitudes to public and world affairs. Cassandra voices loudly bewail the perverseness of materialism and social immorality and the feebleness of any education system to reverse this ethical decline. The authority on international relations, K. J. Holsti, estimated over a quarter of a century ago that about 70 per cent of the population were 'apathetic, uninformed and nonexpressive' (Holsti, 1974: 383). There is little reason to expect that matters have improved very much since. Lack of interest has been notorious. Let us take one blatant example, admittedly from half a century ago, but it is so pertinent to the thrust of this chapter that it is worth describing. In 1949 an enormous public information campaign was mounted in Cincinnati, Ohio, to promote understanding of the UN:

> Parent–teacher associations, schools, churches, radio stations and newspapers were deluged for a six-month period with informational posters, pamphlets, slogans, action programme proposals, films, guest speakers and various other devices intended to spread awareness and knowledge of the UN. (Blumler, 1974: 93)

The result? The proportion knowing nothing about the UN before the campaign was about 30 per cent; the proportion knowing nothing about the UN after this saturation campaign: about 30 per cent!

Therefore, although politicians, schools and the mass media are often blamed for failing to encourage, sometimes even for positively discouraging a global understanding among the citizenry, pupils and readers/audience respectively, this neglect cannot be the sole explanation for the state of affairs epitomized by the Cincinnati initiative. Ignorance about world issues often derives from a lack of interest and boredom. This is sometimes because of the very real difficulty of fully engaging in Martha Nussbaum's 'narrative imagination'. Alternatively, it is because of the intrinsic dullness or arcane nature of the subject-matter: the UN and the international economy are examples. On the other hand, politicians, schools and the mass media cannot be entirely exculpated. It is rare for elections to be decided on anything but domestic issues, so it is a rare politician who would concentrate his or her efforts on promoting an understanding of world affairs. Social studies/civic education in schools have traditionally been focused on pupils' learning about their own state. And the mass media, ever conscious of sales figures or listening/viewing ratings, are hesitant to provide wide or deep coverage of world affairs. A notable exception is the category of the best broadsheet newspapers; but, then, in terms of influence, the mass-circulation tabloids, by pandering to the widespread appetite for trivia, more than outweigh the editorial efforts of the quality press.

In 1803, just before he died, Kant published some brief thoughts on education. And in these notes we can find an early expression of concern about the problem we have just outlined. He wrote thus:

> One *principle of education* which those men especially who form educational schemes should keep before their eyes is this – children ought to be educated, not for the present, but for a possibly improved condition of man in the future; that is, in a manner which is adapted to the *idea of humanity* and the whole destiny of man. . . .
>
> Here, however, we are met by two difficulties – (a) parents usually only care that their children *make their way* in the world, and (b) sovereigns look upon their subjects merely as *tools* for their own purposes.
>
> Parents care for the home, rulers for the state. Neither have as their aim the universal good and the perfection to which man is destined, and for which he has also a natural disposition. But the basis of a scheme of education must be cosmopolitan. (Kant, 1960: 14–15)

Summarized in modern terms: parents want the schools to prepare their pupils to obtain good jobs; governments want the schools to prepare their pupils to be good citizens of the state; but the schools should be educating their pupils in world citizenship.

Although these impediments to a competent civic life have been illustrated from the field of world affairs, in many ways they are little more than the weaknesses of national citizenship competence in exacerbated form. After all, apathy, ignorance and the weakness of the political, educational and journalistic influences are discernible also in the low levels of interest and understanding about social and civic matters at the local and national levels. What, we must now therefore ask, are the major obstructions to the cultivation of world citizenship which are particular to the global scope of the enterprise? Three attitudes of mind in particular hinder the acquisition of a world citizenship competence at school or adult level. One is a blinkered patriotism; second is pedagogical conservatism; third is the constraint of poverty.

Those who identify closely with their own country or 'people' have no disposition to think of themselves as world citizens and are resistant to efforts to fit them with the aptitudes for this role. Maybe only those with the narrowest view on patriotism close their minds to a wider horizon; even so, it is often felt that this kind of mentality is very common. Voltaire, for example, contrasted the world citizen with the patriot, saying of the latter that 'it is the human condition that to wish for the greatness of the fatherland is to wish evil of one's neighbours' (Voltaire, 1971: 329). If football hooligans could be as articulate, they would no doubt express the same belief. The demeaning of the ancient and noble citizenly virtue by this vulgarity associates patriotism with the baseness of nationalism, racism and xenophobia. In 1994, Martha Nussbaum wrote an essay in the *Boston Review* in which she argued that the moral ideals of justice and equality are better served by cosmopolitanism than by patriotism and that education designed to oust the latter in favour of the former was an urgent need. This essay and a selection of responses were later published in book form under the telling title of *For Love of Country: Debating the Limits of Patriotism* (Nussbaum *et al.*, 1996; and already cited in Chapter 1 above). Two of the issues were whether patriotism leads inevitably to xenophobia and is therefore inimical to cosmopolitanism and, conversely, whether cosmopolitanism is corrosive of patriotism. Inevitably, those who are fervent patriots and believe that patriotism is still a cardinal virtue anathematize any suggestion of adapting the learning process to accommodate the cosmopolitan ideal.

Governments almost inevitably, if they intervene in curricular matters at all, reinforce the patriotic thrust of civic education. In its extreme, ideological form it has appeared as Nazi indoctrination; in its republican form it has appeared in the syllabuses and ceremonies in American and French schools. Even in England, the quasi-cosmopolitan teaching about and celebration of the British Empire, encouraged by the Board of Education in the past, had an overwhelmingly patriotic purpose.

The concentrated patriotism of the 'my country right or wrong' attitude tends to be associated with conservative thinking in both political and pedagogical spheres. Consequently, educationists who try to reform the content, methods and environment of civic learning to embrace a cosmopolitan vision are prone to criticism from the political Right. Inevitably, if the very notion of world citizenship sends shudders of apprehension down the spines of those who believe that loyal identity with the state is of paramount importance, then one must expect equal hostility from the same quarter towards any attempt at educating the younger generation to be global citizens. Clearly, if the political objections command support, then they will tend to intrude into views about the schools curriculum: ministers of education, local education authorities, school governors and parents who are opposed to the cosmopolitan ideal will wish to deter teachers from introducing work into the classroom designed to alert young minds to this manner of thinking. But even if there is no overt political hostility, objections are often raised about the subject content and teaching methodologies. It was the fate, for example, of numerous Global Studies projects in the USA in the Reagan era and of the World Studies movement in Britain in the Thatcherite ascendancy to fall foul of both political and pedagogical opposition.

But, first, a little historical background. Conscious attempts to teach for international understanding got under way before the First World War. Britain and the USA, in fact, undertook much of the pioneering work (see Bailey, 1938: 104–55). Then, after the War, the League of Nations gave encouragement for teaching about its purpose and activities. In 1926 the distinguished British scholar Charles Webster explained in a League of Nations Union address:

> For a long time after the formation of the League of Nations, governments were very chary in a great many countries of allowing instruction upon it to be brought into their educational curricula. It was, perhaps, the Corfu incident in 1923 which more than anything altered their point of view. (Webster, 1926: 11)

He explained that this teaching revealed extraordinary ignorance and gross misunderstandings about the League and the consequent need of better education in this field to counteract the 'nonsense' purveyed by many newspapers (*ibid.*). However, his optimism that a more positive mood for 'the teaching of world citizenship' (the title of his published address) was evolving was misplaced. Indeed, during the inter-war years, the problems facing the British and American advocates of what in Britain came to be called education for world citizenship were presented with vivid starkness. The American political scientist Charles Merriam explained in 1931:

For the time being, the attempts at international civic training are obstructed by the antagonism between the pacifists and the imperialists and militarists, and between advocates and opponents of the League of Nations. ... The clash between these competing systems has thus far prevented the organization and presentation of any attitude at all, and has left the [human] race at the mercy of the war psychosis. (Bereday, 1966: 361)

After half a century of varied fortunes, there was a resurgence of education for global citizenship in the 1970s and 1980s, only to be countered by a rallying of its opponents, often expressing their hostility quite vitriolically. Let us take three examples. In 1979, Professor James Becker of Indiana University published a book entitled *Schooling for a Global Age*. A plan to implement an 'Indiana in the World' programme in the state's schools based on Becker's ideas was followed by a hostile campaign, his book being described as 'the *Mein Kampf* for creating world-centred schools in the U.S.'. The teachers of Denver, Colorado, who had been in the vanguard in the 1930s (Bailey, 1938: 109), performed that role again. The focus of this work was the Center for Teaching International Relations at the University of Denver, condemned in 1986 as indoctrinatory by a widely circulated report by Gregg Cunningham, entitled 'Blowing the Whistle on Global Education' (see Lamy, 1990). Three years later, a global education programme for the state of Iowa received similar treatment to that given to the Indiana scheme. The Department of Education authorities became worried. A communication to the members of the Global Education Task Force explained:

The hostile attack ... apparently began with a small number of right-wing fundamentalists, whose voices have reached other groups such as farmers and state legislators. ... There seems to be an organized effort out there to undermine what we are trying to accomplish through global education.

Rumors, distortions, and fabrications have all been used to put certain aspects of education in a bad light. For example, it is charged with vegetarianism, Eastern religions, anti-patriotism and a one-world government. (Svengalis, 1991)

At the same time, curriculum development in Britain (see Heater, 1980) triggered similar reactions in the related atmosphere of Thatcherism. The tone may be judged by the following comment by a professor of philosophy, who also believed that teachers could be professionally untrustworthy. He wrote:

> World Studies masquerades as a 'discipline' whose aim is to produce an open mind towards the differing cultures and varying conditions of humanity. In reality, however, ... It is designed to close the child's mind to everything but the narrow passions of the radical. (Scruton, 1985: 30)

However, in the UK, there were no organized campaigns and the hostile language was less populist in tone than in the USA. During the 1970s and 1980s, schools, encouraged by many educationists, were introducing a variety of new subjects and styles of teaching. These innovations included Political Studies, World History, World Studies, Development Studies and Peace Studies. They provoked an angry Conservative (and conservative) reaction, because the courses offended the Right's understanding of the nature of politics, their patriotic commitment and their conception of schooling.

The Conservative believes in a minimalist form of politics. Too much government activity and too much pressure from the citizenry to stimulate such activity are to be deplored. It naturally follows that encouraging school pupils to grow up as enthusiastically participative citizens (except at the local, community level) should be discouraged. More than that, teachers, many of whom have 'liberal' leanings, cannot be trusted to avoid indoctrinating their pupils with their own questionable opinions. Now, if these convictions of the Conservative throw into serious doubt the induction of young people into the status of citizenship in the domestic sense, the Conservative's objections are multiplied when this kind of teaching is expanded to incorporate a cosmopolitan frame of reference.

People of a Conservative cast of mind believe that they hold to a sturdier patriotism than those to their left. As one politician declared, 'The notion of national greatness is one that comes naturally enough to Conservatives' (Raison, 1964: 118). Accordingly, the introduction of World History, by diverting time from the study of National History, must be resisted. When the English National Curriculum was being implemented in the early 1990s, the draft syllabus for History was criticized for giving insufficient weight to British history. One member of the working party was reported as saying there were 'inexcusable' omissions, explaining that 'children would not be required to study a single British monarch, but there would be a legal obligation to teach topics such as Islamic civilisation, Benin or black peoples of the Americas' (*Guardian*, 6 May 1994). The balance was changed in order to place Britain at the core of the syllabus. However, what really riled the Right in the 1980s was the introduction of Peace Studies. In the atmosphere of the New Cold War, this development appeared to be little short of a treasonous undermining of NATO; showing a Peace Studies document to a Conservative was tantamount to displaying a red rag to a John Bull.

In addition, educational as well as political objections were voiced against extending school curricula to a global perspective. A survey of practices in Western Europe led one researcher to comment: 'teaching objectives ... are often too grandiose and thus fail to provide the needed connections between rhetoric and classroom practice' (O'Connor, 1982: 225; see also O'Connor, 1980: 17–24). And he was a sympathetic observer. In contrast, Roger Scruton, the particularly vocal opponent already cited, declared, 'The World Studies movement ... seeks ultimately to take over every area of the curriculum. And to replace serious knowledge and formal scholarship with political posturing and infantile, manipulative games' (Scruton, 1985: 39). The last three vituperative words refer to the use of role-play exercises to cultivate an empathetic understanding, which will be explained below. Insofar as these lessons reduced the time available for learning facts, this kind of teaching contributed to the alarm of conservative commentators (including some teachers). Scruton continued by accusing the proponents of World Studies of creating a 'stampede' in support of 'a single mendacious idea (the idea that the North is responsible for the South's immiseration)' (*ibid.*: 39).

This equation of World Studies with Third World or Development Studies, though inaccurate, leads us to the third of our obstacles to the spread of world citizenship competence, what we have called the constraint of poverty. This impediment exists in two forms – as a causative factor of xenophobia and extremist nationalism and of inward-looking parochialism.

Economic difficulties, unemployment or fear of unemployment can lead to a hatred of established or immigrant minorities who are perceived as 'stealing' wealth and opportunities from the 'true' nationals of a state. Extreme right-wing nationalist parties both ride on and buoy up this popular animosity. The experience of inter-war Europe in the Great Depression and, most notably, the rise of Nazism exemplify this interpretation. Eric Hobsbawm has put it starkly: 'fascism. Which the slump transformed into a world movement, and more to the point, a world danger' (Hobsbawm, 1994: 108). And, currently, it is no coincidence that neo-Nazism is most virulent in the eastern *Länder* of the Federal Republic of Germany, where the difficult task of raising the living standards of the former Communist Democratic Republic is so slow as to cause envy and resentment. What can be a more obvious antithesis to cosmopolitanism than xenophobic nationalism? What chance, in an atmosphere like this, of teachers persuading their pupils of the validity and virtue of world citizenship?

But, of course, poverty is relative. The economic troubles of the Weimar Republic in 1930 and the eastern *Länder* in 2000 have scarcely been comparable with the abject poverty of hundreds of millions of African, Indian and Chinese peasants, for example. When one is barely scraping a subsistence level of income, daily fearful of malnutrition and disease, imagining oneself as a world citizen is an unaffordable luxury, even in the unlikely event that the concept is known or comprehensible. One's village *is* the world, as the two meanings of the Russian word *mir*, for example, indicate. If any among these great numbers of the world's population are aware of the globe they inhabit, it might well be in the form of the contribution that capitalist globalization is making to their continuing degradation.

Schools' Potential

'Education for world citizenship', 'education for international understanding' and 'global education' are terms that became increasingly widely used in the twentieth century. The first is particularly associated with teaching and related activities in schools in the UK; the second has been used by UNESCO; and the third has been the favoured term in the USA. The basic objective was and, in some respects, still is to ameliorate the world's troubles by cultivating in the younger generation an understanding of global issues and other peoples, 'understanding' to be taken to mean both comprehension and empathy. It is this role of the schools that commands our attention for most of this chapter. However, education has a more complex function in relation to world citizenship than this obvious contribution. Both education as a human right and literacy as a means of communication and of raising indigent peoples from their impoverished lives must also be included in our notion of education for world citizenship.

In 1963, the Director-General of UNESCO presented a report on the urgent need to eradicate illiteracy. He pointed out that 'The strictest economic realism . . . demands as insistently as do morality and justice, that a major effort be made in this essential field.' And he concluded by asking: 'who does not see the permanent threat to peace . . . implicit in a fast-growing inequality which daily widens the gap between those who enjoy the benefits of education' and those who are deprived of them? (quoted in Burnet, 1965: 6). If world citizenship exists or is to exist, then, in the words of the Universal Declaration of Human Rights, 'Everyone has the right to education' (Article 26.1). It follows that anyone who is denied this right cannot be considered a world citizen in the fullest sense. Moreover, if, as was argued above, poverty is an impediment to the achievement of world citizenship, and if the acquisition of literacy is a route by which to rise out of the condition of destitution, then world citizenship is potentially enhanced by the eradication of illiteracy.

Indeed, the linkage between the right to education as a universal human entitlement and its function in cultivating a sense of world citizenship is recognized by the Universal Declaration of Human Rights, which states:

> Education shall be directed . . . to the strengthening of respect for human rights and fundamental freedoms. It shall promote understanding, tolerance and friendship among nations, racial or religious groups, and shall further the activities of the United Nations for the maintenance of peace. (Article 26.2)

Nevertheless, to advocate the use of schools to spread and deepen a sense of world citizenship requires the treading of a careful road between utopian optimism and a pessimistic infirmity of purpose. There is such abundant evidence of hatred, injustice and violence in this world that one would properly court ridicule by naïvely suggesting that schools could readily replace this condition with a cosmopolitan harmony. Yet, at the same time, one would be rightly condemned for weakly suggesting that schools can make no contribution at all nor improve upon what contributions they may already be making. As so often, a *via media* is most apt. This middle way has, in fact, two paths. One leads teachers to an appreciation that they must avoid totally accepting or rejecting the polarized interpretations of the human condition: neither innate sin, selfishness and violent territoriality nor the potential for salvation, humane behaviour and the acceptance of a universal ethic should be thought of as sets of absolutes. The second path is the route to a firm and modest understanding that schools are not insulated institutions. In so far as schools can be considered as institutions of some effectiveness for instilling an awareness of world citizenship, the attitudes of their pupils are also shaped by their parents, friends, mass media and the social and political milieux in which they live. These influences may counteract the schools' efforts; or, with energy and ingenuity, the schools and the education system may be able to recruit these other socializing forces to their cosmopolite purpose. Indeed, that schools can and should have such a purpose has been accepted by an impressive number of educationists.

Zeno founded his *stoa poikelē* as a school. He and his successor, Chrysippus, were teachers; those attending the painted porch were students. Thus, from its Stoic origins, cosmopolitanism was associated with the assumption that this way of thinking should be taught. Evidence of this view can also be discerned in the Neostoic revival. In his essay 'On the Education of Children', Montaigne wrote: 'This great world ... a mirror into which we must look if we are to behold ourselves from the proper standpoint. In fact, I would have this be my pupil's book' (Montaigne, 1958: 63–4). In England, Francis Bacon, also using the essay genre, wrote of 'a citizen of the world ... [whose] heart is no island cut off from other lands, but a continent that joins to them' (Bacon, 1906: 39). In 1627 Bacon published his utopian *New Atlantis*, in which he advocated the establishment of a 'Solomon's House' for the advancement of learning. This proposal attracted a number of English educationists, notably the Puritan MP Samuel Hartlib, who, with a view to establishing such an institution with a cosmopolitan staff, invited to London a prospective principal from the continent. This was the Moravian bishop Comenius, whose ideal of *pansophia* (universal knowledge) seemed so akin to Bacon's plan.

The first half of the seventeenth century was an age of bitter political and religious conflict, which considerably affected Comenius' life and, perhaps, his thought. The Thirty Years War forced him to flee his native Bohemia and made him a refugee; and the outbreak of the English Civil War precluded the foundation of the Baconian college.

Comenius is a crucial figure in the history of education for world citizenship, for three reasons that may be discerned in his multi-volume and separately titled *General Consultation Concerning the Improvement of Human Affairs*. The first reason is his evident absorption of the Stoic ethic. In the *Panegersia* (Universal Awakening), for instance, he asks, 'Since ... we are all co-citizens of one world, who shall prevent us from joining in one republic, under the same laws?'; he also states that 'we are all one body' and 'we are basically all one blood' (quoted in Lange, 1919: 484 n.8, author's translation). Second, in *Panpaedia* (Universal Education) and *Panorthosia* (Universal Reform) Comenius sets out a more thorough exposition of a concept of education for world citizenship than was to be available before the twentieth century. He envisaged a College of Light, a universal administrative structure to ensure that the schools are the workshops of light, that the headteachers are the light-bearers, that the teaching methods are the purifiers of light and that the books are the vessels of light. Comenius' inspiration was the teaching of Christ, 'the fount of light'; his objective was universal peace. This objective is, indeed, the third reason for Comenius' significance. He is the bridge between world citizenship education as the instilling of a Stoic awareness of the oneness of humankind and its prime function as the pacification of humankind. Comenius' political system, the Dicastery, parallel with his educational structure, was to have the function of ensuring 'that no swords or spears shall be left that have not been beaten into ploughshares and pruning hooks' (Piaget, 1967: 203). When education for world citizenship (though not always named thus) was revived as an ideal around 1900 and was episodically revivified throughout the twentieth century, Peace Studies became a major feature of the proposals.

These educational developments grew out of the nineteenth-century peace movements in the USA, the UK and continental Europe. Congresses of concerned citizens to mobilize the force of public opinion for peace were mirrored by proposals by and occasional meetings of educationists who believed in the power of education to achieve the same end. Notably, during the late 1880s, the Dutchman Herman Molkenboer organized an international network of teachers committed to believing in the beneficent potential of teaching the virtue of universal disarmament. This nineteenth-century eirenic mood reached its apogee in the period 1899 to 1914, that is, from the first Hague Peace Conference to the start of the First World War. One feature of this period was the creation of School Peace Leagues in the USA, the UK, France and The Netherlands. The objectives were:

> to promote, through the schools, international peace, arbitration, and friendship; to study ... the problems of racial relationships and the best means of eliminating prejudice ... to promote through lessons in civics, the development of a rational and humane national life and patriotism, and a sense of the corresponding duties to humanity. (Scanlon, 1960: 7–8)

During the two decades between the World Wars, commitments to education for international understanding derived from two quite distinct developments. One was the belief in child-centred education; the other was teaching that sprang from the existence of the League of Nations.

The ideas of the New Education Fellowship (founded by Beatrice Ensor) and Maria Montessori's principles, which she expounded from the first decade of the century, spread to many countries. Contained in their messages was the conviction that children, unspoiled by traditional pedagogical methods and unmoulded by national purpose, can be naturally peaceful and understanding of other peoples. It is notable, for example, that the Montessori schools were closed down in Nazi Germany and Fascist Italy.

Perhaps the greatest commitment to teaching about the League of Nations, already mentioned, was made in the UK, where the Education Committee of the League of Nations Union (LNU) had already been created in 1919. In its heyday, some 1,400 schools were using its wide-ranging support for what was now coming to be called the teaching of or education for world citizenship. Moreover, by the 1930s even some official recognition of the importance of this kind of school work was forthcoming. Two examples may be cited. The first is a proposition from a statement made in 1934 by Arthur Henderson, a former cabinet minister, who decided that 'Perhaps the most vital element in our peace crusade is the adequate education of the young in world citizenship' (quoted in League of Nations Union, 1937: 23). The second is taken from the Board of Education's *Handbook of Suggestions for Teachers*, 1937 edition, which explained that conditions 'in the modern industrial world ... have made it necessary that peoples of the world should combine with their natural sense of local patriotism a conception of their common interests and duties' (quoted in *ibid.*: 7–8). Two years later, however, the outbreak of the Second World War seemed to crush the implied hope of that sentence.

The onset of two World Wars interrupted two initiatives for educating young world citizens. Perhaps the School Peace Leagues and the teaching inspired by the New Education and by the League of Nations were too frailly infant to have had any impact on the powerful forces impelling the world to conflict? Or perhaps education could never have any real influence of this political kind? However, optimistic determination revived as the Second World War was in its early phases.

By this time, the term 'education for world citizenship' was firmly established, certainly in Britain among the fraternity of the LNU. Accordingly, when it was decided, in 1939, to divorce the work of the Education Committee from its parent body, it is not surprising that the metamorphosed organization should have been named 'the Council for Education in World Citizenship' (CEWC). The LNU Education Committee/CEWC enjoyed a continuous life as national bodies for over eighty years (1919–2001), surely unrivalled by any other comparable association committed to the fostering of world citizenship (see Heater, 1984).

Looking ahead to the end of the War, CEWC played a major role in Britain, in parallel with similar activity in the USA, in planning for the creation of an international organization which, in due course, emerged as UNESCO. UNESCO was created on the Comenian principles of international collaboration in education for the purpose of preserving peace – indeed, UNESCO recognized its debt to the Moravian bishop by marking the tercentenary of his death in 1970. There is little wonder that UNESCO's emphasis, like that of Comenius, should have been placed on the pacific purpose of education – after all, it emerged from the most horrendous war since the Thirty Years War of Comenius' own age. Thus UNESCO's Constitution makes the famous epigrammatic statement: 'That since wars begin in the minds of men, it is in the minds of men that the defences of peace must be constructed.'

The question, however, arises – and it is well to face it here – what is the relationship between education for peace and education for world citizenship? They are assuredly not synonymous. Three comments may form a pertinent response to this question. One is, as we have seen, that the desperate practical need to abate man's warlike temperament has brought far more support for a global perspective to education than the less urgent Stoic insight of the oneness of humankind. On the other hand, and this is the second response, harmony or peace can be the expected outcome of comprehending and accepting that all human beings are at root born of the same stock, and that all should therefore be treated with equal justice and dignity. Wars are often started or exacerbated by contempt for or hatred of another, alien country, people or group. Learning and acknowledging that these human divisions are relatively minor in the cosmopolitan context, it is thus argued, may well both breed a consciousness of world citizenship and temper the will to conflict. And, third, there are hints that the founding fathers of UNESCO appreciated this connection; they asserted in the Constitution, for example, that 'peace must ... be founded, if it is not to fail, upon the intellectual and moral solidarity of mankind'.

Education for world citizenship is, in truth, a complex business, as the publications of UNESCO confirm. Its favoured term, 'education for international understanding', came to be seen as inadequate, so that when, in 1974, it issued an authoritative document, it was given the extraordinarily cumbersome title of 'Recommendation concerning Education for International Under-standing, Co-operation and Peace and Education relating to Human Rights and Fundamental Freedoms'. Twenty-one years later came the 'Declaration and Integrated Framework of Action on Education for Peace, Human Rights and Democracy'. So, 'international understanding' was dropped from the 1995 formula (though it is to be found in the text); and none of the three documents contained the words 'world citizenship' – indeed, UNESCO could not use that term because of the possible arousal of the kinds of hostile responses we have already noted in this book. Even so, these three documents are important: they are the nearest we have to universally accepted statements on education for world citizenship; the decisions to publish them represent an unshakeable conviction that schools are expected to play a key role in the promotion of international understanding; and, *pace* the absence of the term 'world citizenship', much of their contents would need to appear in any comprehensive statement on education for world citizenship.

That education for world citizenship is implicit in these documents may be illustrated by quotations from the 1995 Integrated Framework of Action:

The ultimate goal of education for peace, human rights and democracy is the development in every individual of a sense of universal values and types of behaviour on which a culture of peace is predicated. It is possible to identify even in different socio-cultural contexts values that are likely to be universally recognized (II.6).

To strengthen the formation of values and abilities such as solidarity, creativity, civic responsibility, the ability to resolve conflicts by non-violent means, and critical acumen, it is necessary to introduce into curricula, at all levels, true education for citizenship which includes an international dimension. (IV.17)

The wording of the documents makes it clear that schools have both the ability and responsibility to contribute to international understanding. Even so, the Recommendation recognized (indeed, its very purpose was to rectify) the small proportion of the world's schools that were engaged in this task; and the Declaration and the Integrated Framework of Action were produced because of the obsolescence of teaching methods in this aspect of school curricula. The latter two documents speak of the need for 'innovative strategies' and 'transformation of the traditional styles of educational action' in order to respond to the powerful forces at work in the contemporary world that are undermining universal peace, freedoms and rights. After all, rhetorical statements about duty and potential may stimulate new endeavours, but these efforts might well be little more than a waste of time if teachers are untrained in new, well-tested methods.

Fostering Competence

Although UNESCO tried to encourage a global perspective in education through its Associated Schools Project (ASPRO), launched in 1953, it was the quarter-century from about 1965 to about 1990 that was the era of notable curriculum development in individual countries – in Finland and the Federal Republic of Germany, for example, and especially in the USA and the UK. These last two, therefore, had been in the forefront of the movement to create UNESCO and, later, were to undertake work of especially high quality in Global Studies and World Studies (as they were called in the USA and UK respectively). So it is ironic that both these states withdrew from membership of UNESCO for some years in the 1980s and 1990s and that criticism of international education should have been particularly virulent there also.

The oscillation was probably more marked in the USA than in the UK. We have already noticed in the first section of this chapter the hostility in the USA; we must now look at the positive work. In 1966 Congress passed the International Education Act and, subsequently, many other related pieces of legislation. The 1966 Act was followed in 1969 by a seminal document identifying the objectives, needs and priorities for this work, compiled by James Becker and Lee Anderson, and known as the Becker/Anderson report. It has been described as 'truly a landmark' (Buergenthal and Torney, 1976: 34): it defined a properly global, as distinct from an inter-national, education; it persuaded much larger numbers of teachers than hitherto to engage in this work; and it influenced the approach adopted in the UNESCO Recommendation. Although no comparable government support was forthcoming in the UK, two important initiatives did come in the 1970s and 1980s. The first was the World Studies Project, directed by Robin Richardson. From this there emerged the innovative and successful *Learning for Change in a World Society* (1976). The second was the World Studies Teacher Training Project at the University of York, directed by Graham Pike and David Selby. From this there emerged *Global Teacher, Global Learner* (1988, and since published in seven translations). In 1992, Professor Selby became Director of the International Institute for Global Education in the University of Toronto. Through workshops, conferences, consultancies and the recruitment of overseas students, this institute has become a most influential global centre for global education.

Educators who are committed to helping young people to grow into world citizens face a complex task. We may identify some half-dozen of the major issues. These are: an understanding of the basic teaching objectives; the relevant evidence of children's psychological development; guidelines for a coherent curriculum; the special issue of the History syllabus; practical problems of implementation; and the laying of foundations for a lifelong global consciousness.

Education for world citizenship is Janus-faced. Looking back-wards, that face sees ingrained attitudes and pedagogical habits that, from the global educator's point of view, are at best parochial and at worst xenophobic. The task, therefore, is to bring the pupils to an understanding that their own country, religion, language and culture are not the only ones, that others are to be respected, but to do this without alienating the pupils or undermining their justifiably positive loyalties. Moreover, associated with this questioning of traditional syllabuses are doubts concerning the effectiveness of didactic, rote-learning methods of teaching: memorizing facts does not necessarily lead to an understanding of their significance, and certainly does not generate the sense of values and attitudes conducive to international understanding as a willingness and capacity to appreciate other customs and points of view. The forward-looking Janus-face sees the positive virtues of pupils learning a global perspective in their subject-studies. In particular, the young should come to know that their own lives are and will increasingly come to be inextricably shaped by events, forces and developments in the rest of the world. Furthermore, the teacher must recognize that learning in the school about matters and values far beyond its confines requires the cultivation and exercise of the skills of imagination. Lessons involving discussion and role-play, for example, are therefore essential supplements to the acquisition of factual knowledge (see, e.g. Richardson, 1976; Heater, 1980: 108–16).

Research on how young people learn about the wider world and how and when they acquire attitudes has, in fact, thrown light on the crucial importance of flexible and innovative teaching methodologies. These investigations have probed pupils' attitudes to their own and other countries, war and peace (see, e.g. *ibid.*: 41–56). Much of this research, it must be said, has taken great pains to reveal the obvious. However, two main conclusions are of importance for education for world citizenship. One relates to the optimum age for focusing on this work and this has been summarized by Judith Torney-Purta:

> middle childhood (i.e. before the onset of puberty) should be recognized as a time of important development changes in many attitudes, a period during which certain barriers to a global perspective have not yet been erected, and therefore one which is especially appropriate for beginning international education programs. (Buergenthal and Torney, 1976: 107)

The other significant evidence relates to teaching methods. This indicates that the school and classroom climate are more important than factual learning for the development of tolerant, empathetic attitudes, a reduction in apathy and the creation of a feeling of efficacy, that is, confidence and willingness to try to achieve something, however little, to make the world a more peaceful and just place for all its peoples.

How, then, are schools best able to achieve these complex aims? Considerations of subject content, learning objectives and teaching methods to embrace such a vast and intricate area of study have inevitably led to many different solutions to the task. We shall take just three possible approaches.

One is to identify the key concepts that the teacher might believe the pupils should grasp. This is the starting-point favoured by the British Central Bureau for International Education and Training, which, in 2000, identified eight key concepts. These are:

> Democracy and citizenship; sustainable development; social justice and a commitment to gender and racial equality; informed perceptions and appropriate images; intercultural understanding and the appreciation of diversity; personal and global interdependence; the resolution of conflict and the promotion of harmony; and human rights (quoted in Gardner, 2000: 238)

A second approach is to divide the subject-matter into themes, which, in our example, are called categories. This example is the recommended world core curriculum devised by Robert Muller and for which he was awarded the UNESCO Peace Education Prize in 1989. The course has been taught in schools in a number of countries. His four categories, subdivided into full lists of topics, are: I. Our Planetary Home and Place in the Universe; II. Our Human Family; III. Our Place in Time; IV. The Miracle of Individual Human Life (see Muller, 1994).

A third approach has been especially concerned to identify the kinds of learning experiences young people should be given in order to prepare them for the integrating, complicated, fast-moving world that we now inhabit. This approach tends to commend a radical reshaping of teaching. An influential example of this is to be found in the work of Pike and Selby already cited, where they identify 'five aims which together constitute the irreducible global perspective'. The following are their five aims expressed in skeletal form:

Systems consciousness
Students should: acquire the ability to think in a systems mode; acquire an understanding of the systemic nature of the world; acquire an holistic conception of their capacities and potential. . . .

Perspective consciousness
Students should: recognise that they have a worldview that is not universally shared; develop receptivity to other perspectives. . . .

Health of planet awareness
Students should: acquire an awareness and understanding of the global condition and of global developments and trends; develop an informed understanding of the concepts of justice, human rights and responsibilities and be able to apply that understanding to the global conditions and to global developments and trends; develop a future orientation in their reflection upon the health of the planet. . . .

Involvement consciousness
Students should: become aware that the choices they make and the actions they take individually and collectively have repercussions for the global present and the global future; develop the social and political action skills necessary for becoming effective participants in democratic decision-making at a variety of levels, grassroots to global. . . .

Process-mindedness
Students should: learn that learning and personal development are continuous journeys with no fixed or final destination; learn that new ways of seeing the world are revitalising but risky. (Pike and Selby, 1988: 34–5)

Having become acquainted with such options as these three, teachers of world citizenship are faced with three matters for resolution. One is to decide which framework to use as a basis for their syllabuses. The second is how to shape the framework for world *citizenship*, i.e., to stress the moral, legal, political and social elements. Third, a choice must be made between teaching either through the established school subjects or as an integrated,

174

interdisciplinary course. This is a difficult and controversial issue, which we have no space to explore here.

However, the particular matter of World History does deserve at least a brief mention. The reason for this is that, with the introduction and spread of mass popular education, History has been very largely taught with a national content and nationalistic purpose. As a consequence, young people have emerged from school with an extremely slender knowledge of the history of the rest of the world (at least, before the twentieth century) and a view of the past biased in favour of their own state. History textbooks have been notoriously partisan. A British historian provides some vivid evidence:

> If anyone doubts whether British accounts of the Armada may not be entirely valid and true, let him look at Spanish accounts which make no mention of Sir Francis Drake and sometimes none of the English, but make much of the untimely storm. ... An East German account of the Second World War does not mention England. (Thomson, 1969: 28–9)

And, surveying the history of History textbook reform, a professor of comparative education tartly commented on the failure of a League of Nations effort in this field: 'All proposals for actions were defeated on the grounds that national sovereignty included the right of each nation-state to deceive and mislead its citizens' (Lauwerys, n.d.: 7). Nor have professional historians been innocent of partiality, as the title of R. A. Billington's *The Historian's Contribution to Anglo-American Misunderstanding* (1964), for instance, clearly demonstrates. Needless to say, such History teaching is scarcely conducive to a sense of world citizenship. Gross bias in History textbooks can be corrected, and improvements in this manner have been very noticeable over the past half-century. However, the other matter, namely, the revision of syllabus content to introduce a world perspective, is not so straightforward. As we have seen in Chapter 3, even historians are divided on what can or should be meant by world history, so the teacher, once again, has the problem of deciding which model of selection and structure to choose.

As world citizenship is becoming increasingly recognized both as a respectable concept for academic investigation and as a status and attitude that are desirable of wider and deeper application, so its acceptability as a topic or perspective for incorporation in school curricula is reviving in many countries. Having outlined the cons and pros, however, we are still left with a few issues concerning the implementation of programmes of World Studies to which the reader should be alerted.

The first relates to the basic meaning of citizenship. It is reasonable to expect that any definition should incorporate the principle that citizens form a community of individuals treated as persons equal in law and in the respect to which they are due. That community has in practice meant the collective membership of a state. The question therefore arises, and has been raised notably by Eamonn Callan in his *Creating Citizens* (1997), whether schools can effectively prepare their pupils for citizenship only if the educational institutions are collectively microcosms of the state. This argument implies that pupils should not be segregated, either by intellectual ability, religious affiliation, sex, ethnicity or social class; for if (and indeed where) such segregation does occur, pupils grow up with assumptions and behaviour patterns pertinent to their limited group, not as citizens of a variegated society.

Now, if this argument is valid in a national context, how much more is it not true of an education for world citizenship? A number of international schools do exist which recruit their students from numerous countries; most distinguished of all are the United World Colleges. In the words of Lester Pearson, the former Canadian prime minister, after whom the college in Vancouver is named,

> These could provide, in many countries, dedicated men and women with a genuinely international education, who are needed so acutely to staff growing international organisations and companies. In addition, each nation needs its own cadre of ranking businessmen, administrators, civil servants and so on, who have a real sense of loyalty and dedication to the international community. This is one of the great needs of our age and one which the United World Colleges would help meet. (quoted in Heater, 1980: 106–7)

But, as this quotation reveals, these are elite institutions and therefore they do not meet all the requirements for schools of world citizenship. Nevertheless, the increasing rate of migration in recent decades has transformed many a state into a multicultural country. Depending on settlement patterns, of course, an increasing number of state schools are similarly multicultural and accordingly offer realistic opportunities for cosmopolitan education.

The second issue for further consideration derives from the

fragmentary nature of our knowledge about what provision is already made in the countries of the world and what success the schools are achieving. An extremely thorough research project got under way in 1996 on the initiative of the International Association for the Evaluation of Educational Achievement (IEA) to study civic education in twenty-four countries. But this is investigating citizenship education in the state, not the world, meaning of the term. What is needed, though it would be a formidable undertaking, is a comparable study of world citizenship education.

Such a study would provide, among other data, what has been found to be practicable in the broadest meaning of that word. Practicability involves compromise between the ideal and the realistic, between the innovative and the traditional. One must recognize the power of the conservative viewpoint as expounded in the first section of this chapter. Some ministries of education, governors of schools, headteachers, teachers, parents and pupils might find some, even all, of the newer teaching techniques advocated by the vanguard educationists barely acceptable or utterly unacceptable. Therefore, in so far as the vanguard is marching along the most appropriate route, the motif on its banner should, prudently, be *festina lente*. To take one example: proponents of world studies lay great stress on 'activities' – games, simulations, role-playing – partly in response to the adage, 'I hear and I forget; I see and I remember; I do and I understand', and partly because of their claimed greater efficacy in promoting attitude-formation than traditional learning of factual content. At the root of this second argument is the belief that global education should rightly be as much about affective learning as cognitive learning, as much about acquiring appropriate attitudes and behaviour patterns as about acquiring knowledge. We have already noted Scruton's scorn for 'infantile, manipulative games'. Some of these 'experiential activities' have been, it is true, totally lacking in content; others, however, successfully combine both cognitive and affective objectives. One such is the Model United Nations General Assembly (MUNGA). This involves pupils being presented with a hypothetical though feasible international problem, then, in teams representing the interested state-parties, formulating 'their' state's likely position. Having prepared their briefs, they present and defend them in a simulated General Assembly arena. The usefulness of this style of learning is reasonably evident even for the critics to see.

What is more, the skills that are required and developed in this kind of activity are relevant and transferable to many adult situations. In fact, curriculum developers in the field of World Studies insist that they are educating for the future and that some factual knowledge gained at school is likely to become decreasingly relevant; whereas learning to understand shifting global issues, to assess their relative importance and to be equipped with the skills to obtain and use the pertinent data is a set of educational objectives most needed for life in the twenty-first century.

The key is competence. Schools are able effectively to discharge their responsibilities for educating for world citizenship only if they grasp this fundamental point. Knowledge and understanding about developing countries, which is sometimes almost equated with education for world citizenship (see, e.g., Gardner, 2000), misses the very heart of the matter. Admirable as such programmes might be in themselves, they not only offer just a limited interpretation of the global, they severely limit the development of competence. And a citizen without competence is barely a citizen at all. To cite an American work in this field, Lee Anderson's *Schooling and Citizenship in a Global Age* (1979) emphasized the crucial importance of competence and listed four 'competencies' exactly comparable with those required for effective local or national citizenship. These are: competence in perceiving one's involvement in a global society; competence in making decisions; competence in reaching judgements; competence in exercising influence.

This curricular philosophy also leads naturally to the belief that, having acquired the elements of world citizenship competence, citizens need their competence to be sustained and built upon as a lifetime activity. Support is therefore required for adults comparable with, albeit perhaps of a different kind from, the initial help given by schools to novice world citizens. References to the main kinds of knowledge acquisition and participative involvement have appeared in earlier chapters. What is needed, however, is an enhancement of the quality of news media coverage, enlargement of participative opportunities and encouragement from governments for their citizens to behave in more cosmopolitan ways. Scanty media coverage of world affairs, the trivialization of much of the coverage that is provided, and negative commentary on the failings of foreign states and peoples and of inter- and transnational institutions are discouragements to holding fast to a world citizenship mode of thinking and behaviour. Governments are starting to take more seriously the advantages of the populations of their states being adequately educated as citizens. If internal democracy and stability benefit from this preparation, then it is time for governments to heed the benefits for the world as a whole of expanding civic education at all age levels to embrace a global dimension.

Conclusion

World citizenship is an enigma. It is an allusive, puzzling term with no fixed, universally accepted meaning, nor does it refer to a recognized status. This is tantalizing, because there is surely an essence that can be brought from behind the enigmatic veil into a real and universally accepted existence. How should one proceed in order to achieve this clarification and realization? Three approaches are needed, which we may classify as philosophical, institutional and psychological. By philosophical we mean the encouragement of tolerant and sympathetic modes of political thinking with the objective of resolving the conflict between cosmopolitanism and communitarianism, so rendering them mutually compatible. By institutional we mean the development of methods by which individuals can have the opportunity to participate in a democratically ordered world. And by psychological we mean the deepening among many more individuals of a sense of being a world citizen.

The task of political philosophers is to build on what we described in Chapter 2 as the revival of classical compatibilities, so that state citizenship, nationhood and world citizenship can be held in an equilibrium of mutual toleration. Fundamentally, this means an abatement of the antagonism between cosmopolitans and communitarians by the surrender of extremist positions on both sides and acceptance that the principles of each have values that can and do contribute to the needs of mankind. The great Indian writer and educator Rabindranath Tagore expressed through one of his characters the belief that 'man's history has to be built by the united effort of all the races in the world, and therefore this selling of conscience for political reasons – this making a fetish of one's country, won't do' (Tagore, 1985: 165–6). And recently the Canadian academic Kai Nielsen has asserted that 'it will not do to try to root our self-identification *just* to [sic] our humanness. ... Cultural membership and group identity is a fundamental need of all human beings' (Nielsen, 1999: 543). These are merely two examples of the manifold appeals for the two sides to refrain from claiming total control of the individual's political identity. Cosmopolitan thinking needs to be more firmly consolidated, but this can be securely achieved only if the wisdom of these commonsense observations is widely understood and accepted. What, then, are the implications of the pleas for moderation and reconciliation for the patriotic, nationalistic and cosmopolitan modes of thought?

Patriotism, the deeply felt allegiance to the state, is integral to the concept of citizenship, the prime virtue in the republican strand of civic thinking. If, in the layers of multiple citizenships, the individual has to accommodate both the state and world versions, how can the patriotism of state citizenship be reformulated in order to prevent, or at least limit, tension with the differently focused virtues of cosmopolitanism? A common line of thinking is that patriotism must be preserved but should be uncoupled from nationalism. After all, the political virtue of patriotism was not in origin connected to the cultural identity of nationhood. Or, as Habermas has asserted, 'there is only a historically contingent connection between republicanism and nationalism' (Habermas, 1996: 499). Furthermore, detaching patriotism from nationalism is becoming both more feasible and even desirable as mounting immigration further weakens the assumption of nation-states' cultural cohesion. Benjamin Barber, for example, talks of the necessity to 'render tribalism safe' and urges that 'a civic patriotism that eschews exclusion but meets the need for parochial identity can provide an alternative to the many pathological versions of blood kinship that are around today' (Nussbaum *et al.*, 1996: 36). To make the same point, Habermas uses the term 'constitutional patriotism'. And Maurizio Viroli takes the recommendation one stage further, arguing that such a cleansed patriotism can be used as an 'antidote' to nationalism, to 'fight' it (quoted in Canovan, 2000: 277).

By thus liberating patriotism from the closed-mindedness of nationalism it could become more receptive to the idea of world

181

citizenship. Charles Taylor is quite adamant about this. He claims that 'we have no choice but to be cosmopolitans and patriots, which means to fight for a kind of patriotism that is open to universal solidarities against other more closed kinds (Nussbaum *et al.*, 1996: 121). Habermas perceives the possible emergence of a constitutional patriotism of an open-minded and democratic kind in the EU, distinct from the national cultures of the constituent states, and by this process signposting a pathway from state to world citizenship. Thus, he writes that 'Only a democratic citizenship that does not close itself off in a particularistic fashion can pave the way for a *world citizenship*.... State citizenship and world citizenship form a continuum whose contours, at least, are already becoming visible' (Habermas, 1996: 514–15).

Yet it is unrealistic to suppose that a reformulated patriotism would totally replace nationhood as a source of local identity, so we still need to face the question of how nationalism can be adapted to be more compatible with cosmopolitanism. We saw in Chapter 2 how some nineteenth-century thinkers denied their incompatibility. This notion is again being considered by the reiteration of the traditional rough distinction between liberal and aggressive nationalism, the former being interpreted as reconcilable with cosmopolitanism, the latter not. The case can be pursued along the following lines. Liberal nationalism in the form of national self-determination is a human good and a human right. Since this good and right should be capable of being enjoyed universally, all human beings must be considered equal in this regard and their national rights equally respected. Its moral principles therefore look remarkably akin to cosmopolitan principles. Nielsen indicates this in the following passage:

> A liberal nationalism will ... be tolerant of all other nationalisms that ... are similarly tolerant. As a social liberalism it will have substantially egalitarian principles of justice that acknowledge the equal human standing of all human beings, the importance of coming to have the necessary means actually to have that equal standing ... and to recognise as well the deep value of a commitment to equal respect for all human beings. (Nielsen, 1999: 449)

And he adds the further argument that enjoying a national identity is universally essential – it is a 'primary good'. It follows, therefore, that 'We will not, and morally speaking cannot privilege (whoever

we are) our own people with respect to [primary goods] ...
recognising that the people of our nation are not relevantly different
from anyone else in this respect' (*ibid.*: 450).

So, it is possible for a patriot to be comfortable with the thought
of being a world citizen; and an individual who identifies with his or
her cultural group may similarly feel at ease. But if patriotism and
nationhood can be expressed in modes that render them consonant
with cosmopolitanism, then cosmopolitanism, in turn, should be
defined in a manner that is consonant with a civic patriotism and a
liberal nationalism. Two approaches to achieving this may be
identified: these have been termed 'rooted cosmopolitanism' and
'civic cosmopolitanism'. Drawing on national analogies of multiple
loyalties and identities such as hyphenated Americans (e.g. Irish-
Americans) in an essay which he has entitled 'Rooted Cosmopolitanism' (see Walzer, 1995b), Mitchell Cohen condemns what he
calls 'unidevotionalists', and argues for what we may aptly term a
hyphenated world citizenship (e.g., American-world citizens).
Another expressive essay title is 'Cosmopolitan Patriots', by Kwame
Anthony Appiah. Appiah's thesis is that patriotism is an expression
of local identity, differentiating one people from another, and that
this chimes well with the notion of world citizenship because 'The
cosmopolitan ... celebrates the fact that there are different local
human ways of being' (Nussbaum *et al.*, 1996: 25). Unlike
humanism, which, he insists, seeks to emphasize a universal
sameness, cosmopolitanism in the moderate, cultural sense actually
depends on the existence of a multiplicity of political states as
containers of mankind's cultural heterogeneity. This is the frame of
mind of the cosmopolitan patriot.

Whereas the likes of Appiah see cosmopolitanism reconciling
itself with a liberal patriotism, Gerard Delanty sees cosmopolitanism reconciling – indeed needing to reconcile – itself with a liberal
nationalism in a formula he calls 'civic cosmopolitanism'. He
conceives this as a dual process. First, it is necessary to stand up to
and temper strident nationalism. He writes:

> Civic cosmopolitanism is necessary in order to combat
> ethnonationalism and state nationalism. ... The problem with
> many varieties of cosmopolitanism is that they are conceived as
> discourses that transcend the nation and are therefore impotent
> in the face of nationalism. (Delanty, 2000: 143)

Second, cosmopolitanism must create its own kind of community, especially through the development of 'a cosmopolitan public sphere' (*ibid.*: 145). This would be the nurturing of cosmopolitan forms of culture and communication at every level, from local to global. This, he maintains, is an essential precondition to the construction of effective legal and political institutions for the articulation of world citizenship.

Yet, although, because of loose common usage or an academic focus on socio-cultural changes, one must accept a cosmopolitanism that is deficient of legal and political dimensions, a citizenship without legal and political dimensions is properly speaking a contradiction. Of these dimensions, the political is the more important because the conferment of a legal status of citizenship is the function of a political authority. For example, even EU passports, which are legal documents, are issued by the individual political member states. On the other hand, it is generally recognized that the creation of an effective and acceptable network of institutions through which individuals could participate as democratic world citizens would be no easy undertaking, largely because of political inertia. It took the horrific experience of the Second World War to create the UN and the European Community; without a comparable cataclysmic event (which Heaven forfend) an extremely gradual, long period of adaptation is all that can realistically be expected.

The question therefore arises concerning the relationship between institutional creativity and cosmopolitan consciousness. This is our second, institutional approach to the matter of consolidating world citizenship. Influence can work in both directions. Popular pressure can install or reform institutions and the very existence of institutions can persuade individuals to participate in their operation. Nevertheless, the common argument today on the issue of cosmopolitan institutions favours the former. The case can be simply put. Effective institutions do not exist, yet they are needed both to make world citizenship a fully recognized status and because the current *ad hoc* arrangements for global governance conspicuously suffer from a 'democratic deficit'. But a reformed system is unlikely to evolve because of resistance embedded in the jealous protection of state sovereignty and the absence, because of the feebleness of cosmopolitan democratic consciousness, of any momentum for change. Therefore, the enhancement of cosmopolitan consciousness is essential in order to overcome this condition of stagnation.

Appreciative commentary on David Held's pioneering exposition of the concept of cosmopolitan democracy has sometimes included a recommendation that the element of the individual's awareness of a world community should now be developed as a crucial supplement. Janna Thompson, for instance, writes: 'What needs to be added to this account is how global problems and opportunities to develop transnational associations affect individual consciousness, and how these associations can become part of individuals' understanding of who they are' (Thompson, 1998: 194). Similarly, Kymlicka and Straehle urge the need to develop an understanding of the 'preconditions' for cosmopolitan democracy through an under-girding of global 'collective identity and social justice' (Kymlicka and Straehle, 1999: 82).

We have now, as will be evident, intruded into our third approach, the psychological – the development by human beings of an understanding of the nature and significance of world citizenship to the point where it is not questioned, ignored or derided, but accepted as a normal feature of one's social life. To adapt Cicero, the attitude could be expressed with the proud Latin tag, 'civis mundi sum'. We must examine a number of facets to this issue.

First, there is the oft-repeated assertion that world citizenship cannot properly exist unless there is a world community of which the individual can feel a member. If there is no such thing as a world community there is little purpose in the individual's trying to think of him- or herself as a world citizen. Now, there is in fact, despite denials, a fair amount of evidence that the notion of a world community is widely accepted in broad terms, and under whatever name – world society, human family, human brotherhood. As Chris Brown has noted, the term 'world community' 'is never employed with pejorative connotations' (Brown, 2000: 453). None the less, compared with national communities, for example, world commu-nity solidarity, it must be said, is rather feeble. We therefore return to the attitude of individuals and the need for more people to think more deeply that they belong to a global community and to accept the moral implications of that membership. Ultimately, perhaps, this might lead, in Stanley Cohen's words, to a global community in which 'the obligation to assist others in danger or distress was a powerful imperative' (quoted in *Guardian*, 7 April 2001).

Accepting one's status as a member of the world community is a psychological step that brings the individual to the point where the issues of priority and balance must be faced. The problem of priority relates to the widely accepted view that, in conducting themselves as citizens, individuals should treat their compatriots with greater favour than the rest of humankind who are not their co-nationals. The issue contains two main questions. One is whether and on what grounds the argument for priority is justified; the other, partly dependent on the answers to the first question, is how one should calculate the relative sacrifice one should make in terms of outlays of time, energy and resources on behalf of one's fellow state citizens and world citizens. Responses to the first question would take us too deeply into the realms of political philosophy for our purposes (but see, e.g., Beitz, 1983: 593–9), so let us settle for the commonsense view that persons acting as world citizens will also have a prior commitment to their nation or state – 'prior' understood here in the temporal sense, by virtue of birth and upbringing in such a community. Therefore, by diverting a portion of their commitment to needs beyond their nation or state, individuals are presented with the task of establishing a balance of responses to these different moral demands.

This task, like any other movement from a social or political *status quo*, requires both an understanding of the suggested changes and a will to bring them about. Two analyses will help to illuminate what is being asked. One is to examine the nature of conflicting views concerning human nature and political purpose; the other is to recall from Chapter 1 Samuel Scheffler's conditions for the viability of world citizenship.

The ancient debate on whether humans or, rather, men are innately evil and aggressive and the pertinence of this issue for our purpose are encapsulated in this excerpt from that sturdy advocate of toleration, Pierre Bayle, taken from his *Dictionnaire historique et critique* (1697):

> That men should hate one another ... that they should range themselves in armies to butcher one another ... one can understand because men are, we suppose, different from one another, and because 'What is yours' and What is mine' excite warring passions among them. But if men are but modes of one and the same being, if the God that changes himself into a Turk is one and the same God that changes himself into a Hungarian, then that there should be wars and battles between them is the most outrageous idea ever thought of. (quoted in Hazard, 1964: 175)

The conflicting views on political purpose relate to the assumption that local loyalty, national identity and so forth are the stuff of everyday life, concerned with the individual's pursuit of the good, whereas the cosmopolitan ideal is just that, an ideal, concerned with the pursuit of right and justice in the abstract (see, e.g., Freeman, 1994: 85; Nussbaum *et al.*, 1996: 93, 97). Rob Walker shows how this kind of assumed dichotomy has led us into a paradox. He explains that the cosmopolitan agenda requires the reversal of the priority of citizenship over humanity. But:

It has long been conventional political wisdom that this reversal can never happen. It has been our conventional ethical wisdom that it must. In politics, at least, it is also conventional wisdom that conventional wisdom is not to be trusted. (Walker, 1999: 191)

To resolve the issue of human nature one needs a spirit of optimism that educative redemption is possible; and, to resolve the issue of political purpose, one needs to recognize how common it is becoming in various spheres of thought that so many of us are now 'engag[ing] with multiple subjectivities' (*ibid.*: 197).

This need for more widely spread Protean flexibility and adaptability brings us to our second suggested analysis, namely, Scheffler's. He urges that human beings should keep in harmonious balance: justice and loyalty; tradition and choice; past and future; and ourselves and others. Learned loyalty is to the local community, primarily the state, yet justice demands relaxing that allegiance to some degree in order to give consideration to those more distant. Tradition binds individuals to the cultural inheritance of their natal or adopted soil, yet desire to have the opportunity to choose their identity or identities leads them to a wish to loosen the tightness of those bonds. Similarly, being linked to the past preserves the mentalities and institutions formulated into a *status quo*, whereas changes required to prepare for the future must question the validity and utility of this inheritance. And, while it is seductive to give the needs of oneself and one's kin priority, the needs of others will dilute this moral selfishness. Justice, choice, future and others are cosmopolitan considerations, which must be given their due place, but in mutually tolerant acceptance of the loyalty, tradition, past and ourselves of communitarian considerations.

And yet, even when world citizens have managed this programme of delicate balances, there is still a further judgement to make. That is, whether the status should be kept at the vague and figurative level of self-identification, or should be advanced to a true citizenly status of legal and political meaning, confirmed as the apex of the pyramid of multiple citizenship.

References

Anderson, Lee (1979), *Schooling and Citizenship in a Global Age*. Bloomington, IN: Social Studies Development Center, Indiana University.

Andrews, Geoff (ed.) (1991), *Citizens*. London: Lawrence & Wishart.

Annas, Julia (1993), *The Morality of Happiness*. New York: Oxford University Press.

Archibugi, Daniele (1992), 'Models of international organization in perpetual peace projects'. *Review of International Studies*, 18, 295–317.

Archibugi, Daniele (1995), 'Immanuel Kant, cosmopolitan law and peace', *European Journal of International Relations*, 1(4), 429–56.

Archibugi, Daniele and Held, David (eds) (1995), *Cosmopolitan Democracy: An Agenda for a New World Order*. Cambridge: Polity.

Archibugi, Daniele, Held, David and Köhler, Martin (eds) (1998), *Re-imagining Political Community: Studies in Cosmopolitan Democracy*. Cambridge: Polity.

Aristotle (trans. and ed. E. Barker) (1948), *Politics*. Oxford: Clarendon.

Augustine, Saint (trans. W. C. Green) (1969), *The City of God against the Pagans*, vol. VI. London: Heinemann.

Bacon, Francis (1906), *Essays*. London: Dent.

Bailey, S. H. (1938), *International Studies in Modern Education*. London: Oxford University Press.

Baldry, H. C. (1965), *The Unity of Mankind in Greek Thought*. Cambridge: Cambridge University Press.

Bańkowski, Zenon and Christodoulidis, Emilios (1999), 'Citizenship bound and citizenship unbound', in K. Hutchings and R. Dannreuther, pp. 83–104.

Barnaby, Frank (ed.) (1991), *Building a More Democratic United Nations*. London: Cass.

Becker, James A. (1979), *Schooling for a Global Age*. New York: McGraw-Hill.

Beetham, David (1998), 'Human rights as a model for cosmopolitan democracy', in D. Archibugi, D. Held and M. Köhler, pp. 58–71.

Beiner, Ronald (ed.) (1995), *Theorizing Citizenship*. Albany, NY: State University of New York Press.

Beitz, Charles, R. (1979), *Political Theory and International Relations*. Princeton, NJ: Princeton University Press.

Beitz, Charles R. (1983), 'Cosmopolitan ideals and national sentiment'. *Journal of Philosophy*, 80, 591–600.

Beitz, Charles R. (1999), 'International liberalism and distributive justice: a survey of recent thought'. *World Politics*, 51, 269–96.

Bereday, George Z. F. (ed.) (1966), *Charles E. Merriam's The Making of Citizens*. New York: Teachers Press, Columbia University.

Billington, R. A. (1966), *The Historian's Contribution to Anglo-American Misunderstanding*. London: Routledge.

Blumler, Jay G. (1974), 'Does political ignorance matter?' *Teaching Politics*, 3(2), 91–100.

Bréhier, Émile (1951), *Chrysippe et l'ancien Stoïcisme*. Paris: Presses Universitaires de France.

Brierly, J. L. (1928), *The Law of Nations*. Oxford: Clarendon.

Brown, Chris (1992), *International Relations Theory: New Normative Approaches*. Hemel Hempstead: Harvester Wheatsheaf.

Brownlie, Ian (1990), *Principles of Public International Law*. Oxford: Clarendon.

Buergenthal, Thomas and Torney, Judith V. (1976), *International Human Rights and International Education*. Washington, DC: US National Commission for UNESCO.

Bull, Hedley (1977), *The Anarchical Society*. London: Macmillan.

Burke, Edmund (ed. A. J. Grieve) (1910), *Reflections on the French Revolution*. London: Dent.

Burke, Edmund (ed. J. M. Robson) (1962), *An Appeal from the New to the Old Whigs*. Indianapolis, IN: Bobbs-Merrill.

Burnet, Mary (1965), *ABC of Literacy*. Paris: UNESCO.

Callan, Eamonn (1997), *Creating Citizens: Political Education and Liberal Democracy*. Oxford: Clarendon.

Canovan, Margaret (2000), 'Patriotism is not enough', in C. McKinnon and I. Hampsher-Monk, pp. 276–97.

Carr, E. H. (1966), *The Bolshevik Revolution 1917–1923*, vol. 1. Harmondsworth: Penguin.

Cassesse, Antonio (1991), 'Violence, war and the rule of law in the international community', in D. Held (1991).

Cheah, Pheng and Robbins, Bruce (eds) (1998), *Cosmopolitics: Thinking and Feeling beyond the Nation*. Minneapolis: University of Minnesota Press.

Cicero (trans. W. Miller) (1956), *De Officiis*. London: Heinemann.

Cicero (trans. C. W. Keyes) (1959), *De Re Publica*. London: Heinemann.

Clark, Grenville and Sohn, Louis B. (1958), *World Peace through World Law*. Cambridge, MA: Harvard University Press.

Cohen, L. Jonathan (1954), *The Principles of World Citizenship*. Oxford: Blackwell.

Cohn, Mitchell (1995), 'Rooted cosmopolitanism', in M. Walzer (1995b).

Commission on Global Governance (1995), *Our Global Neighbourhood*. Oxford: Oxford University Press.

Crawford, James and Marks, Susan (1998), 'The global democracy deficit: an essay in international law and its limits', in D. Archibugi, D. Held and M. Köhler.

Dahrendorf, Ralf (1994), 'The changing quality of citizenship', in van Steenbergen.

Dann, Otto and Dinwiddy, John (eds) (1988), *Nationalism in the Age of the French Revolution*. London: Hambledon Press.

Delanty, Gerard (2000), *Citizenship in a Global Age*. Buckingham: Open University Press.

Donnelly, Jack (1985), *The Concept of Human Rights*. Beckenham, Croom Helm.

Durkheim, Emile (1961), *Moral Education*. Chicago: Free University Press of Glencoe.

Epictetus (trans. W. A. Oldfather) (1961), *The Discourses as Reported by Arian*, vol. I. London: Heinemann.

Erasmus, Desiderius (ed. A. Grieve) (1917), *The Complaint of Peace*. London: Headley Bros.

Falk, Richard (1994), 'The making of global citizenship', in van Steenbergen.

Falk, Richard (1995), *On Humane Governance*. Cambridge: Polity.

Fichte, J. G. (ed. G. A. Kelly) (1968), *Addresses to the German Nation*. New York: Harper & Row.

Freeman, Michael (1994), 'Nation-state and cosmopolis: a response to David Miller'. *Journal of Applied Psychology*, 11(1), 79–87.

Gardner, Roy (2000), 'Global perspectives in citizenship education', in D. Lawton, J. Cairns and R. Gardner.

Gewirth, Alan (1982), *Human Rights: Essays on Justification and Applications*. Chicago: University of Chicago Press.

Glossop, Ronald, J. (1993), *World Federation? A Critical Analysis of Federal World Government*. Jefferson, NC: McFarland.

Glover, T. R. (1944), *The Ancient World*. London: Penguin.

Green, L. C. (1987), 'Is world citizenship a legal practicality?' *Canadian Yearbook of International Law*, 25, 151–85.

Guardian (1994) 6 May.

Guardian (1999) 28 March.

Guardian (2000) 22 June, 29 September, 28 December, 30 December.

Guardian (2001) 8 February, 7 April.

Habermas, Jürgen (1996), *Between Facts and Norms: Contributions to a Discourse Theory of Law and Democracy*. Cambridge: Polity.

Hague Appeal for Peace (1999), *The Hague Agenda for Peace and Justice for the 21st Century*. London: World Goodwill.

Hale, John (1994), *The Civilization of Europe in the Renaissance*. London: Fontana.

Hassner, Pierre (1998), 'Refugees: a special case for cosmopolitan citizenship?', in D. Archibugi, D. Held and M. Köhler.

Hazard, Paul (trans. J. L. May) (1964), *The European Mind 1680–1715*. Harmondsworth: Penguin.

Heater, Derek (1980), *World Studies: Education for International Understanding in Britain*. London: Harrap.

Heater, Derek (1984), *Peace through Education: The Contribution of the Council for Education in World Citizenship*. Lewes: Falmer Press.

Heater, Derek (1990), *Citizenship: The Civic Ideal in World History, Politics and Education*. London: Longman.

Heater, Derek (1996), *World Citizenship and Government: Cosmopolitan Ideas in the History of Western Political Thought*. Basingstoke: Macmillan.

Heater, Derek (1999), *What Is Citizenship?* Cambridge: Polity.

Held, David (ed.) (1991), *Political Theory Today*. Cambridge: Polity.

Held, David (1995), *Democracy and the Global Order: From the Modern State to Cosmopolitan Democracy*. Cambridge: Polity.

Held, David, McGrew, Anthony, Goldblatt, David and Perraton, Jonathan (1999), *Global Transformations*. Cambridge: Polity.

Herodotus (trans. A. de Selincourt) (1954), *The Histories*. Harmondsworth: Penguin.

Hettne, Bjorn (2000), 'The fate of citizenship post-Westphalia'. *Citizenship Studies*, 4(1), 35–46.

Hill, Lisa (2000), 'The two *Republicae* of the Roman Stoics: can a cosmopolite be a patriot?' *Citizenship Studies*, 4(1), 65–79.

Hirst, Paul and Thompson, Grahame (1999), *Globalization in Question*. Cambridge: Polity.

Hobbes, Thomas (1914), *The Leviathan*. London: Dent.

Hobsbawm, Eric (1994), *The Age of Extremes: The Short Twentieth Century*. London: Michael Joseph.

Hoffmann, Stanley (1981), *Duties Beyond Borders*. Syracuse, NY: Syracuse University Press.

Holsti, K. J. (1974), *International Politics*. Englewood Cliffs, NJ: Prentice-Hall.

Hutchings, Kimberly and Dannreuther, Roland (eds) (1999), *Cosmopolitan Citizenship*. Basingstoke: Macmillan.

InterAction Council (1998), *A Universal Declaration of Human Responsibilities*. London: World Goodwill.

Isin, Engin F. and Wood, Patricia K. (1999), *Citizenship and Identity*. London: Sage.

Jelin, Elizabeth (2000), 'Towards a global environmental citizenship?' *Citizenship Studies*, 4(1), 47–63.

John XXIII (trans. H. Waterhouse) (1980), *Pacem in Terris*. London: Catholic Truth Society.

Jones, Charles (1999), *Global Justice: Defending Cosmopolitanism*. Oxford: Oxford University Press.

Jones, Steve (1999), *Almost Like a Whale: The Origin of Species Updated*. London: Doubleday.

Kant, Immanuel (trans. A. Churton) (1960), *Education*. Ann Arbor: University of Michigan Press.

Köhler, Martin (1998), 'From the national to the cosmopolitan sphere', in D. Archibugi, D. Held and M. Köhler.

Kohn, Hans (1961), *The Mind of Germany*. London: Macmillan.

Krause, Jill and Renwick, Neil (eds) (1996), *Identities in International Relations*. Basingstoke: Macmillan.

Kymlicka, Will and Straehle, Christine (1999), 'Cosmopolitanism, nation-states, and minority nationalism: a critical review of recent literature'. *European Journal of Philosophy*, 7(1), 65–88.

Lamy, Steven L. (1990), 'Global education: a conflict of images', in D. Tye.

Lange, C. L. (1919), *Histoire de l'internationalisme*, vol. I. Kristiani a: Aschehoug.

Lauwerys, J. A. (n.d.), *Cyprus School History Textbooks*. London: Education Committee of the Parliamentary Group for World Government.

Lawton, Denis, Cairns, Jo and Gardner, Roy (eds) (2000), *Education for Citizenship*. London: Continuum.

League of Nations Union (1937), *Teachers and World Peace*. London: League of Nations Union.

Linklater, Andrew (1982), *Men and Citizens in the Theory of International Relations*. London: Macmillan.

Linklater, Andrew (1998), *The Transformation of Political Community*. Cambridge: Polity.

Locke, John (1962), *Two Treatises of Civil Government*. London: Dent.

McKinnon, Catriona and Hampsher-Monk, Iain (eds) (2000), *The Demands of Citizenship*. London: Continuum.

Marcus Aurelius Antoninus (trans. C. R. Haines) (1961), *The Communings with Himself*. London: Heinemann.

Marshall, T. H. (1950), *Citizenship and Social Class*. Cambridge: Cambridge University Press.

Marx, Karl (ed. H. J. Laski) (1948), *Communist Manifesto*. London: Allen & Unwin.

Maser, Werner (1979), *Nuremberg: A Nation on Trial*. London: Allen Lane, Penguin Press.

Mayne, Richard and Pinder, John (1990), *Federal Union: The Pioneers*. Basingstoke: Macmillan.

Mazlish, Bruce and Buultjens, Ralph (eds) (1993), *Conceptualizing Global History*. Boulder, CO: Westview Press.

Mazzini, Joseph (1891), *Life and Writings of Joseph Mazzini*, vol. III. London: Smith, Elder & Co.

Mazzini, Joseph (1961), *The Duties of Man and Other Essays*. London: Dent.

Meinecke, Friedrich (trans. R. B. Kimber) (1970), *Cosmopolitanism and the National State*. Princeton, NJ: Princeton University Press.

Miller, David (1999), 'Bounded citizenship', in K. Hutchings and R. Dannreuther.

Montaigne, Michel de (trans. J. M. Cohen) (1958), *Essays*. Harmondsworth: Penguin.

Muller, Robert (1994), *A World Core Curriculum*. London: World Goodwill.

Nathan, Otto and Norden, Heinz (eds) (1960), *Einstein on Peace*. New York: Simon & Schuster.

Neff, Stephen C. (1999), 'International law and the critique of cosmopolitan citizenship', in K. Hutchings and R. Dannreuther.

Nielsen, Kai (1999), 'Cosmopolitan nationalism'. *The Monist*, 82(3), 446–68.

Nussbaum, Martha C. (1997a), *Cultivating Humanity: A Classical Defence of Reform in Liberal Education*. Cambridge, MA: Harvard University Press.

Nussbaum, Martha C. (1997b), 'Kant and Stoic cosmopolitanism'. *Journal of Political Philosophy*, 5(1), 1–25.

Nussbaum, Martha C. *et al.* (1996), *For Love of Country: Debating the Limits of Patriotism*. Boston: Beacon.

O'Connor, Edmund (1980), *World Studies in the European Classroom*. Strasbourg: Council of Europe.

O'Connor, Edmund (1982), 'Global Education: a report on developments in Western Europe'. *Theory into Practice*, 21(3), 224–7.

O'Neill, Onora (1991), 'Transnational justice', in D. Held (1991).

Oakeshott, Michael (ed.) (1940), *Social and Political Doctrines of Contemporary Europe*. London: Basis Books.

Paine, Thomas (ed. I. Kramnick) (1976), *Common Sense*. Harmondsworth: Penguin.

Perez de Cuellar, Javier (1989), *Promoting a Universal Human Rights Culture*. London: World Goodwill.

Piaget, Jean (intro.) (1967), *John Amos Comenius on Education*. New York: Teachers College, Columbia University.

Pike, Graham and Selby, David (1988), *Global Teacher, Global Learner*. London: Hodder & Stoughton.

Pogge, Thomas W. (1992), 'Cosmopolitanism and sovereignty'. *Ethics*, 103, 48–75.

Raison, Timothy (1964), *Why Conservative?* Harmondsworth: Penguin.

Rawls, John (1971), *A Theory of Justice*. Cambridge, MA: Harvard University Press.

Rawls, John (1999), *The Law of Peoples*. Cambridge, MA: Harvard University Press.

Reiss, Hans (ed.) (1991), *Kant: Political Writings*. Cambridge: Cambridge University Press.

Richardson, Robin (1976), *Learning for Change in a World Society*. London: World Studies Project.

Roberts, John C. de V. (1993), *Why Human Rights Need World Law*. London: Association of World Federalists.

Robertson, Geoffrey (1999), *Crimes against Humanity: The Struggle for Global Justice*. London: Allen Lane, Penguin Press.

Robinson, Mary (1999), *The Mortal Power of Affirmation*. London: World Goodwill.

Rousseau, Jean-Jacques (trans. B. Foxley) (1911), *Émile*. London: Dent.

Scanlon, D. G. (ed.) (1960), *International Education: A Documentary History*. New York: Teachers College, Columbia University.

Scheffler, Samuel (1999), 'Conceptions of cosmopolitanism'. *Utilitas*, 11(3), 255–76.

Schlereth, T. J. (1977), *The Cosmopolitan Ideal in Enlightenment Thought*. Notre Dame, IN: University of Notre Dame Press.

Schmidt, Helmut (1999), 'It is time to talk about responsibility' (mimeo).

Scholte, Jan Aart (1996), 'Globalisation and collective identities', in J. Krause and N. Renwick.

Scruton, Roger (1985), *World Studies: Education or Indoctrination?* London: Institute for European Defence and Strategic Studies.

Seneca (trans. J. W. Basore) (1958), 'On the Happy Life', in *Moral Essays*, vol. II. London: Heinemann.

Seneca (trans. R. M. Gunmere) (1961), *Epistolae Morales*, vol. I. London: Heinemann.

Shue, Henry (1988), 'Mediating duties'. *Ethics*, 98, 687–704.

Sidgwick, Henry (1966), *The Methods of Ethics*. New York: Dover Publications.

Sieyès, E. J. (trans. M. Blondel) (1963), *What Is the Third Estate?* London: Pall Mall.

Singer, Peter (1981), *The Expanding Circle*. New York: Farrar.

Smith, Adam (ed. D. D. Raphael and A. L. Macfie) (1982), *The Theory of Sentiments*. Indianapolis, IN: Liberty Classics.

Smith, Anthony D. (1991), *National Identity*. Harmondsworth: Penguin.

Smith, Anthony D. (1995), *Nations and Nationalism in a Global Era*. Cambridge: Polity.

Stanton, G. R. (1968), 'The cosmopolitan ideas of Epictetus and Marcus Aurelius'. *Phronesis*, 13, 183–95.

Steward, Fred (1991), 'Citizens of planet earth', in Andrews.

Stockholm Initiative on Global Security and Governance (1991), *Common Responsibility in the 1990s*. Stockholm: Prime Minister's Office.

Streit, Clarence K. (1939), *Union Now*. London: Cape.

Sugamini, Hidemi (1989), *The Domestic Analogy and World Order Problems*. Cambridge: Cambridge University Press.

Svengalis, Cordell (1991), Letter to global education task force members, Iowa (mimeo).

Tagore, Rabindranath (1985), *The Home and the World*. Harmondsworth: Penguin.

Thompson, Janna (1998), 'Community identity and world citizenship', in D. Archibugi, D. Held and M. Köhler.

Thomson, David (1969), *The Aims of History*. London: Thames and Hudson.

Turner, Bryan S. (1986), *Citizenship and Capitalism*. London: Allen & Unwin.

Tye, Kenneth A. (ed.) (1990), *Global Education from Thought to Action*. Alexandria, VA: Association for Supervision and Curriculum Development.

UNESCO (ed.) (1949), *Human Rights: Comments and Interpretations*. London: Allan Wingate.

United Nations (2001), *The Millennium Summit*. London: World Goodwill.

van Steenbergen, Bart (1994), *The Condition of Citizenship*. London: Sage.

Voltaire (trans. T. Besterman) (1971), *Philosophical Dictionary*. Harmondsworth: Penguin.

Walker, R. B. J. (1999), 'Citizenship after the modern subject', in K. Hutchings and R. Dannreuther.

Walzer, Michael (1994), *Thick and Thin: Moral Argument at Home and Abroad*. Notre Dame, IN: University of Notre Dame Press.

Walzer, Michael (1995a), 'The civil society argument', in R. Beiner.

Walzer, Michael (ed.) (1995b), *Toward a Global Civil Society*. Providence, RI: Berghahn Books.

Ward, Barbara and Dubos, René (1972), *Only One Earth: The Care and Maintenance of a Small Planet*. Harmondsworth: Penguin.

Webster, C. K. (1926), *The Teaching of World Citizenship*. London: League of Nations Union.

Wells, H. G. (1940), *The Rights of Man: or What Are We Fighting For?* London: Penguin.

Wight, Martin (1991), *International Theory: The Three Traditions*. London: Leicester University Press.

Wise, Steven M. (2000), *Rattling the Cage: Towards Legal Rights for Animals*. London: Profile Books.

World Commission on Environment and Development (1987), *Our Common Future*. Oxford: Oxford University Press.

Zolo, Danilo (1997), *Cosmopolis: Prospects for World Government*. Cambridge: Polity.

Index